ENDS OF CINEMA

Center for 21st Century Studies

Richard Grusin, Series Editor

ENDS OF CINEMA

RICHARD GRUSIN *and*
JOCELYN SZCZEPANIAK-GILLECE
EDITORS

Center for 21st Century Studies

UNIVERSITY OF MINNESOTA PRESS
MINNEAPOLIS
LONDON

Portions of chapter 8 were originally published in French as
"La résilience du 'cinéma' . . . ," in *Anais—2018 (Annales du SIIMI 2018),*
Universidade Federal de Goiás Media Lab.

Published by the University of Minnesota Press
111 Third Avenue South, Suite 290
Minneapolis, MN 55401-2520
http://www.upress.umn.edu

Library of Congress record available at https://lccn.loc.gov/2020023732

Printed in the United States of America on acid-free paper

The University of Minnesota is an equal-opportunity educator and employer.

25 24 23 22 21 20   10 9 8 7 6 5 4 3 2 1

Contents

Introduction

Jocelyn Szczepaniak-Gillece

B y the time you read this, cinema will have died. That's a certainty no
matter what year it is that you're opening this book. Cinema has
definitely ended, because cinema has ended many, many times and will
surely end again in the near future. In fact, cinema's ends have been so
endless that, depending on the company you keep, even referring to such
a well-worn cliché can result in theatrical eye-rolling and a quick escape
for the hors d'oeuvres table. Bringing up the end of cinema can be a very
effective way to end a conversation.

But we urge you not to cast aside this volume quite so fast. Maybe a little
perversely, what this book sets out to do is not to terminate but to enliven
conversation by unpacking the histories and theories of ends. Those questions that seem overwrought or answered or finally put to bed—or, simply, ended—are sometimes the very ones that beg to be reawakened.

In spring 2018, the Ends of Cinema conference sponsored by the Center for 21st Century Studies at the University of Wisconsin–Milwaukee
sought to do just that. We started with some simple questions: Are we
now, as many scholars have proclaimed, in an age of "post-cinema"? Has
the massive global wave of digital production, distribution, and exhibition finally eradicated cinema as we've known it? Martin Scorsese seemed
to think so, declaring in an interview with the Associated Press in the last
days of 2016 that "cinema is gone . . . the cinema that I grew up with and
that I'm making, it's gone."[1] Scorsese's mournful tone echoed Ridley Scott
and Peter Greenaway as well as articles in popular publications, such as

GQ, the *New Yorker,* and *Vanity Fair,* that blamed prestige television, high ticket prices, and, mostly, streaming platforms and digital technologies. Similar elegies for cinema have saturated academic discourse over the past fifteen years, from Paolo Cherchi Usai to D. N. Rodowick to Alexander Zahlten.[2]

Whatever the object "cinema" was, it often seems to have been summarily executed in the digital era. Yet, as John Belton has more recently noted, "predictions of the death of cinema have been with us as long as the cinema itself," while declarations of cinema's ends are in part a function of its beginnings.[3] But whose cinema is ending? If "cinema" implies a universal canon built on default ideologies, has its "death" been a response, in part, to deeper investigations into diversities made possible by increased access to the means of production? Did 2015's #OscarsSoWhite predict an end to white, male, and Western-centric cinema? Are cinema's many deaths bound to another kind of end: what we understand to be the goal of cinema, whether political, aesthetic, representational, theoretical, or technological?

Over visual media's long century, the emergence of new technologies, both filmic and otherwise, has repeatedly elegized cinema's ruin and celebrated its rejuvenation. Early on, sound seemed a sure eradication of the universality of the image's language. In 1930, Benjamin Fondane wrote on silent cinema at the dawn of synchronized sound, noting its "sudden death, certainly, but also sudden birth and feverish life, tormented, restless.... The mystery of its death can only be investigated in the light of the mystery of its life."[4] The collapse of the studio system—and its contemporary rebirth—upended all manner of production practice. In the 1950s, widescreen and 3D destabilized the very dimensions and depths of the image. From the 1940s through the 1970s, as Lynn Spigel, Frederick Wasser, and Joshua Greenberg, among many others, have shown, cinema found itself threatened by the emergence of television and then by the development of the VCR.[5] For Thomas Elsaesser, Jean-Louis Baudry's theory of the apparatus in the 1970s mourned the disappearance of a particular cinematic practice—interest in which has been reinvigorated recently with returns to the *dispositif.*[6] Girish Shambu refuted Susan Sontag's "end of cinephilia" in the 1990s by examining the new cinephilia of global networks.[7] Blockbusters threatened any attachment film had to art. The mall theater wrecked cinephilia. Home video destroyed exhibition. The digital killed the index. Postcinema fractured form. And Marvel Studios eradicated platform-specific media along with global cosmopolises, planets, mythical dimensions, and, depending on the day, half the life in the universe. Considered historiographically, these concerns with cinema's ends both breathed life into a discipline and exemplified a kind of millennial anxiety around technology, nostalgia, and vague threats of apocalypse. But the cinema never actually ended, or, at least, it always came back. Its ends are sources of both panic and secret desires, or even simply moments when something else is needed to shake up the standards and reconfigure what seemed natural.

What has become abundantly clear is that cinema's ends are quite endless: multiple, messy, untenable, and fascinating. Moreover, at the moment of cinema's emergence, it already bore within itself these many kinds of ends. In reenvisioning what these ends might be in a contemporary moment, the Ends of Cinema conference and the essays you are about to read insist that cinema's end should never be limited merely to discarding one aesthetic or technical form for another. Instead, ends can and should be reframed. In that sense, cinema's end is not the division between analog and digital photography or effects or the dissolution of indexical relationships to the real. Rather, cinema's ends can be teased out to include multiple discursive constellations. This volume considers the ends of cinema in four main ways—none of which, we are pleased to say, laments the loss of celluloid or grieves for an idealized nostalgic past. Instead, the ends of cinema discussed here reflect the blind-spot effect that a single term can induce: how the restriction of *end* to an indelible and idiomatic meaning has derailed so many thrilling trains of thought and how careful interrogation of some of the many possible ends of cinema can upend what appeared to be complete. These ends are not, of course, the only potential ends. But the Ends of Cinema conference was conceived in the spirit of convivial discourse. Following that model, the writers gathered here provide inspiration for the ways in which multifaceted conversation can create exhilarating new approaches to shared disciplinary thought.

This collection deliberately takes up the ends of "cinema," not film. In this sense, we want to encourage an understanding of cinema as audiovisual text plus spatial organization, scale, and the limits of cinema's physical presence. Thus an end of cinema is not an end of film; the end of a film is when the credits roll, but the end of cinema might instead be the limits of the auditorium structure, or the edge of the screen, or the fluidity of those boundaries that formerly seemed so stable. Mary Ann Doane's discussion of scale and bodies from cinema's beginnings to now questions the spatial ends of cinema when its limits have become boundless. If screens have proliferated to such a dramatic extent that architecture, cities, and quotidian experience are now enmeshed in networks of repeated and multiple mediation, what of the miniscule and the infinite projected on-screen? Where the infinite was once contained in a version of secular sublimity, multiplying formats and their concurrent aesthetics insist that cinema's ends can no longer be found at those screen edges. Cinema, here, has not ended and will not end. Perhaps the nostalgia for its loss was entirely misplaced and the widespread mourning was, instead, for the dissolution of its boundaries and the certainty that it was a single, enclosed thing.

Yet screens serve an additional function architecturally and technologically, and that is to hide or filter what might otherwise be seen. Once we return this aspect of the screen's *dispositif,* Francesco Casetti argues, a countergenealogy emerges whereby cinema becomes an environmental medium. This countergenealogy developed over the course of the twentieth century, both tracking and interrogating the ongoing technical development of screens and exhibition. Insofar as cinema has always been a medium of space, it is also a landscape. Still, the screen's performance of its vanishing function has similarly obfuscated this characteristic. If we can uncover all of the screen's mechanical skeletons, we can recognize that new media and cinema have commonalities that have also been left to the shadows. In its function as a spatial construct both built and naturalized, Doane and Casetti argue, cinema has concealed its subtle defining features and its ends. In these new considerations of cinema's spatial limits, cinema becomes something less on its way out than it became on its way in: seeping between the lines that divide old from new, insisting that a focus on scale and surround reanimates film form, removing built environments and exhibition from the fringes and placing them in the center, and demonstrating that an object that seemed stable and complete is anything but. To consider this end of cinema, then, is to reveal that not only has cinema not ended in the wake of new media and screen proliferation but its boundaries have become energized and electrified. There is, still, so much to be discovered in what at first appeared to be a shuttered archive.

Another end of cinema can be found in the moment of burgeoning extinction that it shares with its creators: the end of nature, of humanity, of Earth as we know it. Cinema thereby acts as a marker of the Anthropocene and its apocalyptic dimensions: cinema's end is also our own. But cinema's documentary function might serve as an archive of a disappearing world, which it has done at least since Albert Kahn's grand experiment of the Archives de la Planète, and so its end might also be considered a goal: to preserve, to note, and to study what might otherwise degrade into refuse. Jennifer Lynn Peterson takes on a remarkable set of educational nature films dating from the 1920s through the 1930s and currently held at the Hugh M. Hefner Moving Image Archive at the University of Southern California. These films' "endangerment sensibility" promote a particularly affective relationship between film, biological life, and spectator. And by insisting on tracing the provenance of these films, Peterson uncovers the ways by which the archive itself takes on a melancholic residue of ends at once human, natural, and cinematic. In turn, the mutual ephemerality of animal life and filmic archives hints at how cinema's ends are present from the moment celluloid is shot. It is always immediately decaying and thereby turning to both detritus and newfound objects of aesthetic astonishment. One end—an unprojectable strip—results in another beginning: an unexpected new beauty. With breathtaking analog images of discarded celluloid, EYE Filmmuseum curator Mark Paul Meyer elucidates cinema's paired figures of waste and grace and elegizes the value of tangible filmmaking from the perspective of the archivist. And these twinned characters of cinema, its trash and its treasure, its ancestors and its orphans, its living breath and its dying spirits, twist up the spine of James Leo Cahill's elegy for cinema's "garbage and ghosts." "Finitude and return" echo here through readings of Siegfried Kracauer's and Georges Bataille's negative discussions of photographic media, and where such endings and renewals might remain even in the haunted era of the Anthropocene. Cinema has always been ending, because it has always borne the burden of nature's—and humans'—ghosts.

When attending to the ends of cinema, it is a political imperative to question whose cinema and which cinema. If cinema can be said to end, or to be in the process of ending, is it simply a certain mode of cinema by certain specific practitioners? What are we mourning when we mourn the ends of cinema? And how might violence and death signify additional modes of cinematic ends? The linkages between Blackness and death find new—and imperative—resonance when interrogated alongside the deaths and ends of cinema. Violence at (rather than in) the movies draws a long trajectory of moral panic that, as Caetlin Benson-Allott articulates, has always been racialized. As Benson-Allott's incisive research proves, movie theater violence is categorized as "tragic" and "random" only when it happens to white people. Exhibition is thereby implicated in a larger system of sensationalism and stereotyping that resists an accurate depiction of cinema violence's racialization. Unbraiding the entanglements of Blackness, death, and cinema can also guide us to a version of Christina Sharpe's "wake work," which Michael Boyce Gillespie poignantly argues through an analysis of four short films by Black women filmmakers. Works by Leila Weefur, Frances Bodomo, Ja'Tovia Gary, and A. Sayeeda Clarke constitute powerful rejoinders to the universal end of cinema by asserting the need to examine "circuits of knowledge related to Blackness, death, and film form." What Gillespie calls "cinema in the wake" provides essential tools for considering how one of cinema's ends—in this case, one of its goals—is to critique the structures of racial capital under which we live.

Finally, our last two contributors take up the potential limitations or wild tangles of possibility inherent in the words we use when we discuss media, film, and cinema. In titling the conference and volume "Ends of Cinema," we meant to draw attention to the many potential ends that cinema has and will continue to experience. For both André Gaudreault and Amy Villarejo, this focus on cinema's multiple ends offered an opportunity to contemplate the ways in which language configures subjects, especially cinema and media. A term, after all, terminates; thus the lexicon itself represents another end of cinema. Gaudreault reminds us that the word *cinema,* like *ends,* is polysemous, especially when put in the context of bilingual scholarship as well as global distribution. How does "cinema" call upon its viewers, researchers, and profiteers to understand it?

The question of cinema's ends here becomes less one of ontology and more one of the vocabularies of organizations, academies, institutions, and, of course, capital. Both Netflix and Cannes grapple with what to call their product: Cinema? Film? Something strange and in between? Whatever it is, it is multiple and multidirectional, and as Villarejo's essay exhorts both rigorously and playfully, it can be held together only with the tenuous mark of the ampersand. An ampersand belongs to language and not to speech; it joins and separates; it is bodily and abstract. It is an imperfect mediation, and it is, in its own weird way, a conclusion that doesn't quite end: a typographical mark lacking meaning on its own that can engender a thought experiment on assemblages and the messiness of lived critical theory. Media, cinema, postcinema, television, and digitality become less discrete formal constructs and more dimensions of how collectivity and thinking can reenchant our engagement with each other.

It is, we hope, fitting that this volume finds its own end with a dialogue between the editors: a call to take what has seemingly been secured and reopen it together. When you reach the end of this volume, take heart. Even what appears to have ended hasn't always really done so. Sometimes coming to the end of a thing leads back, again, to the beginning. That beginning, we hope, could be one of many models for reworking histories and theories that were already decided and embarking on reformed pathways in the spirit of intellectual community. With that in mind, we invite you to explore some of the many potential ends of cinema and see for yourself whether what seemed like a dead end might also prove to be a way forward into a welcoming—and collective—unknown.

Notes

1. See Jake Coyle, "Martin Scorsese: 'Cinema Is Dead,'" *Boston Globe*, December 29, 2016, https://www.bostonglobe.com/arts/movies/2016/12/29/martin-scorsese -cinema-gone/s4ekJjONfrxyjZO4pkONqL/story.html.

2. See Paolo Cherchi Usai, *The Death of Cinema: History, Cultural Memory, and the Digital Dark Age* (London: BFI, 2001); D. N. Rodowick, *The Virtual Life of Film* (Cambridge, Mass.: Harvard University Press, 2007); and Alexander Zahlten, *The End of Japanese Cinema: Industrial Genres, National Times, and Media Ecologies* (Durham, N.C.: Duke University Press, 2017), among many others.

3. John Belton, "If Film Is Dead, What Is Cinema?," *Screen* 55, no. 4 (2014): 460.

4. Benjamin Fondane, "From Silent to Talkie: The Rise and Fall of the Cinema," in *French Film Theory and Criticism: A History/Anthology, 1907–1939*, ed. Richard Abel (Princeton, N.J.: Princeton University Press, 1993), 2:45.

5. See, e.g., Lynn Spigel, *Make Room for TV: Television and the Family Ideal in Postwar America* (Chicago: University of Chicago Press, 1992); Frederick Wasser, *Veni, Vidi, Video: The Hollywood Empire and the VCR* (Austin: University of Texas Press, 2002); and Joshua M. Greenberg, *From Betamax to Blockbuster: Video Stores and the Invention of Movies on Video* (Cambridge, Mass.: MIT Press, 2010).

6. Thomas Elsaesser, "What Is Left of the Cinematic Apparatus; or, Why We Should Retain (and Return to) It?," *Recherches Sémiotiques* 31, no. 1–3 (2011): 33–44.

7. Susan Sontag, "The Decay of Cinema," *New York Times*, February 25, 1996, and Girish Shambu, *The New Cinephilia* (Montreal: Caboose, 2014).

1

Scale and the Body in Cinema and Beyond

Mary Ann Doane

In Jim Campbell's works *Portrait of My Father* (1994–95) and *Photo of My Mother* (1996), two photographs are connected to machines that record the artist's own bodily functions (heartbeat and rate of breathing) and use these recordings to regulate the visibility of the photographs (Figure 1.1). In *Portrait of My Father*, the frequency with which the photograph appears and disappears is determined by the rate of Campbell's heartbeat, recorded over an eight-hour period one night while the artist slept. A one-hour digital recording of Campbell's breath similarly regulates the fogging and clearing of the glass in front of the photograph of his mother. The machines that control the temporality of these effects are labeled and dated ("My Heartbeat 12 am to 8 am, January 12, 1995" and "My Breath January 1996 1 hour"). The photographs are clearly old photographs, instances of an already obsolete medium that contrast with the sophisticated digital and electronic technologies of the installation. But they are also eerily reminiscent of Siegfried Kracauer's analysis of an old photograph as the glimpse of a moment of time past or Walter Benjamin's "tiny spark of contingency . . . with which reality has so to speak seared the subject."[1] Part of a larger series entitled *Memory Works*, the two pieces articulate the son's body—its unconscious and life-sustaining movements and temporalities—with the indexical traces, the past–present of the parents' historical inscription—producing a form of technologically mediated Oedipal drama. Subject to a seemingly endless literary metaphoricity, the heart and the breath determine the appearance and

1

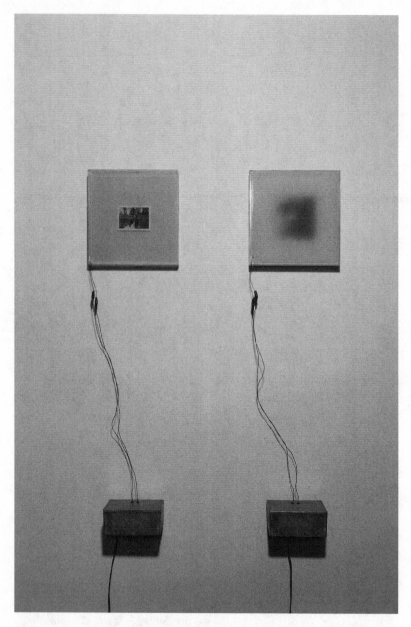

Figure 1.1. Jim Campbell, *Portrait of My Father* (1994–95) and *Photo of My Mother* (1996). Courtesy of the artist.

disappearance of ephemeral memory here. The photographs seem to live, to breathe themselves, trembling in their opacity. Memory, as in Proust, is physical—involuntary and contingent. Its clarity fluctuates, and the past is revealed as always beyond our grasp, although tantalizingly close, flickering intermittently.

Assuming the rigidity of the formal pose, the father composes his face, which is close, filling the frame, harshly confronting, facing-off the camera and viewer: this is the "*Portrait* of My Father." The mother, on the other hand, is relaxed, exuding spontaneity, situated in the bucolic mise-en-scène of the countryside, signifying—although not achieving—the contingency thought to be proper to amateur photography: this is the "*Photo* of My Mother." Visible wires connect the registration of the son's bodily functions, separately, to the representation of the mother and father, who, in turn, are connected only invisibly, through the electrical circuitry of the building itself—the nuclear family, reproduced for the museum. This work—to which I return later—produces the legibility of the body in a unique and quite specific way in relation to both time and space, presence and absence. Historically, the human body has been used as a measure, primarily of scale, and it is this phenomenon that I would like to investigate here, some of whose complexities are signaled by Campbell's conflation of measuring the body with the body as measure.

Campbell's works are part of an installation, viewable in a museum setting. They reference photography and, to some extent, cinema, but they belong in neither category. Beyond the increasing appearance of time-based media in the museum, arguments about the end or death of cinema often circulate around the accelerating proliferation of different venues or platforms for the exhibition and reception of films. Films can now be viewed on phones, laptops, tablets, desktop computers, and television screens as well as in traditional or IMAX theaters. So it is not simply or primarily the loss of celluloid as material base and the perceived dematerialization of the digital that contribute to a nostalgia for a lost cinema but also its delocalization/displacement from the theatrical sites that have been its historical support. Images are mobile and transportable, savable and recyclable, called up at will and often ephemeral. The cinematic object is no longer "site-specific," which contributes to the sense of its heavy physical being vanishing into a vaporous and elusive network for which the "cloud"—continually malleable, shape-shifting, evanescent—emerges as the perfect trope. The 35mm film, in cans, on reels, requiring projectors, transported on trucks, trains, or planes, is the bearer of a terrestrial weight that we barely remember.

In architectural theory, scale has always been a vexed category, eliciting arguments that circulate around the human body as measure. The classical or conventional view is aligned with the insistence on a calibration of scale by the body so that the built environment comfortably accommodates it. With the advent of modernity and, in particular, expanding technological mediation, space and scale with it are projected into the realm of the virtual, and the body becomes an avatar whose inhabitation of space is similarly virtual, imagined. Space has expanded its purview—what would it mean to activate the human body as a measure of phenomena described as on a "global scale"?

Scale's complicity with the body has generally worked as support and guarantee of humanism. Tall skyscrapers, monumental urban structures that exceed thinkability in relation to the body as measure, are often thought to be "dehumanizing." In this vein, E. M. Forster has written very tellingly of the body's sense of distance as hostile to technology:

> "Near" is a place to which I can get quickly on my feet, not a place to which the train or air-ship will take me quickly. "Far" is a place to which I cannot get quickly on my feet.... Man is the measure. That was my first lesson. Man's feet are the measure for distance, his hands are the measure for ownership, his body is the measure for all that is lovable and desirable and strong.[2]

"Near" and "far" in the media have, however, been conceptualized outside of the question of where my feet will take me. In the cinema, nearness and farness are ineluctably linked with the scale of the shot—close-up, medium shot, long shot—insofar as size becomes the signifier of distance (close-ups are not simply huge or monstrous [though they are that as well]—they are close, intimate). Yet this correspondence between size and distance in representation is not an invention of the cinema but can be traced back to Renaissance perspective, which precisely and mathematically calculates and maps this diminution and enlargement of things proportionally, on a two-dimensional surface, in relation to a place that is both there and not there—the vanishing point. Scale, perspective, proportion, and the body are ineluctably bound together in classical representation.

Contemporary urban landscapes are often populated with gigantic screens, emphasizing the monumentality of the image. Projected onto buildings, or screens on buildings, these images call out to a mobile spectator, an occasional spectator, a spectator who is often distracted by the countless other stimuli of the modern city. The most densely populated metropolises—New York, Hong Kong, Tokyo, Shanghai—seem to exhibit most strikingly this culture of colossal screens (Figure 1.2). In most cases, but not all, the images bear the transparent messages of a rampant commodification.

A seemingly more subtle example of this commodification would be the transformation of a corporation's office building into a prestigious aesthetic object, flaunting the concepts of "taste" and "value." On December 4, 2004, Chanel opened its largest boutique on the elite Chuo-dori Avenue of the Ginza district of Tokyo (designed by American architect Peter Marino). During the day, the building seems to be an ordinary office

Figure 1.2. Tokyo's screens. Photograph by the author.

building with transparent windows allowing workers to see outside, but at night, the two-hundred-foot-tall, ten-story facade becomes an enormous screen, a high-tech version of Chanel's signature tweed. Abstract patterns, figural images and messages, all in a tasteful black and white, glide across the surface of the building. Matthew Tanteri, a collaborating architect, claims, "The important thing it had to achieve was becoming

Figure 1.3. Chanel building in Ginza, Tokyo. Photograph by the author.

media, rather than a fixed graphic. So while the facade also acts as lighting for the building, it's a communication tool with imagery, logos, and branding" (Figure 1.3).³ Becoming media. While architecture has always been a medium, this exhortation situates the screen as the quintessential support of media, a screen that increasingly permeates both domestic and public space.

From January 16 through February 12, 2007, New York's MoMA projected Doug Aitken's *Sleepwalkers* on five large screens on the sides of the museum. The work was advertised as a "Large-Scale Cinematic Installation to Be Projected onto the Facades of The Museum of Modern Art" and a "Major Public Artwork." Aitken himself spoke of turning the museum inside out. What strikes me about this installation is its uncanny formal resemblance to the massive screens of commodification discussed earlier. The overwhelming size of the images seems to situate them unconsciously within the framework of a genre whose conventions are already known and overly familiar. The installation attempts to occupy a site that is already crowded, already dictates its own urban and architectural logic. What determines—or overdetermines—this representational proximity, this affinity between the realm of aesthetics and the forms of commodification, particularly in relation to scale? I return to this question later.

The cinema was also understood at the time of its emergence in terms of scale—it was "bigger than life." The twentieth century will undoubtedly be seen as the era of the *cinematic* screen, a restricted and localized screen (situated primarily within a theatrical space). And this cinema was also characterized by a surprisingly stable screen and frame size throughout that century (the dominant frame ratio being that used by Thomas Edison for the Kinetoscope in 1889 and later standardized for the entire industry—1.33:1). In contrast, screen culture now has become strikingly heterogeneous and pervasive. Screen sizes now range from the miniature touch screen of the iPhone and iPad to the immense scale of IMAX. The small size of the iPhone is associated primarily with ideologies of individual agency and ownership as well as transportability, but with IMAX, size is the central and defining characteristic, so much so that the films themselves must entail subjects of a certain grandeur and ungraspability, self-reflexively conjuring narratives of magnitude. IMAX seems to have fulfilled the early cinematic aspirations associated with the phrase "bigger than life." The early history of IMAX was hence dominated by nature and exploration films, seemingly transcending the comparatively minute human scale of characters and plots. IMAX emerged from and originally found a home in world fairs and expositions as a performance of the capabilities of image technologies—the films were less about subjects than the very fact of the technology. Migrating to specialized venues associated with museums and science centers, the films were presented as an educational experience, often touristic (and imperialistic).[4]

The advertising rhetoric for IMAX reiterates and refashions that for wide screen in the 1950s and focuses on the concept of "immersion." "You," that is, the spectator, are not observing the space revealed on the screen—you are inside of it. For John Belton, the "illusion of limitless horizontal vision" in Cinerama and Cinemascope intensified the spectator's sense of immersion or absorption in the space of the film (much of the advertising for these processes emphasized the spatial relocation of the spectator from her seat to the world provided by the cinema).[5] IMAX ads as well insist that the spaces of film and spectator are confused and entangled. Objects or persons in the film reach out of the screen into the space of the audience, or the spectator is sucked into the world of the film, erasing all borders between representational space and the space of the viewer. In this scenario, there is no "offscreen space." All of the world has become media, and as a consequence, there is no mediation.

The paradox of IMAX is that its development and expansion in theaters coincided with the accelerating minimization of screen size—on computers, with QuickTime media player, laptops, and notepads, culminating in handheld mobile devices such as the iPhone. The iPhone is often seen as the descendant of the Newton MessagePad that emerged in the mid-1990s, and clearly the movement is toward diminutive size. But it is the touch screen that provided the true technological breakthrough, along with mobility and portability. Films are now viewable on the smallest of screens as well as the largest. Although David Lynch, in defense of the large screen, has categorically insisted (using various expletives) that if you view a film on an iPhone, you simply haven't seen the film,[6] the mobility of images is a pervasive cultural phenomenon that must be confronted. Perhaps it is not so much a question of whether it is the "same image" as of how technologies with such extreme differences of scale can inhabit the same media network. What is the work of "scale" in contemporary media, and how does it configure or reconfigure space, location, and subjectivity?

At first glance, the iPhone, unlike IMAX, would not seem to provide an immersive experience. Immersion connotes a transport of the subject into the image, and the iPhone appears to give its user an unprecedented control over the screen. But if immersion, with its alliance with water, fluids, liquidity, indexes an absorption in a substance that is overwhelming and all-encompassing, there is a sense in which the user of the iPhone could be described as immersed. In fact, this has been the social anxiety concerning iPhones—young people, absorbed in their iPhones, are lost to the world. They no longer have face-to-face conversations; they are no longer where they are. They have fled the real. This fear of the danger of iPhones is reminiscent of historical diatribes against the movies for their irresistible influence on young and malleable minds, particularly in relation to images of sex and violence. In the case of the iPhone, what is feared is a form of temporal and spatial immersion, absenting oneself from a specific time and location. The geography of the iPhone is that of "elsewhere," the elsewhere of an unmappable, uncognizable network.

Yet immersion is a very vague, imprecise analytical concept, and we should be suspicious of its easy transfer between advertising and journalistic discourses and critical theoretical discourses on the media. Immersion is used to describe the experience not only of IMAX but of new technologies, such as virtual imaging. It is the lure, the desire, the alleged fascination of the industry itself. But what does it mean to be immersed? And why is it the focus of a contemporary desire? Obviously figural, the tropology denies the physical location of the spectator. I propose to read the concept of immersion as symptomatic, as a claim that points to a work of spatial restructuring in a screen-saturated social economy.

IMAX is about excess—one of its movie theater intros deploys the traditional movie countdown from ten to one (which gradually enlarges the numbers until they become gigantic) and inserts the words "See more, hear more, feel more," ending with the IMAX slogan "Think Big." The largest IMAX screen is in Sydney, Australia, and is approximately eight stories high. IMAX screens can be ten times the size of a traditional cinema screen. The clarity and resolution of the image are made possible by a frame size that dwarfs that of conventional 70mm film (three times larger). With the perforations placed horizontally rather than vertically, the film must run through the projector at extremely elevated speeds. The very high resolution of the image allows spectators to be positioned closer to the screen. In a typical IMAX theater, the seats are set at a significantly steeper grade, and all rows are within one screen height, whereas in a conventional movie theater, all rows can be within eight to twelve screen heights. As Allan Stegeman points out in an article claiming that IMAX and other large-screen formats can compete effectively with high-definition television, "the large-screen format effectively destroys the viewer's awareness of the film's actual frame line."[7]

It is this annihilation of the frame line on which I would like to focus here. Whereas Cinemascope claimed to compete with the spectator's peripheral vision, IMAX and other large formats attempt to exceed the eye in all dimensions so that the image appears to be uncontained. The frame in cinema is not only a technical necessity adjudicating the relation to temporality (24 fps) and the production of an illusion of motion but also a link between cinema and the history of Western painting, particularly in its inscription of perspective as a rule of space. The frame demarcates the space of the representation as a special place, one that obeys different dictates for legibility. Or, as Jacques Derrida has pointed out, the frame as parergon is neither part of the work nor outside the work but gives rise to the work.[8] The frame is the condition of possibility of representation. In the history of cinema, the frame lends to the film's composition a containment and a limit that rivaled the limit of the two-dimensional surface of the screen. Both could be contested, but the frame and the screen were themselves activated to produce the concepts of off-screen space and depth of field as domains of the imaginary.

If the frame constitutes a limit—a fully visible limit—in the experience of the spectator in conventional cinema, what does it mean to remove that limit by using technology to exceed the physiological limits of the spectator's vision? IMAX clearly has limits, but they are not of a visible order in the spectator's experience. It strives against limits, as seen in an ad from the IMAX corporation: "People say our screen curves down at the edges. It doesn't. That's the earth." The limit of the IMAX screen merges with that of the earth, which is to say that it has no artificial or cultural limit. What is the lure of this idea of boundlessness?

In the history of aesthetic theory, this concept has been most frequently associated with that of the sublime in its philosophical formulation, and that term has been resuscitated in discussions of IMAX. In Edmund Burke's analysis, in which "sublime objects are vast in their dimensions," the eye is given a privileged position, standing in metonymically for the entire body ("as in this discourse we chiefly attach ourselves to the sublime, as it affects the eye").[9] For Burke, the sublime is associated with passion, awe, and terror and with a pain that proves to be pleasurable. And this abstraction of pain from pleasure is in many instances a bodily phenomenon—both terror and pain "produce a tension, contraction or violent emotion of the nerves."[10] This is the sublime, as long as any possibility of actual danger is removed. In a section of the book entitled "Why Visual Objects of Great Dimension Are Sublime," Burke buttresses his argument with a detailed discussion of the physiology of the eye, particularly its susceptibility to a kind of violent stimulation, a forceful impression on the retina produced by the light emanating from all points of the object seen.

Hence the sublime, in one of its earliest formulations, is conceptualized as an assault on the eye. Paul Virilio has referred to IMAX as "cataract surgery," designed to rescue the cinema from the proliferation of small screens by, in effect, welding the eye to the technology.[11] From another point of view, the visual field of the IMAX film, overwhelming that of the spectator, is an assault on the eye, exceeding its capacities in a sheer demonstration of imagistic power. But why should pain and even terror produce the particular pleasure associated with the sublime? For Kant, it is a pleasure that can only be produced through a detour, and it is the detour that causes pain preparatory to the pleasure of discovering the power and extension of reason.

Pain is produced as a result of a striking impression of human inadequacy, finitude. Nature—the ocean, a vast mountainous landscape, a tremendous thunderstorm—may be the occasion for the sense of the sublime, according to Kant, but none of these can be designated as a "sublime object" because the sublime is an attribute of subjectivity. And it is, ultimately, a correlative of the realization of the simultaneous possibility and impossibility of a finite representation of the infinite. Apprehension falls short, and while the subject cannot comprehend the notion of the infinite—imagination is inevitably inadequate—it grasps its own sensuous and imaginative inadequacy as a failure that is nullified by reason—the ability, that is, to form a concept of infinity as totality. It is the faculty of the subject that is unlimited, so that infinity resides not in the world—which would be threatening and incomprehensible—but instead as a power within the subject. This is entirely consistent, as I try to demonstrate later, with the representation of the subject's relation to infinity within the system of Quattrocento perspective. Hence the sublime is produced under the pressure to hold the infinite in thought, to conceptualize it as a totality. The fact that this is possible is for Kant a validation of the superiority of reason, of its movement beyond the sensuous—it is "supersensual." This, in turn, is a validation of the human, of the ability of human reason to exceed the boundaries or limitations of its spatiotemporal localization. Infinity, in a sense, resides within the subject. But the "unlimited faculty" (i.e., reason) is based on lack/inadequacy.

Hence the concept of the sublime grapples with the notion of infinity and its representability, although this is not the term Kant would have used. Yet there is another way of thinking and representing infinity that is not usually articulated with the sublime. Renaissance perspective, inherited by the cinema, constitutes infinity as a point—a perpetually receding point, the vanishing point—which mirrors the position of the subject contemplating the painting. Like Kant's reason in at least one respect, it acts as an imprimatur of a mastery that takes form by going beyond, even annihilating, the subject's sensory and spatiotemporal localization, all the singularities/particularities of embodiment in a finite body limited by the reach of its senses. At least this reading of perspective is that of apparatus theory in film studies, the legacy of Jean-Louis Baudry, Jean-Louis Comolli, and others in the 1970s. And it is that of Erwin Panofsky as well. Panofsky analyzed Renaissance perspective as the symptom and instantiation of a new concept—that of infinity, embodied in the vanishing point.[12] Yet this was a representational infinity that confirmed and reassured the human subject, replacing a theocracy with an individualizing humanism. In a way, it could be seen as a secularization of the sublime.

Perspective produces an illusion of depth in the image—potentially endless depth guaranteed by the vanishing point marking the "place" of infinity. It allows for the simulation of the three-dimensional on a two-dimensional surface. However, both modernity and postmodernity have been characterized as a regime of the surface, a decimation of depth. As Fredric Jameson has famously written, "a new kind of flatness or depthlessness, a new kind of superficiality in the most literal sense [is] perhaps the supreme formal feature of all the postmodernisms."[13] How, or is, the infinite thought or represented in such a context? Where is the sublime? In a provocative essay entitled "Notes on Surface: Toward a Genealogy of Flatness," David Joselit has argued that, in the case of painting, illusionistic recession has been transposed into lateral extension. He cites Clement Greenberg, who claims that the abstract expressionists utilized huge canvases to compensate for the spatial loss of illusionistic depth.[14] And, indeed, this lateral extension can be seen in the movement toward larger and larger screens culminating in IMAX but also in the embedding of smaller screens, such as the iPhone, in complex and extensive networks whose scope and scale are challenges to individual comprehension. The intricacy of these networks contributes to what Jameson has labeled the problem of cognitive mapping. This suggests that infinity is no longer conceptualizable in relation to depth and recession, as in a humanist perspectival system, but instead in relation to questions of scale, extension, and uncognizable networks. For a network, in theory, has no closure. This heralds not a break with the disembodiment or delocalization of perspectival illusionism but a shifting or displacement of the subject's relation to space, scale, and location that shares with Kant's sublime a lack in relation to knowledge and imagination. From Joselit's point of view, the increasing emphasis on surface and flatness in aesthetic representation cannot be divorced from late capitalism's production of the self as image, as a commodity of surfaces. In other words, there is a conflation of psychological and optical flatness that generates a politics of the visualizable self and motivates the incessant work of the stereotype (whether racial, sexual, ethnic, etc.).

The *Oxford English Dictionary* defines *sublime* as "set or raised aloft, high up" and traces its etymology to the Latin *sublimis,* a combination of *sub* (up to) and *limen* ("lintel," literally the top piece of a door). The sublime is consistently defined by philosophers in relation to concepts of largeness, height, greatness, magnitude. For Burke, visual objects of "great dimension" are sublime. Kant claims, "Sublime is the name given to what is absolutely great" and "the infinite is absolutely (not merely comparatively) great." The sublime is associated with formlessness, boundlessness, and excess beyond limit. It is not surprising in this context that IMAX has been analyzed by invoking the concept of the sublime (Haidee Wasson and Alison Griffiths refer to Burke's sublime in particular), especially insofar as the terror associated with the sublime, for both Burke and Kant, must be experienced from a position of safety.[15] The sublime is an aesthetic category, and it is inevitably chained to affect—whether awe, terror, pleasure, or fear, and most frequently a combination of these. The advertising and the analysis of IMAX are obsessed with its involvement of the subject in a gripping experience—hence the discourse of immersion. IMAX is described as above all a visceral experience, requiring a form of bodily participation. Unlike the disembodiment of the classical perspectival system, the body seems to be what is above all at stake in discourses on IMAX. The IMAX sublime, if there is such a thing, here deviates from Kant's, for whom the sublime was sublime only on condition that it exceeded the sensuous, proclaimed the irrelevance of the subject's spatiotemporal presence in favor of the infinite grasp of reason. The discourse of immersion would seem to rescue the body from its nullification by both Renaissance perspective and the Kantian sublime, making us once again present to ourselves.[16]

But I would like to argue that immersion as a category is symptomatic, and one has to ask what this body is. The body here is a bundle of senses—primarily vision, hearing, and touch. But this appeal to the body as sensory experience, as the satiation of all the claims for its pleasure, does not revive an access to spatiotemporal presence or localization. Instead, it radically delocalizes the subject once again, grasping for more to see, more to hear, more to feel, in an ever-expanding elsewhere. IMAX emerged from the world fairs and expos that constituted exhibitionistic displays of the expanding powers of technology (what David Nye has called the "technological sublime"). It is telling that one of the works of this early tendency toward magnification of the scale of the image and proliferation of screens was the Eameses' iconic *Powers of Ten* (1977). This pedagogical film illustrates a movement from a couple having a picnic in Chicago to the edge of the universe and back to the interior of the body by exponentially increasing the "camera's" distance from the couple, reversing the trajectory, and decreasing that distance to the point of inhabiting the body itself, delimiting its cells, its atoms, and their quarks. The human body would seem to be central to this demonstration, primarily as a marker of scale and as the threshold of a trajectory from the gigantic to the infinitesimally small. Yet the film is instead an allegory of the nullification of the body and its location, acting only as a nostalgic citation of a time when the human body was the ground and reference for measurement, replacing it with a mechanical mathematical formula for the progressions of scale. The limits of the "camera's" trip in both directions are, of course, the limits of human knowledge—at the moment. But the film suggests that this movement is infinitely extendable, and it is not accidental that technologies of knowledge and technologies of the image are inseparable here. Human vision, with the aid of imaging technologies, is infinitely extendable, and knowledge is embedded in that vision. But I have spoken only of the represented body, not of the spectatorial body. The spectatorial eye is fully aligned with the technological eye—not with the vision of the represented "characters," the man and the woman—and its travels are limited only by the current state of technologies of imaging/knowledge. Yet there is a sense not only that it is disembodied or delocalized but that it is potentially everywhere.

I would like briefly to discuss here another, quite different film, one that is also not an IMAX film but could be said to have IMAX aspirations and at the same time struggles with earlier modes of representation. Like *Powers of Ten*, Terence Malick's *Tree of Life* (2011) strives to articulate the everyday with the grandeur and sublimity of the universe. Sections of *Tree of Life* were filmed in IMAX and originally designed to be exhibited separately in IMAX theaters. But the film was released in traditional theaters and included these sections, whose only gain from IMAX filming was increased resolution but not scale. The film makes ample use of what I would call the "IMAX shot," inevitably a point-of-view shot moving forward toward the horizon, over a cliff, or down a waterfall, and so on. This is in effect a simulation of a point-of-view shot, an impossible point-of-view shot that is thereby depsychologized. It is also one of the primary generators of the discourse of immersion. In *Tree of Life,* it is accompanied by shots reminiscent of educational nature IMAX films but clearly deployed here to evoke the sublime. These are the "birth of the universe shots," often accompanied by moving and swelling classical or religious music—here, Zbigniew Preisner's *Requiem for My Friend.* Malick refused to use computer-generated imagery (CGI) to produce his cosmic special effects and instead achieved them by returning to techniques reminiscent of those utilized in the early years of the cinema: milk through funnels, various chemicals, fluorescent dyes, CO_2, smoke, unidentifiable objects shot so closely that they seem gigantic and overwhelming.[17] Similarly, *Battle of Manila Bay* (1898) was shot with toy boats in a bathtub. This is a form of special effect that exploited the spectator's inability to ascertain dimension, her failure to negotiate imagistic space with respect to the scale of everyday life. The illegibility of the distance between camera and object is translated into that between spectator and image. *Tree of Life* is in many ways about scale—both temporal and spatial. Eons in the life of the universe are juxtaposed with memories of a single lifetime. In the sense that they strive to represent the unrepresentable, they inhabit the problematic of the sublime. But this is not the sublime of Burke or Kant, though it has affinities with them. Malick's sublime is also lodged within the family scenes, which are curiously decontextualized. Within the diegesis of memory, time is fractured in the service of a significant condensation often aimed toward the production of affect. Jump cuts are consistently deployed, the film's dialogue is truncated and inarticulate, and the images sometimes seem as impossible as those of the cosmic sequences. The cinematic techniques of the narrative partake of the same condensation of time and evocation of awe as those of the cosmic sequences—to make individual memory as sublime as the infinite wonder of the cosmos. As an effect of this, the narrative scenes seem dislocated, derealized, but nevertheless, or perhaps as a consequence, sublime.

Yet these images, in their sublimity, are not far removed, particularly at certain points in the depiction of the mother, from those of commercial advertising, which also strives to package life into moments of condensed bliss. Movement becomes life in a form of instantaneous gesture that aims at reproducibility, distributability, and a common consensus of the good life. At these moments, the sublime appears to be in collusion with the commodity form. According to Jean-François Lyotard,

> there is something of the sublime in capitalist economy . . . It is, in a sense, an economy regulated by an Idea—infinite wealth or power. It does not manage to present any example from reality to verify this Idea. In making science subordinate to itself through technologies, especially those of language, it only succeeds, on the contrary, in making reality increasingly ungraspable, subject to doubt, unsteady. . . . Hidden in the cynicism of innovation is certainly the despair that nothing further will happen. But innovating means to behave as though lots of things happened, and to make them happen. Through innovation, the will affirms its hegemony over time. It thus conforms to the metaphysics of capital, which is a technology of time.[18]

Capitalism's collusion with the sublime, particularly in its insistent innovation in the realm of technology, and especially technologies of imaging, does not mean that the concept of the sublime is inevitably complicit. Malick, in *Tree of Life*, is no doubt attempting to resist the capitalist logic of innovation as well as commercialism's hollowing out and abstraction of the image. The film resuscitates a heavily theological discourse, locating its thinking of infinity there, grasping for a way to deal with indeterminacy and to produce a sublime that is outside of capitalism's hegemonic hold over time. Yet the veering of its images toward those of advertising should act as a warning of the vulnerability of the logic of the sublime—especially of attempting to locate the sublime in everyday life—to the spatiotemporal coordinates of commodification. For the logic of the IMAX sublime—perhaps the technological sublime par excellence—is also harnessed to that of capitalism in another way, insofar as it operates under the umbrella of the discourse of immersion, producing an illusion that depth and ready access to the body are still with us and concealing its radical delocalization and dislocation of a subject seemingly empowered in the face of a world defined as infinite extension.

Jim Campbell's *Portrait of My Father* and *Photo of My Mother* give the photographic image a central role, but only in its juxtaposition or clash with another mode of recording—one previously viewed not as aesthetic but perhaps as medical: that of the breath, the heartbeat. The work's temporality becomes that of the body, or perhaps the body becomes a kind of medium (in a manner quite different from that of French performance artist Orlan). In this sense, the work is witness to (and a participant in) the hemorrhage of the aesthetic, its transfer to any-material-whatever.

This crisis of the aesthetic has been remarked by Jameson, who claims that any notion of the image as art has been assimilated by the logic of commodification and, in tandem with this, everything in daily life has become aestheticized, leaving the concept no effectivity whatsoever in an "age of the world picture."[19] Everyday life is saturated with images, screens, and recorded sound. Donald Judd and Robert Morris have spoken of the exhaustion of the rectangle of painting. There was only so much one could do within its confines, and therefore it was crucial to expand the concept of the work to include real space. The screen is a rectangle as well—one whose aspect ratio has remained remarkably standardized for decades. But in screen culture, as opposed to museum culture, the response is not to frame art differently, to expand or surpass its frame or renegotiate its objects, but to disengage the screen from the theatrical space and disseminate it everywhere. So here we are dealing not with the exhaustion of the rectangle but with its transport—the screens of YouTube, of cell phones, of television and computers, and even the gigantic screens of the walls of buildings in Tokyo, Hong Kong, New York. The anxiety attached to medium saturation points to a critical realignment of the concept of infinity—in which everything is infinitely representable, screenable. For Panofsky, Renaissance perspective was a sign of the historical emergence and dominance of a new way of thinking about space in relation to infinity, in which a single point—the vanishing point—took on a critical importance.[20] This was the condition of possibility of a reassuring stabilization of the human subject as point of view, as agent of the seen. In an age of the proliferation of screens, the concept of infinity has been reconfigured—it exists not in the depths of the image but in its expansion, its seemingly endless extension, its occupation of almost any site. This representational infinity, far from reassuring, provokes an anxiety about the body and its difficult negotiation of space.

Campbell's *Portrait of My Father* and *Photo of My Mother* intervene in this mediatic network. The artist's pulse and rate of breathing are not any-material-whatever. They are traces of the body—that which feels and senses. For Clement Greenberg, the medium is the point of contact with the real, the physical, that which makes art *sensual,* that is, aesthetic. Another reading of Campbell's work would situate it as a demonstration that the body is the medium par excellence, always already implicated in the deciphering of photography as a trace of time—there and not there, in the image. For the body of the viewer of Campbell's work is necessarily involved in its temporality (which is the temporality of the artist's body)—with the appearance and disappearance or alternate blurring and focusing of the image the work forces its viewer to *strain* to see. And in that straining, the viewer is made cognizant, again, of the work, the very presence of the body, not as immersed in a simulated sensory universe but as a resistance and as subject itself to technological measure/recording, as part of a network that is only legible in flickering moments.

Notes

1. Siegfried Kracauer, "Photography," in *The Mass Ornament: Weimar Essays,* trans. and ed. Thomas Y. Levin (Cambridge, Mass.: Harvard University Press, 1995), 49; Walter Benjamin, "A Small History of Photography," in *"One-Way Street," and Other Writings,* trans. Edmund Jephcott and Kingsley Shorter (London: NLB, 1979), 243.

2. E. M. Forster, *Collected Tales of E. M. Forster,* cited in John Raskin, *The Mythology of Imperialism: A Revolutionary Critique of British Literature and Society in the Modern Age* (New York: Random House, 1971), 36.

3. Matthew Tanteri, quoted in C. C. Sullivan, "Design Focus: Chanel Ginza, Tokyo," *Architectural Lighting,* June 27, 2007, http://www.archlighting.com/retail -projects/chanel-ginza--tokyo.aspx.

4. See Charles Acland, "IMAX Technology and the Tourist Gaze," *Cultural Studies* 12, no. 3 (1998): 429–45.

5. John Belton, *Widescreen Cinema* (Cambridge, Mass.: Harvard University Press, 1992), 197.

6. Brittney Gilbert, "David Lynch on iPhone," January 4, 2018, YouTube video, 0:30, https://youtu.be/wKiIroiCvZo.

7. Allan Stegeman, "The Large-Screen Film: A Viable Entertainment Alternative to High Definition Television," *Journal of Film and Video* 26, no. 2 (1984): 24.

8. Jacques Derrida, *The Truth in Painting,* trans. Geoffrey Bennington and Ian McLeod (Chicago: University of Chicago Press, 1987), 23.

9. Edmund Burke, *A Philosophical Enquiry into the Origin of Our Ideas of the Sublime and Beautiful* (Oxford: Oxford University Press, 1990), 113, 128, Kindle.

10. Burke, 120.

11. Paul Virilio, "Cataract Surgery: Cinema in the Year 2000," trans. Annie Fatet and Annette Kuhn, in *Alien Zone: Cultural Theory and Contemporary Science Fiction Cinema,* ed. Annette Kuhn, 169–74 (New York: Verso, 1990).

12. See Erwin Panofsky, *Perspective as Symbolic Form,* trans. Christopher S. Wood (New York: Zone Books, 1997).

13. Frederic Jameson, *Postmodernism, or the Cultural Logic of Late Capitalism* (Durham, N.C.: Duke University Press, 1990), 9.

14. See David Joselit, "Notes on Surface: Toward a Genealogy of Flatness," *Art History* 23, no. 1 (2000): 19–34.

15. See Haidee Wasson, "The Networked Screen: Moving Images, Materiality, and the Aesthetics of Size," in *Fluid Screens, Expanded Cinema,* ed. Janine Marchessault and Susan Lord (Toronto: University of Toronto Press, 2007), 85, and Alison Griffiths, *Shivers Down Your Spine: Cinema, Museums, and the Immersive View* (New York: Columbia University Press, 2008), 108.

16. In one of the most extended and detailed studies of IMAX to date, Alison Whitney, "The Eye of Daedalus: A History and Theory of IMAX Cinema" (PhD diss., University of Chicago, 2005) argues strenuously that the spectator's body is very much involved in IMAX. She links this to a number of factors, including the fact that the heads of other spectators are continually visible, acting as a measure of scale and reminding the spectator of her own body's location in a theater. In the case of IMAX 3D, the space of the screen invades that of the spectator so that the only measure of scale becomes the spectator's own body. And finally, there is a kind of self-consciousness or self-awareness built into IMAX and IMAX 3D: "Just as the design of IMAX theaters asks you to contemplate your position and role as a spectator, the 3D film asks you to question the precise nature of your binocular visual experience, and consider the extent to which your senses must work to render an intelligible image of the world. This notion of perceptual labor being part of the viewer's responsibility relates closely to IMAX's notion of the involved, active spectator" (126). Whitney is insistent that the spectator is always aware of being both in the diegetic world and in the auditorium, "in the IMAX theater itself, where viewers are continually reminded of their roles and responsibilities in the production and reception of images" (132). It strikes me as unlikely that spectators have any sense of "roles and responsibilities in the production and reception of images," and this and her invocation of an "involved, active spectator" are part of a larger strategy in the discipline to resist any notion of ideological positioning by the apparatus. I would argue, on the contrary, that whether or not the spectator is aware of being in an auditorium (and this is inarguable but not really what is at issue), the work of the film and of discourses about IMAX is to lure the spectator into another space, to delocalize her in the interests of an "absorbing" diegesis, not to provoke any critical analysis. It is interesting that while Whitney insists on the spectator's continual awareness of her location in the

theater, she speaks of the other "there" of the diegesis in much the same terms. She also treats 3D as though its effects were always "emergent" (out of the screen rather than into it). See Kristen Whissel on positive and negative parallax in "Parallax Effects: Epistemology, Affect and Digital 3D Cinema," *Journal of Visual Culture* 15, no. 2 (2016).

17. Douglas Trumball, cited in Hugh Hart, "Video: *Tree of Life* Visualizes the Cosmos without CGI," *Wired,* June 17, 2011, http://www.wired.com/underwire/2011/06/tree-of-life-douglas-trumbull/.

18. Jean-François Lyotard, *The Inhuman* (Stanford, Calif.: Stanford University Press, 1991), 105–7.

19. Fredric Jameson, "Transformations of the Image in Postmodernity," in *The Cultural Turn: Selected Writings on the Postmodern, 1983–1998*, 99–113 (New York: Verso, 1998).

20. See Panofsky, *Perspective as Symbolic Form.*

2

A Countergenealogy of the Movie Screen; or, Film's Expansion Seen from the Past

Francesco Casetti

About Cinema and Its Lineages

When we discuss cinema's future—its possible death, its current trans-formations, and its potential afterlife—we tend to think of cinema as a visual medium. We focus on images and the alleged consequences of their digitalization at the expense of other, versatile aspects of the cine-matic dispositive.[1] This is especially true when we speak of the movie screen. Despite the fact that the optical connotation of the word *screen* is quite recent—it emerged only in the second half of the eighteenth cen-tury in connection with devices like the microscope, the magic lantern, and the Phantasmagoria[2]—we often consider the screen as a mere back-ground or support to visual data.[3] In doing so, we marginalize other and early meanings of the word *screen*—which could describe a shelter pro-tecting against fire and air, a partition dividing a room, a device sieving grain, or a wall masking a facade[4]—as if these meanings had long disap-peared behind the horizon of the movie screen. Likewise, we also forget the fact that the movie screen is a physical object whose material proper-ties (texture, size, allocation) affect both the quality of images that spec-tators perceive and the configuration of the setting in which spectators dwell—including their mode of physically accessing a film. Traditional film theories—especially the Western theoretical canon—have favored these omissions. The screen was generally seen as ancillary to images and was consequently excluded from the key elements that define film's essence; the French critic Élie Faure did so openly in his influential 1920s volume *The Art of Cineplastics*.[5] And when it was mentioned, the screen was usually associated with one of two metaphors, the *window* or the *mirror*. Both metaphors refer to an object that is at the service of the eyes and that vanishes under what it displays.[6]

Against this backdrop, I retrace some lateral, but not necessarily marginal, film theories that speak of the screen in very different terms. Mostly European, and dated between the second and eighth decades of the twentieth century—a period coincident with film's golden age—these theories contend that the screen is a *slate* that physically inscribes a peculiar kind of trace, an *installation* that organizes a space around it, a porous surface that actively *filters* the represented world, a *protection* that keeps audiences safe from dangers, a *partition* separating the actual and the fictional worlds, and a surface that *conceals* a hidden reality. By recovering these alternative definitions—which were often presented in utopian tones, and yet which uncovered still latent or still unnoticed modes of the screen's existence—we can construct a new *genealogy*[7] of the movie screen: one whose foundation depends not only on the need to let an image be shown but also on functions and practices related to the screen's materiality and setting, and which consequently keeps its door open to the primitive meanings of the word.

Such a countergenealogy of the screen has two main implications. On one hand, it can regain what has been long denied: normally thought of as a purely visual art, cinema can now be seen as a spatial medium as well. Indeed, as spectators well know, whenever and wherever they watch a movie, they define a center of attention, they take place in front of it, they outline (and challenge) edges beyond which the vision changes mode, they create privileged (and unprivileged) zones of attendance, and so on. The creation of "viewing positions"[8] is not the only way in which cinema works within and upon the space. The ideas of installation, filter, protection, partition, and cover-up precisely help to unearth the full range of actions that film performs toward the environment in which it operates.

On the other hand, this countergenealogy allows us to reconsider the current explosion of screens. Many of them clearly move beyond the merely visual dimension. Surveillance monitors reinforce the division between an exterior and an interior and control passage from the former to the latter. Handheld devices help to create an existential bubble where users can find an intimacy and a refuge, even in public. The Global Positioning System parses the territory and identifies right and wrong routes. Pixelated media-facades envelop entire buildings and hide them from view. Contemporary screens restore the original functions of the screen; they are again a kind of filter, shelter, spatial divide, or camouflage. The very fact that these basic functions were never completely alien to cinema suggests some links between cinema and more recent media. This does not mean that cinema is the "father" of all the new media:[9] lineages are not based on sole and direct causes; they are instead rhizomatic connections that involve several and disparate points, without necessary primacies. This means that cinema, sometimes against any evidence, is nevertheless part of the new media's roots. As a consequence, not only can new media regain a new perception of their own descent but cinema can also find itself in unexpected devices. The screen's countergenealogy provides some good reasons for film's expansion.

The Variable Screen

We can find a first deviation from the dominant theoretical canon in an ironical short essay published in 1918 in the elegant film magazine *In Penombra* by the Italian critic Emanuele Toddi.[10] Toddi noted that frames change their content but not their ratio: their size on the filmstrip is always 25 × 19 millimeters. This proportion is completely arbitrary, since the human eye narrows or widens the perceptual field according to our interest in observed reality. The camera's lenses are a substitute or an "emissary" of the human eye—referring to the civil law, Toddi calls them a sort of *longus oculus*, a "long eye." Consequently, he argues, movies should be able to offer the audience different kinds of ratios: "a car racing through a twisting street" demands an oblong frame to correspond to the long stretches of the road, instead of the usual square. Different kinds of ratios imply a *variable screen*: the canvas has to be larger, but the rays must hit different portions of it. This would give to the filmmaker the opportunity to express his own vision: "the perimeter that he gives to a particular scene can essentially be an interpretation of it."[11] At the same time, the screen would become more functional: "There are frames for which the

entire screen has a desolate, Saharan vastness, while for others it is nar-
row: the first want to be enclosed in a small, intimate frame, the others
want to be projected beyond the walls of the theater or to descend, down
to the viewers' feet."[12] Spectators would gain in enjoyment and truth. And
the screen would acquire an active role.

Toddi's suggestion would find a sequel in the famed lecture given by
Sergei M. Eisenstein in front of the Academy of Motion Picture Arts and
Sciences in 1930.[13] Eisenstein, who likely did not directly know of Toddi's
essay, partly followed his steps: he too proposed a variable screen ready
to adjust itself to the content of the frame. Leaving aside the comparison
between the two contributions, Toddi's and Eisenstein's suggestions of a
variable screen matter because they highlighted a characteristic that the
classical film theories tended to deny: far from being a simple "accessory," as Faure called it, the screen owns an agency that enables it to play
a crucial role.

The Page, the Slate—and Other Kinds of Surfaces

Another step toward a full recognition of the screen's role was brought
about by the French Italian critic Ricciotto Canudo—one of the key figures
in the early film theories. In his "Reflection on the Seventh Art," written
in the early 1920s, Canudo retraced the origins of cinema in the act of
writing. Moving images, he suggested, are ultimately an attempt "to arrest
the fleeting aspects of life," as letters of the alphabet do, "so others could
know them."[14] Hence a consequent metaphor: "the screen, this single-
paged book as unique and infinite as the life itself, permits the world—
both internal and external—to be imprinted on its surface."[15] The screen
is where we record in its singularity and completeness what otherwise we
lose, in an attempt to "triumph over the ephemeral and over death."[16]

At the time, other voices associated film with the act of writing:[17]
Canudo's metaphor had the merit of making clear that we need a physical "medium" for film, in the same sense that Greenberg speaks of canvas
as a "medium" of painting.[18] An image needs a surface that supports it: if
we write with light, as movies do, we cannot avoid dealing with a screen.[19]
Yet the metaphor also carried more radical connotations. In 1926, the surrealist critic Robert Desnos devoted a striking passage to the movie screen:

"a true masterpiece would be the one in which a spectator shoots the canvas instead of the villain character, or one, unfortunately utopian, in which the projectionist is able to reveal traces of kisses on the screen."[20] Here the screen is still a surface that retains traces of reality—a *slate* more than a page of a book. What changes is the extension of its action. On one hand, the screen can ideally record the presence of the environment in which the film is screened—in this case, spectators' kisses. It can even be scratched by these environmental presences—the bullets that pierce the canvas. On the other hand, the screen's own presence can be integrated into the story that the movie tells: the spectator's violent reaction is ultimately part of the action orchestrated by the filmmaker—as Desnos claims in another passage, where he includes the audience among the means of expression in the hands of a true director.[21] In this sense, Desnos's screen is not just a repository; it is the centerpiece of an apparatus that can take unexpected and extreme directions. The Surrealists' pleasure consisted exactly of this unexpectedness and extremism.[22]

We can find equally radical proposals, though differently oriented, in the work of the theorist-artist Lázló Moholy-Nagy. I will limit myself to just a few remarks. In his *Painting, Photography, Film,* Moholy-Nagy envisioned new arrangements for the screen, all aimed at underscoring its presence and action.[23] A first proposal consisted in the transformation of "the normal projection plane . . . into differently obliquely positioned planes and cambers, like a landscape of mountains and valleys."[24] The image projected on such a surface undergoes unexpected and expressive distortions. A second proposal included a screen "in the shape of a segment of sphere instead of the present rectangular one. . . . More than one film (perhaps two in the first trials) would be played on this projection screen; and they would not, indeed, be projected on to a fixed spot but would range continually from left to right or from right to left, up and down, down and up, etc."[25] The image projected on this screen is not only deformed; it is also unstable.

Moholy-Nagy's subsequent volume, titled *The New Vision* in English,[26] brought things even further. What if a screen were called to reflect not a beam of light directed to it but everything that comes from the surroundings? Moholy-Nagy was fascinated by this idea of a sensitive screen. He found an antecedent in Kazimir Malevich's *Suprematist Composition:*

White on White (1918): "Malevich's last picture, the plain white surface, . . . constituted an ideal plan for kinetic light and shadow effects which, originating in the surroundings, would fall upon it. In this way, Malevich's picture represented a miniature cinema screen."[27] Hence a final step: if a screen can or even must reflect its environment, many components of an environment can become a screen. Two kinds of artworks may exemplify such a possibility. On one hand, we can conceive of "projections on the clouds or other gaseous backgrounds through which one can walk, drive, fly, etc." On the other hand, we can use "simultaneous displays, either by means of an increased number of projectors concentrated on a single screen, or in the form of simultaneous image sequences covering all the walls of a room."[28] The screen explodes and becomes ubiquitous.

It is easy to read in Moholy-Nagy's proposals the anticipation of some of the works that characterize our current art landscape. What matters here is something else: in Moholy-Nagy, as well as in Desnos and at least partially in Canudo, the screen is still a surface that supports the images, but its action implies an increasing interplay between it and the environment in which it operates. On one hand, the screen is affected by the human environment (Desnos); on the other hand, the screen transforms and appropriates the physical environment (Moholy-Nagy). As a consequence, the screen has not only an agency, it also possesses its own sphere of action.[29]

An Altarpiece and an Installation

An iconic metaphor proposed in the same years by the Italian film theorist Antonello Gerbi casts further light on the reevaluation of the screen that we are examining. Published in 1926, Gerbi's "Introduction to the Delights of Cinema" is an extraordinary meditation on film experience and an extensive analysis of the movie screen.[30] When not hit by the beam of light, Gerbi writes, the screen is meaningless: "Devoid of images, the screen is so stupid and useless that it is irritating. It doesn't justify itself. It doesn't explain itself."[31] Once the projection starts, a true transformation occurs. "What was a large bandage strewn with talcum powder is reborn as an altarpiece for the liturgies of the new times." Spectators, like believers, follow the spectacle in awe. "The entire altarpiece miraculously and restlessly, varies color, trembles, grows pale, flees into the background, comes up close right under the nose of the worshipper in the close ups, passes through a number of hurried and temporary reincarnations, and modifies its face and soul a hundred times a minute."[32] Immersed in such an intense vision, the audience is prone to images: "we are ready to receive the new Epiphany."[33]

Gerbi offers other provoking allegories to define the screen.[34] Yet the idea of the *altarpiece* is quite striking. Indeed, while keeping the visual dimension of the screen, the metaphor changes the screen's usual meaning. Compared, for example, with the window, the altarpiece is something to be looked *at,* not *through*; something that orients observers toward the interior of a building or a room, not toward an external space; and something that spreads images around, more than letting them come in. Visibility depends on a point of attraction, against which the other components of the situation define their own position, and ultimately the entire configuration of the space takes shape. This very nature of physical insertion in a context makes the screen a true *installation,* that is, an element located in a space and aimed at organizing its sensorial, physical, and behavioral structure.

The metaphor can also recall a minor yet revelatory text by Sergei M. Eisenstein. In a personal note, dated from December 28, 1927, on the failed film project *Glass House,*[35] Eisenstein wished for an opening night when his movie would be projected on a gigantic screen: "May be for the opening /// Let's try—Écran monstre. A screen surface four times as large. Why not???"[36] This *écran monstre* has some qualities of an installation: it imposes its presence on the space of screening, and it reshapes its usual layout. The meaning and functions of such a screen become clear when we look at the entire project of *Glass House*. The film intended to depict the social life of a building whose walls were transparent: after the first moment of excitation, as inhabitants shed their mutual indifference and start looking at each other, the situation becomes progressively unbearable. There are people who go unnoticed and die alone, passions that spring out of control, and an increasingly "panicked desire to hide oneself": the only solution is to destroy the building.[37] Keeping the film's plot in mind, we can interpret Eisenstein's fantasy for the film's opening night as an attempt to redouble the tension between a total transparency and an impending blindness. The gigantic screen may have provided a condition of enlarged visibility, but it also would have made viewing the film difficult—if not impossible—because of the excessive size of the screen's surface. The experience of spectatorship was to emulate both the excitement and the frustration of the Glass House's residents. In this process, the screen, once again, would bear witness to the contradictions elicited by any optical device: in displaying a world in plain sight, it becomes a black hole for our eyes.

The Porous Surface

So far, I have covered theoretical interventions that, while still focusing on the screen as the background or the support to images, tried to give back to the screen an active role within the cinematic dispositive and an ability to interact with the environment. The recognition of these two characteristics resulted in a reconsideration of the film's visibility: the screen is not only necessarily a transparent surface. In the next pages, I explore a number of contributions—sparks of theory more than theories in a proper sense—that made an attempt to go beyond the idea of support, on behalf of other roles that the screen can play, as a filter, a divide, a shelter, or a camouflage. These roles—which recall the traditional functions covered by the preoptical screen—make the film's visibility even more controversial.

The Austrian writer Joseph Roth, who during the 1920s had a brilliant career as a film critic, wrote many essayistic pieces privileging his own experience of being at the movies over the film he had seen. A recurring sensation was that the fictional world was able to intrude in the real world through the porous fabric of the screen. In "Praterkino," he described how the fictional characters literally move toward the auditorium. "An inexplicable event did happen: the woman sitting on my left side now holds a smoking gun, she sprays bullets, she is the waitress in a saloon of the wild west, her boss is the cinema's doorman, the one with the cap with the golden ribbon—is he no longer at the entrance?—no, he is an innkeeper in the region of the golden mines."[38] The same situation characterized a movie about a group of outlaws in the Abruzzi mountains, which was screened in front of an audience of dock workers in Marseilles: "The men from the harbor have more or less the same habits and morals as the men from the mountain."[39] The story begins to spill out of the screen, as spectators start to perform the same actions as the characters: in a playful game, they challenge each other, they fight, they brag. "As a result, one sees in the movie theatre not only the deeds of the men from the Abruzzi but also those of the men from Marseille." This idea of a porous surface found its most radical formulation in Roth's extraordinary book *Antichrist*. Recalling a documentary about the Russo-Japanese War that depicts regiments moving toward the foreground, Roth wrote, "The first double file of marching troops were already raising their clumsy feet to press them down upon our necks, and we began to duck before the oncoming heels."[40] At the very last moment the soldiers disappear, as shadows generally do. Yet, later in the book, we discover that the widespread success of cinema makes shadows able to penetrate our world; even more, we are becoming shadows, instead of flesh-and-blood creatures. Cinema has already taken possession of reality.

Roth's image of a "fibrous surface" endorses an idea of screen as a *filter* that allows large portions of the fictional world to drop into the actual one. The metaphor was frequent in the collective imaginary between the wars, and often it took the form of a two-way point of passage: as the fictional world can breach ours, so we can penetrate into the world depicted on the screen. A 1926 short story by the Italian writer Camillo Mariani dell'Anguillara, which described a group of riders on horseback spilling out of the screen, abducting a spectator, and transforming him into a character, can exemplify the genre.[41] After World War II, the emphasis on the process of identification would provide a psychological foundation to the metaphor.[42]

Its ultimate instantiation can be found in one of the last writings of Sergei Eisenstein, devoted to early experiments in stereoscopy. Thanks to 3D technology, the image at once "pours out of the screen into the auditorium" and "pierces through to the depth of the screen, taking the spectator into previously unseen distance."[43] Hence an unexpected spectacle: "birds fly out of the auditorium into the depths of the screen, or perch submissively over the very heads of the spectators on a wire palpably extending from the area which used once to be the surface of the screen up to . . . the projection booth." The auditorium becomes a risky space: "panthers and pumas leap out of the screen into the arms of the spectators."

The Divide

As opposed to the idea of the filter that allows the fiction to leak into the auditorium, and spectators to get into the fiction, in the late 1940s and early 1950s, the scholarly movement called filmology promoted the metaphor of the *divide.* The reality depicted on the screen and the reality in which spectators live tend to overlap, yet they never actually meet.

Filmology was widely interested in the screen. Its "vocabulary" provided one of the first attempts at a coherent conceptual framework for the study of film. In it, "screenic reality" (in French, *réalité écranique*) referred to what specifically appears on the screen, as opposed to "non- or pre-filmic realities" *(réalité a-filmique or pro-filmique)* that designed the physical world independent from, or prior to, being filmed, and to the "diegesis" *(diégèses),* which is the fictional world that spectators build in their minds while watching a movie.[44] To what extent do these three realities communicate with each other? Etienne Souriau, to whom we owe the "vocabulary" of filmology, offered a preliminary answer. Describing spectators' experience, he wrote, "The lobby, the auditorium. A door: the rectangle of the screen. And beyond this door, a world. This world undoubtedly looks like the real one, due to the great number of traits they have in common; and yet it is deeply different from it, due to some less numerous but nonetheless constitutive characteristics."[45] Indeed, the fictional world that spectators enjoy has nothing of the real world in which spectators live. It possesses neither depth nor relief; distances, temperatures, and density are only suggested; we approach it only through sight and hearing and not with our whole bodies. Despite the recurring invitation for spectators to join the fictional world,[46] there is no means to get into it. The screen, with its images and sounds, attracts and holds off. It is not a door; it is a barrier.

The psychologist Albert Michotte, another leading figure of filmology, went deeper into the problem. In his pioneering study on the impression of reality at the movies, he admitted that spectators mostly experience the reality depicted on the screen as if it were a factual reality, and yet they

do not perceive it—nor do they respond to it—in the same way they perceive and respond to factual reality.[47] "It is quite clear that we do not react
to the events that we see at the movies in the same way we bear witness
to the everyday life."[48] Indeed, one thing is to take a reality "as if" it were
true, another is to "know" and to "believe" that it is true: our cognitive processes and our behavior change from one condition to another. Sometimes
we fall prey to an excess of confidence in "purported" reality, and yet we
always are aware of its difference from what we "feel" is reality as such.
The distinction is crucial, not only because it keeps us safe from the dangers of illusion, but moreover because it creates two distinct spheres of
action, the one in which we can imagine or pretend to live and the one
in which we actually live. In a movie theater, the two spheres coexist: not
by chance, the spectator's visual field is partly occupied by the projected
images and partly by the persistent perception of the environment that
surrounds her. The two spheres sometimes look similar, but they are always
split. The screen is what ideally marks the distinction: its borders perform a radical "segregation of spaces," letting the fictional world come
close to the real world but ultimately avoiding any effective overlapping.
The screen is a line of separation between two divergent spaces.[49]

A third consideration came from Eric Feldman, in his still-illuminating
phenomenology of film attendance.[50] Examining the process of identification with film characters, Feldman noticed that, despite their desire to
be part of the fictional world, spectators are perfectly aware that they will
never be able to change the course of the depicted events. "The stronger
the images offered by the film, the more intensely spectators imagine that
the dramatic action of the film must be accepted as a predetermined
destiny and that the situations must be left to play themselves out."[51] This
lack of spectators' agency raises a further barrier between the fictional
world and the everyday reality: the former does not respond to the latter,
and the latter cannot touch the former. Their separation is due to their
intransitivity.

In the 1960s, the idea of separation found new impulse in Stanley Cavell.
In a brilliant passage of his *The World Viewed*, Cavell—who never mentions filmology—states, "The screen is not a support, not like a canvas. . . .
A screen is a barrier. What does the silver screen screen? It screens me
from the world it holds—that is, makes me invisible. And it screens that

world from me—that is, screens its existence from me."[52] Here the separation is essentially exemption. On one hand, spectators are alienated from the depicted world—they are pulled apart. This means that they are no longer responsible for what this world represents or tells. On the other hand, the fictional world hides itself from spectators' eyes—it does not even require somebody to look at it. This means that it has no longer to respond to spectators' desires. The movie screen literally seals two universes: in doing so, it exempts them from their mutual obligations. Quite paradoxically, Cavell's interpretation of the filmic situation brings me to Guy Debord. In his *The Society of the Spectacle*—a book not about film but in which film plays the role of implicit model—he speaks of "separation perfected." In contemporary society, "all that once was directly lived has become mere representation."[53] These representations have lost any connections with life, and now they work "as a pseudo-world apart, an object of mere contemplation." As in Cavell, there is no correspondence, in every sense of the word, between parties. Differently from Cavell, the consequence is not exemption but indifference. The ideal screen on which social life is projected sterilizes the universes that it seals.

The Protective Shield

In the last pages of his *Theory of Film*, published in 1960, Siegfried Kracauer recollects the myth of Perseus, who approached the petrifying Gorgon through her image reflected on his shield. Kracauer comments, "The moral of the myth is, of course, that we do not, and cannot, see actual horrors because they paralyze us with blinding fear; and that we shall know what they look like only by watching images of them which reproduce their true appearance. . . . Now of all the existing media the cinema alone holds up a mirror to nature. Hence our dependence on it for the reflection of happenings which would petrify us were we to encounter them in real life. The film screen is Athena's polished shield."[54] Here the screen, more than a filter or a divide, is a protection that keeps spectators safe from the dangers of the actual world.

To better appreciate Kracauer's metaphor, we have to go back to his previous writings. In 1929–30, Kracauer published in the influential *Frankfurter Zeitung* an inquiry about the living conditions of the salaried employees in Weimar Germany. He found these workers in a state of cultural deprivation. "The house of bourgeois ideas and feelings in which they used to live has collapsed, its foundations eroded by economic development." As a consequence, the blue-collar workers have become "spiritually homeless." Such a state ignites the desire for a glamorous existence, characterized by a profusion of lights, entertaining spectacles, brilliant and superficial encounters—what emerges is a need for distraction. This need is filled by special places that offer an abundance of distractions and that consequently work as *shelter for the homeless*. "Shelters in the literal sense are those gigantic taverns in which, as one garrulous fellow once put it in a Berlin evening paper, 'for not much money you can get a breath of the wide world.'"[55] Kracauer focused in particular on Haus Faterland, at the time the most famous pleasure palace in Berlin, with its lobby, its frescoed and richly furnished rooms, its entertainments, its bar; but—as he openly claimed—his description also applied to film palaces, with their lights, their magnificent decorations, their spectacles, and their movies.[56] In the film palace, the climax is reached at the precise moment when the screen "descends and the events of the three-dimensional stage blend imperceptibly into two-dimensional illusions."[57] Likewise, the pleasure palaces provide a "world vibrant with color. The world not as it is, but as it appears in popular hits. A world every last corner of which is cleansed, as though with a vacuum cleaner, of the dust of the everyday existence."[58] Such a reward is clearly unable to feed the real needs of the salaried masses: they are given illusions instead of substantial stuff, so to say.[59] Nevertheless, in these places, blue-collar workers find what they believe they need and think they have lost: resources for living—or for surviving.

Kracauer resumed the metaphor of the "shelter for the homeless" in his American writings, taking greater latitude with the concept and considering the metaphor in a more positive light.[60] This is the case in *Theory of Film*, where the "homeless" is the modern man who faces "the declining hold of common beliefs on the mind and the steadily increasing prestige of science."[61] Deprived of any certitude by the former, and invited by the latter to think in mere quantitative terms, the modern man progressively loses his grip on reality: he lives "with a shadowy awareness of things in their fullness" and falls prey to an abstract idea of the world.[62] The cinema offers him the resources he needs, this time in a substantial way, and no longer as an illusion. Indeed, in a movie theater, one can access the physical reality in its broad expanse and depth: the world, so close and yet so far for the modern man, becomes fully available. "In recording and exploring physical reality, film exposes to view a world never seen before, a world so elusive as Poe's purloined letter, which cannot be found because it is within everybody's reach."[63] The very fact that, at the movies, access to the surrounding world is mediated by images does not diminish the capacity of modern man to regain a full experience of things. Film images provide a perfect testimony, and at the same time, as we have seen, they avoid the risk of being petrified by a direct exposition to actual horrors. This is why the screen must work as a protective shield: because film can rescue the modern man when it is not only faithful but also safe.

The Camouflage

In the 1970s, apparatus theory reversed the idea of film as a faithful and safe reflection. The screen is not a protective surface that gives us back the sense of reality; instead, it is a *camouflage* that hides the only reality that matters, that is, film's mode of production. Let's retrace the way in which images are screened. As Jean Louis Baudry recalls, "projector and screen restore the light lost in the shooting process, and transform the succession of separate images into an unrolling which also restores . . . the movement seized from 'objective reality.'"[64] What in the filmstrip was a series of single opaque frames becomes a luminous and moving reality-like image—an illusion so close to the original that it can be taken for the original. Nevertheless, this illusion has a cost. The camera's work is characterized by the simple "recording of differences of light intensity (and wavelength for color) and the difference between the frames."[65] This is the only way in which film can capture the reality. To get the (illusory) reality back on the screen, both these differences must be denied: the running of the filmstrip in the projector transforms the variation of light in a homogeneous texture and the discontinuity of movement in a developing action. The mere variations become a consistent and continuous world. "Film lives on the denial of difference: difference is necessary for it to live, but it lives on its negation."[66] In this sense, the screen literally masks the work of apparatus—its inner mechanisms and the processes it requires.

In accordance with the dominant ideology, it favors an "effect of reality" against the potential emergence of an "effect of knowledge."

We observe the same kind of operation when we look at the way in which a film is enjoyed. On the screen, spectators find a double source of identification: in a character, in whose shoes they can literally put themselves, or in the ideal gaze that captures and keeps under control the entire scene, in which they can find alter egos of their own action. The identification with a character or the gaze would provide the spectator with a self—an "I" that gives to the onlooker the sense of being able to develop a coherent act of seeing and to master the object of her seeing. And yet, once again, there is a cost in such an operation. The spectator's coherence and mastery are purely illusory: watching a film is to deal with something that is given in dribs and drabs and that resists any attempts at being encompassed by a single, graspable meaning. Put in other (Lacanian) terms, the spectator's "I" is an imaginary one: it is supposed to unite "the discontinuous fragments of phenomena, of lived experience, into unifying meaning,"[67] when in actuality it belongs to a domain characterized by gaps and splits—the symbolic order, where difference reigns. The idea of an imaginary subject that is able to keep the film together and under control is necessary if we want the film experience to appear desirable and enjoyable; but this idea (this ideal?) hides the crude reality of the processes that cinema activates. The screen is where this concealment takes place: it is the playground where a supposedly strong subject masks its weakness. Once again, what gets buried is the apparatus's factual work. Hence an inevitable conclusion: "The cinematic mirror-screen . . . reflects images but not 'reality'; . . . 'reality' comes from behind the spectator's head and if he looked at it directly he would see nothing except the moving beams from an already veiled light source."[68]

A Countergenealogy

So, the movie screen is not just the silent support of moving images. In some decisive way, it still has to do with the original meanings of the word *screen*—it is still a filter, a partition, a shelter, and a camouflage. The sparks of theories that I have retraced not only underscore the materiality and agency of the screen but also capture the persistence of certain functions that the optical connotation of the screen had obscured.[69] These theories do not always have a practical counterpart—after all, they are simply discourses.[70] Yet, by hypotheses, they render such characterizations of the screen thinkable, applicable, and even real. In this sense, once unearthed, the screen's obscured functions appear still alive, and they must be fully taken into account.

Their presence pulls us toward a different *genealogy* of the movie screen. Its foundations do not exclusively rely on the primacy of *visuality*—a primacy that became apparent in Western culture in the early seventeenth century, when it found an ally in what Bruno Latour calls the *process of visualization,* that is, the need to make visual data consistent, transferable, comparable, and combinable to grant intellectual, political, and economic possession of the world.[71] Visuality and visualization undoubtedly exerted a great amount of influence on the emergence and the spread of optical devices like the shadow theater, the Phantasmagoria, the Panorama, the Diorama, and, eventually, the cinema. Consequently, they exerted influence on the new definition of *screen* that emerged alongside these technologies. Yet, as we can recognize from the film theories that I have retraced, the screen is more than a device for visualization. Its presence raises questions regarding not only the availability of the visual data but also the forms and terms of their accessibility; not only the scopic pleasure but also the need of protection from an overexposure to images; not only the transparence of the filmic representation but also the distance that spectators have to keep from it; and not only the density of pictures but also what they hide and what they sieve. In short, the screen asks us to focus not on what is seen but on the conditions of seeing—including spectators' positions and more generally the setting or the environment in which the act of seeing takes place. In this sense, the screen's functions that we have unearthed—a filter, a partition, a shelter, and a camouflage—speak first the language of space and then the language of the eye. They recall the original idea of the screen: a device that keeps at distance, provides protection, rearranges sites, and creates zones of seclusion. Hence arises the necessity to revise the movie screen's genealogy and to keep under consideration the environmental aspects, functions, and practices that the process of visualization put aside, unable as it was to fully appropriate them for its purposes. These elements are still part of the ground from which the silver screen emerged, and they still have a role to play as its constitutive components.

The countergenealogy that comes to the fore calls for a full recognition of this environmental dimension. The movie screen's descent[72] must include all the public exhibitions of changing images, especially for entertaining purposes, be they the magic lantern, stereopticon, amusement parks, fairs and carnivals, music halls, penny arcades, shadow theaters, and so on.[73] Yet it must also include all the spaces in which the visual data created points of aggregation, partition, exclusion, resistance, and obstruction. I am thinking of scientific laboratories, public ceremonies, religious cults, urban squares, and private cabinets. The list must be expanded, taking into consideration what, drawing on Arjun Appadurai, I have described as *mediascapes*—environments defined by a structural presence of media and characterized by their capacity to perform mediations.[74] What matters is that we go beyond the usual suspects in most of the current archaeologies of the screen[75] and move toward an inclusive picture, based not on self-evident lineages, but on a *rhizomatic network* of references.

Rethinking the Cinema

Our lateral metaphors not only suggest a screen's countergenealogy; they also uncover a different intellectual framework in which to insert cinema—better, they reveal a different *cinematic episteme* within which cinema can be thought.[76] Hence a new question: to what extent does the discovery of an environmental dimension change our perception of cinema at large?

First, cinema can regain a dimension that has been largely neglected from the beginning: beyond being a visual art, it can also be an environmental medium. Indeed, cinema implies not only a representation but also a space where the representation is performed—not only a "what" but also a "where." This space is openly influenced by the representation itself: it is designed to make seeing possible and easy, and it often echoes the world depicted on the screen.[77] Nevertheless, it is a physical space, since it is coincident with the actual place where a movie is screened— be it public, private, specialized, temporary, or so on. Not by chance, it is in this double capacity that the space is considered as a key component of the cinematographic situation in approaches like filmology. At the movies, the act of seeing is always spatialized.

Consequently, it is worthwhile to give more room to an analysis inspired by Jacques Rancière's concept of the "distribution of the sensible."[78] Media, including cinema, make content accessible to the senses in different ways: they can do that by addressing the whole social body or selecting a public for a more limited circulation, by making an argument graspable or totally cryptic, by choosing their audiences or building new ones, and so on. In this way, media—and the arts—are at once mirrors and agents of the terms and conditions in which a society "distributes" the meanings that constitute its communal footing. Each form of distribution has a specific political value: it defines which sense must be engaged, by whom, with which kind of personal implication, in which kind of framework, and so forth. And, I would add, each form of distribution has a spatial counterpart: it defines where access is possible, whether there are privileged points of access, which kinds of spatial practices are necessary for gaining access, and so on. That means that both the forms of participation in public life and the geography of power are rooted in the modalities in which the sensible is distributed.[79] Access (or lack of it) to a word or image, if in public spaces or in institutional venues, being reached by messages or having to retrieve them, being a direct addressee or a mute witness, being part of a large conversation or having to keep one's mouth and eyes shut, are all choices that determine the ways in which the political process is performed based on the ways media organize social spaces. Politics, then, has an aesthetic basis: the organization of the senses reveals and establishes the organization of a society, including the distribution of power. In this framework, the aforementioned screen's functions—as a filter, a divide, a shelter, and a camouflage—acquire a concrete meaning: they refer to the diverse ways in which a visual representation can be offered: as a shared or a secluded reality, as a directly or only partially graspable world, as a masked or unmasked entity, as a threatening or safe contact. Film reveals itself to be political not just because of its content but more broadly because of its environmental dimension.

Finally, the very fact that the environmental nature of cinema has for a long time been there, but not in plain sight, helps us to understand cinema's potentiality. Classical film theory's obstinate search for specificity obscured the fact that cinema is a multifaceted and composite entity. It congregates diverse components and aspects, some of which are original, some of which come from other dispositives. Cinema regenerates and transforms the components from outside, yet they bring with them the memory of their previous functions and practices. This memory, no less than the still-unexplored uses of the new components, constitutes a potential that is usually kept "in reserve" but that is also ready to re-emerge and to give cinema a new direction, when circumstances allow or request it to do so.[80] This is the case of the screen's environmental connotations. They remind of the previous functions of the screen that the new optical assemblage had largely silenced but not terminated. Far from being incoherent, these functions were a potential from which cinema could benefit, either covertly or openly. The potential now becomes a plain resource. It already came to the fore every time cinema had to be aware of its environmental nature, as in some of the artistic experimentation of the 1960s addressed to the filmic apparatus.[81] Now this environmental potential is converted into an effective force, partly as an effect of cinema's relocation in museums and galleries, in public squares, at home, and so on, partly under the pressure of more recent media.[82] Cinema discloses a latent side and becomes a visual art that also works as an environmental medium.

The Explosion of Screens

Such a theoretical framework enables us to reconsider the current explosion of screens and the role film has played in it.[83]

There is no doubt that the new screens—be they the components of handheld devices, of laptops, of urban or home design, or of work equipment—perform functions that are quite different from movie screens. They are terminals of constant data flow; stations from which to retrieve documents from virtual repositories; worktables on which to write, to draw, to calculate, to project; meeting points at which we chat with "friends"; proxies for our credit cards, identity papers, or boarding passes; and so on. In this sense, these surfaces are closer to *displays* than to *screens*.[84] On the other hand, these new screens are more explicitly environmental. They monitor geographic and spatial territory, in connection to surveillance

cameras or GPS; they create spaces of intimacy when they project a sort
of bubble around their users; they designate zones where crowds gather,
as megascreens allocated in public squares do when they become points
of attraction; they conceal things behind a superposed surface, as media-
facades do with buildings; they add virtual elements to the actual landscape, as augmented reality and even more so mixed reality do.

Despite new media's apparent discontinuity with cinema, once we recognize that the latter was never simply an optical apparatus but rather a
multisided dispositive that kept some of its aspects "in reserve," we can
create a bridge toward the former. In particular, we can read the new
media's environmental vocation as the coming in plain sight of a potential that for most of its life film kept unrealized. New media screens act
as filters, divides, shelters, and camouflage, not only recalling but also
giving real body to the lateral metaphors for the movie screen that we
unearthed a few pages ago. At the same time, film now is fully aware of
its own environmental vocation thanks to new media. If the movie screen
expounds its nature as a filter with 3D films, or as a shelter in home theaters, or as a subtle divide when used in open spaces, it is because new
media made these conditions familiar.[85] This does not mean that there
is a direct parentage that connects cinema to the more recent media:
descent is more complex than that. As we have seen, descent includes
relations at a distance, lateral influences, random borrowings, and stop-
pages. However, this means that there is a common ground where both
film and more recent media are allocated—a ground on which the action
of the former can be retroactively enlightened but also brought forward
by the latter.

This is also true for the new media's potentialities. Indeed, new media
also keep a few aspects "in reserve" on which film could exert some
influence. Two issues are worthy of attention. First, if cinema had to
negotiate the environmental and the optical, assigning primacy to the
former while keeping the latter "frozen," how will new media negotiate
between the two? Indeed, they perform their spatial functions through
visual data. How, then, will visuality take its revenge? Second, if cinema
provided a distribution of the sensible based on images that were accessible to an entire audience, but which also addressed the single spectator, what kind of distribution will new media develop? Cinema was a

one-to-many medium, holding the one-to-one address in the second row; new media reverse the ratio. Where will the final balance be set?

When we are looking at the end of the cinema—in both senses, as termination and as climax—this common ground, mostly inflected by the presence of potentialities that the other medium can uncover, can provide an answer. There are no direct heirs of the cinema. There are territories that, despite their apparent dissimilarities, retain and develop the dynamics that cinema has faced. In this sense, new media are cinema's second life, if not its afterlife. This paradoxical statement is not so paradoxical, after all. When we consider media transformations neither as a strict determination nor as a brutal leap but as the becoming actual of a potential that was already there, this statement gains its meaning. It is up to us, through a constant monitoring of new media's ways of working, to substantiate and better define this meaning.

Notes

My current research on the screen is deeply indebted to ongoing discussions with Bernard Geoghegan, Craig Buckley, Rudiger Campe, and Weihong Bao. I am also grateful to Ariel Rogers and Jocelyn Szczepaniak-Gillece for productive exchanges. Special thanks to Mal Ahern for our always-inspiring conversations and for her excellent revision of the manuscript.

1. A good example of this kind of approach is D. N. Rodowick, *The Virtual Life of Film* (Cambridge, Mass.: Harvard University Press, 2007).

2. We can capture the sense of this emergence in two notices referring to the Phantasmagoria's patent granted to Paul De Philipsthal on January 26, 1802, respectively published in *Cobbett's Political Register* (1053) and in the *Monthly Magazine* (488). The two notices read "transparent screen," while, quite curiously, the text of the patent published a few months before in *The Repertory of Arts and Manufactures* (303–5) reads "transparent body." The substitution of the old term with the new—justified by the fact that the screen was also intended to hide the source of the light, that is, to *screen* it in the traditional sense—underscores the surfacing of the new visual connotation of the word. Nevertheless, the term *screen* in its new meaning was already circulating: Henry Baker in *The Microscope Made Easy*, 3rd ed. (London: Doldsley, 1744), 23, 25–26, speaks of "screen" and "paper screen" on which the enlarged image appears.

3. The idea of the screen as an optical device still permeates recent collections, such as Dominique Chateau and José Moure, eds., *Screens: From Materiality to Spectatorship* (Amsterdam: Amsterdam University Press, 2016), and Mauro

Carbone, Anna Caterina Dalmasso, and Jacopo Boldini, eds., *Vivre par(mi) les écrans* (Paris: Les Presses du Réel, 2016). A more philosophical approach is Mauro Carbone, *Philosophie-ecrans: du cinéma à la révolution numérique* (Paris: Paris Vrin, 2016). An explicit revision of the visual connotation of the screen is Giuliana Bruno, *Surface: Matters of Aesthetics, Materiality, and Media* (Chicago: University of Chicago Press, 2014).

4. The classical edition of the *Oxford English Dictionary,* edited by James A. H. Murray at the turn of the century, while almost incidentally mentioning the new meaning of *screen* ("a flat vertical surface prepared for the reception of images from a magic lantern or like"), also accurately lists the traditional ones: "a contrivance for warding off the heat of a fire or a draught of air"; "a partition of wood or stone, pierced by one or more doors, dividing a room or building in two parts"; "a wall thrown out in front of a building and masking the façade"; "[a] shelter from heat or wind"; "something interposed as to conceal from view"; "a small body of men detached to cover the movement of an army"; "an apparatus used in the sifting of grain, coal, etc." James A. H. Murray, ed., *A New English Dictionary on Historical Principles* (Oxford: Clarendon Press, 1914), 8:272.

5. "I do not speak of the screen, which is a material accessory, forming a part of the hall, like the setting in the theatre." Élie Faure, *The Art of Cineplastics* (Boston: Four Seas, 1923), 22 (the French original appeared in 1922). Faure's definition discharges the screen from being among the film's key elements (a role reserved to the actor, the camera, and the cinematographer, as intermediaries between the filmmaker and the audience); nevertheless, it recognizes the materiality of the screen and the pertinence of the environment.

6. The two metaphors emerged early in the public debate on cinema. See, for example, two occurrences, both included in *Early Film Theories in Italy, 1896–1922,* edited by Francesco Casetti with Silvio Alovisio and Luca Mazzei (Amsterdam: Amsterdam University Press, 2017). For the mirror, Giovanni Papini, "The Philosophy of Cinematograph," orig. 1907: "sitting before the white screen in a movie theatre we have the impression that we are watching *true events,* as if we were watching through a mirror, following the action hurtling through space" (48). For the window, Luigi Lucatelli, "Families of Soldiers," orig. 1912: "And in that silence, the silent square, which typically shows the vulgarity of the 'comical final scene,' opened up like a strange window into the far-off homeland" (164). Each metaphor had its apex, respectively, in the reference to the Lacanian mirror in Jean-Louis Baudry, "The Apparatus: Metapsychological Approaches to the Impression of Reality in the Cinema," *Camera Obscura* 1 (Fall 1976): 104–26 (orig. 1975), and in Anne Friedberg, *The Virtual Window: From Alberti to Microsoft* (Cambridge, Mass.: MIT Press, 2002).

7. I use the word *genealogy* in reference to Michel Foucault, "Nietzsche, Genealogy, History," in *Language, Counter-Memory, Practice: Selected Essays and Interviews,* ed. D. F. Bouchard, 139–64 (Ithaca, N.Y.: Cornell University Press, 1977).

8. An early exploration of this topic is Linda Williams, ed., *Viewing Positions* (New Brunswick, N.J.: Rutgers University Press, 1994).

9. This is the well-known hypothesis of Lev Manovich, *The Language of New Media* (Cambridge, Mass.: MIT Press, 2000).

10. Emanuele Toddi, "Rectangle Film (25 X 19)," in Casetti, *Early Film Theories in Italy: 1896–1922*, 348–52. Orig. "Rettangolo-Film (25 X 19)," *In Penombra* 1, no. 3 (1918): 121–23.

11. Toddi, 351.

12. Toddi, 352.

13. Sergei M. Eisenstein, "The Dynamic Square," in *Film Essays and a Lecture*, ed. Jay Leyda, 48–65 (Princeton, N.J.: Princeton University Press, 1982).

14. Ricciotto Canudo, "Reflections on the Seventh Art," in *French Film Theory and Criticism: A History/Anthology, 1907–1939*, ed. Richard Abel (Princeton, N.J.: Princeton University Press, 1988), 296. Orig. "Réflection sur la Septiéme Art," in *L'usine aux Images*, 29–47 (Paris: Chiron, 1926).

15. Canudo, 296.

16. Canudo, 296.

17. On the idea of cinema as a form of writing, see in the same years Blaise Cendrars, "L'ABC du Cinéma," in *Aujourd'hui*, 55–66 (Paris: Grasset, 1931). The text is dated 1921.

18. Clement Greenberg, "Towards a Newer *Laocoön*," *Partisan Review* 7 (July–August 1940), then in *The Collected Essays and Criticism: Vol. 1. Perceptions and Judgments 1939–1944*, 23–38 (Chicago: University of Chicago Press, 1986).

19. For the idea that cinema is writing with light, see in particular the section "On Cinematic Truth" of Canudo's "Reflections on the Seventh Art."

20. Robert Desnos, "La Morale du Cinéma," *Paris Journal*, May 13, 1923, later published as *Cinéma* (Paris: Gallimard, 1966), 111. Desnos's translations are mine.

21. "The filmmaker and the screenwriter do not have only actors' availability. They also can count on the crowd of spectators whom they can invite to live the most extreme experiences and plug in the most unusual adventures." Desnos, 111.

22. Desnos is adamant in recalling this surrealist principle: "cinema should allow us to reach the absolute in an action" (109).

23. Lázló Moholy-Nagy, *Painting, Photography, Film*, trans. Janet Seligman (Cambridge, Mass.: MIT Press, 1969). Original, *Malerei, Photografie, Film* (Munich: A. Langen, 1925), published as the eighth volume of the Bauhausbücher series and republished as *Malerei, Fotografie, Film*, 2nd ed. (Munich: A. Langen, 1927). English translation is of the second edition.

24. Moholy-Nagy, *Painting*, 41.

25. Moholy-Nagy.

26. Lázló Moholy-Nagy, *Von Material zu Architektur* (Munich: Albert Langen, 1929). English translation of the fourth edition: *The New Vision, and Abstract of*

an Artist (New York: Wittenborn, 1946). Suggestions from this book will migrate and expand in the posthumous volume *Vision in Motion* (Chicago: Paul Theobald, 1947).

27. Moholy-Nagy, *New Vision*, 39.

28. Moholy-Nagy, 50.

29. It's worth noticing that in Moholy-Nagy, this interaction with the environment directly challenges the very idea of visibility. See the following passage, clearly inspired by Georg Simmel's "The Metropolis and Mental Life" (1903): "The realization of such plans makes new demands upon the capacity of our optical organ of perception, the eye, and our center of perception, the brain. The vast development both of technique and of the big cities have increased the capacity of our perceptual organs for simultaneous acoustical and optical activity. Everyday life itself affords examples of this: Berlin cross the Potsdamer Platz." Moholy-Nagy, *Painting*, 43.

30. Antonello Gerbi, "Iniziazione alle Delizie del Cinema," *Il Convegno* 7, no. 11–12 (1926): 836–48. Gerbi's translations are mine.

31. Gerbi, 839. We find the same sense of uselessness in Maxim Gorky's description of an early Lumière screening: "And suddenly [image] disappears. Before your eyes there is simply a piece of white canvas in a wide black frame, and it seems there never was anything on it." Maxim Gorky, "Lumière's Cinematograph," in Richard Taylor, *Film Factory: Russian and Soviet Cinema in Documents 1896–1939* (Cambridge, Mass.: Harvard University Press, 1988), orig. in *Odesskie Novosti* 3681 (July 6, 1896).

32. Gerbi, "Iniziazione."

33. Gerbi, 842.

34. For example, Gerbi speaks of "the bed of a river of images, the frigid mirror of the most passionate ghosts, of the most erotic dreams" (839). Gerbi even advances some risky gendered allegories: "the screen, which indifferently welcomes all of the images and then completely forgets them, has the versatile cynicism of a man.... Impassable and untiring, the screen is the last incarnation of the spirit of Don Giovanni" (839).

35. Sergei M. Eisenstein, *Glass House*, ed. Francois Albera (Brussels: Les Presses du Reel, 2009). The project was conceived in Berlin in mid-April 1926 (in room 73 of Hotel Hessler, as stated in Eisenstein's journal in a note dated January 13, 1927), then was reworked and finally dropped during his Hollywood period, but never forgotten: in a note in the journal dated May 22, 1946, Eisenstein wrote, "Everybody once in his life writes his secret: mine is *Glass House*." See Albera, 79, to whom we owe an exemplary reconstruction of the project.

36. Eisenstein, *Glass House*, 34. In the original, "Ecran monstre" is in French, and "Why not???" in English.

37. Eisenstein provided several summaries for the movie, but the main plot was clear from the beginning. A note dated September 18, 1927, summarized the

core of the film: "C'est le nouveau paradis ... d'abord la vie dénudée puis le cauchemar des yeux et de la visibilité et le désir panique de se cacher" (28); that same day, in a note for his journal, Eisenstein wrote, "On pourrait construire une ligne générale sur la 'découverte' progressive des habitants qui commencent à se voir les uns les autres, se regarder, faire attention à eux, ce qui, dans le système capitaliste, mène a une haine chaotique, a des méfaits, des abus, des catastrophes. Les passions se déchainent jusqu'à l'éclatement de la maison en mille morceau" (71). It may be interesting to compare Eisenstein's project, with a turn from an early fervor to a final destruction of the house, with Walter Benjamin's appreciation for transparent houses: "To live in a glass house is a revolutionary virtue par excellence. It is also an intoxication, a moral exhibitionism, that we badly need. Discretion concerning one's own existence, once an aristocratic virtue, has become more and more an affair of petty-bourgeois parvenus." Benjamin, "Surrealism: The Last Snapshot of the European Intelligentsia," in *"One-Way Street" and Other Writings* (London: NLB, 1979), 228.

38. Joseph Roth, "Praterkino," in *Drei Sensationen und zwei Katastrophen: Feuilletons zur Welt des Kinos,* ed. Helmut Peschina and Rainer-Joachim Siegel, 32–35 (Göttingen, Germany: Wallstein, 2014), orig. in *Der Neue Tag,* April 4, 1920.

39. Roth, "Ein Kino im Hafen," in Peschina and Siegel, *Drei Sensationen,* 157–60; orig. in *Frankfurter Zeitung,* November 4, 1925.

40. Roth, *Antichrist,* trans. Moray Firth (New York: Viking Press, 1935), 29; orig. Joseph Roth, *Antichrist* (Amsterdam: Albert de Lange, 1934).

41. Camillo Mariani dell'Anguillara, "Una Avventura Cinematografica," *Lo Schermo,* August 23, 1926, 11–12. The author was also a screenwriter, in particular for the Italian epic *Scipione l'Africano* that Fascism heralded as its own manifesto.

42. See in particular Edgar Morin, *Cinema; or, the Imaginary Man* (Minneapolis: University of Minnesota Press, 2005). Orig. *Le cinema ou L'Homme Imaginaire: Essai D'Anthropologie Sociologique* (Paris: Minuit, 1956). A noteworthy reference is Benjamin's comments about the story of the Chinese painter who disappeared into his own painting. See Walter Benjamin, *Berlin Childhood around 1900,* trans. Howard Eiland (Cambridge, Mass.: Belknap Press of Harvard University Press, 2006), 134.

43. Sergei Eisenstein, "About Stereoscopic Cinema," *Penguin Film Review* 8 (1949): 38.

44. Etienne Souriau, "La structure de l'univers filmique et le vocabulaire de la filmologie," *Revue internationale de filmologie* 7–8 ([1950]): 231–40.

45. Etienne Souriau, "Les Grand Caractères de L'Univers Filmique," in *L'Univers filmique* (Paris: Flammarion, 1951), 11. In this essay, Souriau explains why he speaks of a door instead of a window: it is precisely because he wants to underline the (impossible) desire to cross a threshold.

46. "Ce monde, nous y sommes invites. Il est fait pour nous; il nous est dédié. Il s'adresse à nous. Il nous prépare une place." Souriau, 12.

48 Francesco Casetti

47. A[lbert] Michotte, "Le caractère de 'réalité' des projections cinémato-graphiques," *Revue internationale de filmologie* 3–4 (1948): 249–61.

48. "Les représentations cinématographiques donnent à la majorité des spectateurs, et pendant la plus grande partie du déroulement du film, une impressionne très vive de la *réalité* des choses et des aventures qu'ils perçoivent sur l'écran . . . il est manifeste d'autre part que nous ne réagissons pas (et que même les enfants ne réagissent pas) de la même manière aux évènements auxquels nous assistons au cinéma qu'à ceux, analogues, dont nous pourrions être témoins dans la vie courante." Michotte, 249.

49. "L'image n'occupe que une faible partie du champ et l'espace qu'elle represente ne constitue pas le cadre de reference des spectateurs. Il se produit dans ces conditions une veritable ségrégation des espaces. L'un d'eux est celui dans lequel 'vivent' et se meuvent les acteurs, l'autre est celui auquel appartiennent les spectateurs." This segregation results in a "juxtapositions de deux mondes différents." Michotte, 256.

50. Eric Feldmann, "Considérations sur la situation du spectateur au cinéma," *Revue internationale de filmologie* 26 (1956): 83–97.

51. Feldmann, 92.

52. Stanley Cavell, *The World Viewed,* Enlarged ed. (Cambridge, Mass.: Harvard University Press, 1979), 24.

53. Guy Debord, *The Society of the Spectacle* (New York: Zone Books, 1955), 12.

54. Siegfried Kracauer, *Theory of Film* (New York: Oxford University Press, 1960), 305.

55. Siegfried Kracauer, *The Salaried Masses: Duty and Distraction in Weimar Germany,* trans. Quintin Hoare (London: Verso, 1998), 91. Orig. "Die Angestellten. Aus dem neusten Deutschland," serial publication in *Frankfurter Zeitung,* December 1929–January 1930, and then as a book published by Societats, Frankfurt, 1930.

56. The claim is both in *The Salaried Masses* and in his famous essay "Cult of Distraction: On Berlin Picture Palaces." See, e.g., "Like hotel lobbies, [picture palaces] are shrines to the cultivation of pleasure; their glamor aims at edification." Siegfried Kracauer, "Cult of Distraction: On Berlin Picture Palaces," in *The Mass Ornament: Weimar Essays,* ed. and trans. Thomas Y. Levin (Cambridge, Mass.: Harvard University Press, 1995), 323; orig. *Das Ornament der Masse* (Frankfurt: Suhrkamp, 1963). The essay was originally published in 1927.

57. Kracauer, "Cult of Distraction," 324.

58. Kracauer, *Salaried Masses,* 91–92.

59. "All events relating to the unorganized salaried masses, and equally all movements of these masses themselves, are today of an ambivalent nature. . . . Under the pressure from the prevailing society they become, in a metaphorical sense, shelters for the homeless. Apart from their primary purpose, they acquire the further one of binding employees by enchantment to the place the ruling

stratus desires, and diverting them from critical questions—for which they anyway feel little inclination." Kracauer, 94.

60. Interesting is the application of the idea of "shelter" to the art world as such: "Thus Art is assigned the task of providing a shelter for all those in need of a roof above their heads. Improbable as it is that the increasing talk about poetry should reflect an increasing interest in it, it certainly gives the people the pleasant illusion that there is something somewhere which can be believed in if one has the gift of believing. The idolatry for art does, for a moment, away with the fear of the vacuum." Sigfried Kracauer, "Art Today: A Proposal," in *Siegfried Kracauer's American Writings: Essays on Film and Popular Culture*, ed. Johannes von Moltke and Kristy Rawson (Berkeley: University of California Press, 2012), 106.

61. Kracauer, *Theory of Film*, 286.

62. Kracauer, 291.

63. Kracauer, 299.

64. Jean-Louis Baudry, "Ideological Effects of the Basic Cinematographic Apparatus," in *Narrative, Apparatus, Ideology*, ed. Philip Rosen (New York: Columbia University Press, 1986), 287. Orig. "Cinéma: *Effets Idéologiques* produits par l'appareil de base," *Cinéthique* 7–8 (1970): 1–8. On cinematographic apparatus, see also Baudry, "The Apparatus: Metapsychological Approaches to the Impression of Reality in the Cinema," in the same volume.

65. Baudry, "Ideological Effects," 288.

66. Baudry, 290.

67. Baudry, 295.

68. Baudry, 294.

69. An issue that deserves more attention is the fact that the four metaphors of filter, partition, shield/shelter, and camouflage emerge in a context characterized by a fear of cinema. The four terms speak either of a menace from some kind of external reality or of a means for resisting this menace. On the role of cinephobia in shaping film theories, see Francesco Casetti, "Why Fears Matter: Cinephobia in Early Film Culture," *Screen* 59, no. 2 (2018): 145–57.

70. Yet sometimes film production tried to respond to the instances that theories raised. For example, film industry gave body to Toddi's and Eisenstein's ideas of a variable screen with the Magnascope, a dispositive that in the late 1920s paired a screen four times bigger than the twenty- by twenty-two-foot usual size with projector lenses able to substantially enlarge the image during some key scenes and with masks that were moved aside when the image became larger. The Magnascope was short-lived, but it paved the way for future wide-format movies. See John Belton, *Widescreen Cinema* (Cambridge, Mass.: Harvard University Press, 1992).

71. Bruno Latour, "Visualization and Cognition: Thinking with Eyes and Hands," *Knowledge and Society* 6 (1986): 1–40.

72. I follow Foucault in using the terms *descent* and *emergence,* as opposed to the idea of origin. *Descent* refers to the fact that an affiliation to a group does not imply univocal determinations or chronological timelines. Foucault states, "To follow the complex course of descent is to maintain passing events in their appropriate dispersion; it is to identify the accidents, the minute deviations—or conversely, the complete reversals—the errors, the false appraisals, and the faulty calculation that gave birth to those things that continue to exist and have value for us." Foucault, "Nietzsche, Genealogy, History," 146.

73. A useful analysis of the influence of these dispositives on the birth of cinema is Charlotte Herzog, "The Archaeology of Cinema Architecture: The Origins of the Movie Theater," *Quarterly Review of Film Studies* 9, no. 1 (1984): 11–32.

74. For the original concept of mediascape, see Arjun Appadurai, *Modernity at Large: Cultural Dimensions of Globalization* (Minneapolis: University of Minnesota Press, 1996); I redefined the concept in "Mediascapes: A Decalogue," *Perspecta* 51 (Fall 2018).

75. Among the projects aimed at retracing the lineage of the screen, Charles Musser's history of screen practices and Erkki Huhtamo's archaeology of the screen are of particular relevance. See the "inaugural" texts, respectively, Musser, "Toward a History of Screen Practice," *Quarterly Review of Film Studies* 9, no. 1 (1984): 59–69, and Huhtamo, "Elements of Screenology: Toward an Archaeology of the Screen," *Iconics* 7 (2004): 31–82. Musser claims that "the origins of screen practices . . . can be traced to the mid-1600s and the demystification of those magical arts in which observers confused the 'lifelike' image with life itself" (16). In this way, he retraces a clear-cut line of practices centered on seeing but also including belief, disbelief, and knowledge. Huhtamo, in a more recent essay, "Screen Tests: Why Do We Need an Archaeology of the Screen?," *Cinema Journal* 51, no. 2 (2012): 146–50, recognizes the difficulties in retracing a screen archaeology but ultimately provides a definition that matches the traditional ones: the screen is "a blank surface to be filled with visual information by means of luminous projection" (146). Starting from this definition, Huhtamo expands it in a twofold direction: on one hand, we have "cultural objects that have not been identified as screens, but have nevertheless functioned as surfaces for retrieving and transmitting visual information" (Huhtamo mentions enchanted mirrors and the Panorama, especially the mobile Panorama); on the other hand, we have "objects identified as screens in the past [that] have not always functioned as the screens of today" (Huhtamo mentions fire-screens, fans, etc.)—hence an archaeology that goes beyond Musser's "screen practices" and that adds to them peep practices, touch practices, and mobile practices. With respect to Huhtamo, my claim is that we need to go beyond the consideration of the screen as a support and include in a more strategic way the old meanings of the word as threads to be followed.

76. The concept of cinematic episteme has been discussed and explored by François Albera, "First Discourses on Film and the Construction of a 'Cinematic Episteme,'" in *A Companion to Early Cinema*, ed. André Gaudreault, Nicolas Dulac, and Santiago Hidalgo, 121–40 (Malden, Mass.: John Wiley, 2012).

77. For the crucial decades of the 1920s and 1930s, see Ariel Rogers, *On the Screen* (New York: Columbia University Press, 2019), and Jocelyn Szczepaniak-Gillece, *The Optical Vacuum: Spectatorship and Modernized American Theater Architecture* (Oxford: Oxford University Press, 2018).

78. "I call the distribution of sensible the system of self-evident facts of senses perception that simultaneously discloses the existence of something in common and the delimitations that define the respective parts and positions within it." Jacques Rancière, *The Politics of Aesthetics: The Distribution of the Sensible* (New York: Continuum, 2004), 12. Orig. *Le partage du sensible* (Paris: Fabrique, 2000).

79. On the connection between space and politics, see also Peter Sloterdijk, "Atmospheric Politics," in *Making Things Public*, ed. Bruno Latour and Peter Weibel, 944–51 (Cambridge, Mass.: MIT Press, 2005).

80. This process is common to all media. Indeed, media always tend to be dual; they contain in themselves a sort of divergent double, constituted by both the memory of previous functions and open slots for future aggregations. This doubling complements media's life with a set of possibilities that can be developed in the media's further life or afterlife. In this sense, we must rethink McLuhan's famous sentence: if it is true that content of a medium is always another medium, it is even truer that within a medium—in its folds, so to speak—other, hidden media persist, ready to come out and inflect or deflect a medium's way of working.

81. See, e.g., the work of Anthony McCall, Robert Smithson, and Stan VanDerBeek.

82. On the current "relocation" of cinema, see Francesco Casetti, *The Lumière Galaxy: Seven Key Words for the Cinema to Come* (New York: Columbia University Press, 2015).

83. While focusing on film's role in new media's emergence, I forget neither the part played by television in the transition from traditional to new devices nor the influence of other media like radar in establishing different lineages, nor finally the relevance of artistic experimentation in exploring and deconstructing the optical media's traditional practices and consequently in pushing their perimeters farther.

84. On the nature of display of current screens, and on the new form of visibility they imply, see Casetti, *Lumière Galaxy*, 155–78.

85. Of course, we need to answer the question of what concretely triggers the transition from potentiality to actuality in cinema. The short answer: among the factors to consider is the process of media convergence, the turn toward multiuse devices, and the digitalization of the everyday life, of which the "internet of things" is emblematic. The long answer: the passage from a society centered on

discipline to one centered on control implies an accent on the environment where the mobile subjects live—an environment that at once hides possible threats and is in turn threatened by an irreversible deterioration. In this sense, today, we need fewer stories and more maps—or at least stories in the form of mental maps—both to locate ourselves and the others and to escape from a fearsome condition.

3

Cinema, Nature, and Endangerment

Jennifer Lynn Peterson

Instead of taxidermy we have film.
—Gillian Beer, "Darwin and the Uses of Extinction"

Although analog film has become a rarity today, projected on fewer than 5 percent of global cinema screens, moving image media are flourishing like never before, having found new life in the proliferating forms of digital media.[1] Likewise, seemingly outmoded styles of film, such as silent cinema, are finding new life in the digital age.[2] New forms of media perpetually replace older forms, or so the argument goes; the older forms do not really die but persist in new and formerly unimagined ways. According to this line of thinking, the much-heralded death of cinema is not really a death but part of a regular technological life cycle. There is a cyclical nature to this view of media history that bears some resemblance to the idea of natural history. However, the concept of natural history has been knocked on its side by the emergence of the concept of the Anthropocene. What does the concept of life cycles have left to teach us about survival in the age of environmental crisis?

If photochemical film has reached the end of its first life cycle, perhaps film history can help us come to understand another, much larger death now under way: that of natural ecosystems and the animals and plants they support, commonly referred to as the sixth mass extinction.[3] Perhaps film history might even help us understand what we are now facing: the end of livable climate conditions in the twenty-first century and the uneven dispersal of human and nonhuman suffering that entails. It is no wonder that we look away from these horrendous truths as they punctuate our daily news cycle and, increasingly, our lives. Perhaps, in serving as evidence of endangered habitats and species, archival images of nature's past might bear potential to spark new ecological awareness.

This chapter explores some of the ways in which archival films can help us come to terms with the ecological emergency that is being revealed to us more fully each day. I use examples from film history to show how cinema's role as a machine for envisioning ecosystems can help us trace the evolving concept of "nature" across the long twentieth century. Specifically, I take as a case study a set of educational nature films from the 1920s and 1930s held by the University of Southern California's (USC) Hugh M. Hefner Moving Image Archive (HMIA). My goal is to model an ecologically inspired nonlinear historicism that uses the life cycle of cinema to help us think through ecological collapse.

Archival nature films, preserved and re-presented today, have implications for how we envision the future. As Daniel Rosenberg and Susan Harding have observed, "futures today seem to be reproducing themselves faster and more cheaply than ever. At the same time, their shelf lives appear to be getting shorter.... More and more, our sense of the future is conditioned by a knowledge of, and even a nostalgia for, futures we have already lost."[4] This chapter argues that the futurity of old nature footage has two components: first, a nostalgia for a lost Eden in which nature appears unsullied by humanity's influence, and second, a utopian potential for sparking environmental awareness through a process of revitalization and remediation by digital media.[5] This negative and positive antinomy should not be seen as an inhibiting binary but rather as components of a dialectic that holds promise for a process of overcoming. At stake is the struggle to undo the stubborn idea of the telos of nature, which has been challenged by the emergent concept of the Anthropocene. Moving between historical and contemporary perspectives, my emphasis is on how these films can be relevant to present-day concerns.

Archival nature films activate a powerfully affective mode of endangerment. Nature films made before the onset of the popular environmental movement in the mid-twentieth century do not typically present animals and plant species as endangered, but thanks to the passage of time, these films' original meaning has radically changed. Now that some of these films have been saved and are being rediscovered, they have the potential to be revitalized and reconfigured for new uses. This reimagining has been enabled by the establishment and expansion of media archives in recent decades, thanks to the efforts of archivists, scholars, filmmakers, collectors, and fans, and has arguably entered a new phase with the confluence of Web 2.0 and accelerating evidence of global warming and other forms of environmental degradation. I will discuss three specific case studies in this chapter, but first I want to frame their potential within the context of endangerment, which is an increasingly important contemporary structure of affect.

In a generative essay, science historians Fernando Vidal and Nélia Dias coin the term *endangerment sensibility* to describe a "particularly acute" way of understanding the world through an attitude attuned to loss, disappearance, and preservation.[6] Vidal and Dias are interested in endangerment as it applies to a range of entities, not just endangered biological species but also cultural artifacts, places, and languages. Endangerment relies on scientific knowledge: gathering information, making inventories, studying, and ranking. To classify an entity as endangered means to bring about efforts to preserve, archive, and catalog it. Such a classification is a declaration of value, and endangered entities "acquire significant political and moral valence inside and outside science."[7] The endangerment sensibility thus describes an affective response to hard data. Vidal and Dias characterize the endangerment sensibility's central features as "a certain sentimental impulse, empathy extending to animals, landscapes and marginalized humans, as well as attention to one's own affective experience."[8] While awareness of the phenomenon of extinction certainly predates the mid-twentieth century, the current understanding of loss and destruction is new, "fraught with guilty feelings and a sense of responsibility."[9] Not just a sensibility but a "regime," endangerment names both a structure of affect and a set of complexly determined responses. "The endangerment outlook is both proleptic and regretful," anticipating a future in which something is lost and anticipating a mourning process before the loss happens.[10]

The endangerment sensibility is traumatic but also potentially emancipatory; it looks backward and forward at the same time and is thus useful for the larger project of awakening to ecological awareness that is currently needed. Cinema, with its power to freeze time and capture the excess noise characteristic of the photographic image, is an ideal medium for registering this sense of endangerment. But cinema, by which I mean not only analog film but also the old exhibition context these films formerly inhabited, is now itself a relic. These films come alive today not so much in the cinema but on digital screens. As reconfigured in the era of digital media, archival fragments hold a potential to activate unanticipated responses. As it heralds new forms of visualization by remediating outmoded films, perhaps digital media and even film history itself can help us shift into a new mode of thinking to meet the challenge of living within limited possibilities.

Endangerment: An Anthropocene Sensibility

One great paradox of ecological awareness in this moment is the realization that the future of the world and all who inhabit it has been irrevocably shaped by actions in the past. As Bruno Latour puts it, "it seems as though we have become the people *who could have acted* thirty or forty years ago—and who did nothing, or far too little."[11] Rising CO_2 levels, deforestation, pesticides, and plastic pollution, to name just a few symptoms of the ecological crisis, passed the point of large-scale harm decades ago. The so-called Great Acceleration began in 1945, putting into place exponentially greater rates of resource extraction and waste production than ever before seen.[12] These specific conditions, along with the structural inequities of capitalism and continuing forms of imperialism, have brought about a host of unintended consequences to earth systems that we are now witnessing. We learn about the ecological impact of all this when it seems too late to do anything about it (or rather, after the forces of capitalist accumulation and consumption have produced an outcome in which nothing was done). However, as a chorus of voices point out, such an attitude of game-over despair is a barrier to life as it remains. This chapter, and my larger project of arguing for film history as a tool of awakening and adjustment, is indebted to Donna Haraway's approach to ecological crisis. She writes, "I am not interested in reconciliation or restoration, but I am deeply committed to the more modest possibilities of partial recuperation and getting on together. Call that staying with the trouble."[13]

As a sensibility, endangerment is well suited to the Anthropocene epoch. Although its precise moment of emergence would be hard to pin down (a task that lies beyond the scope of the present chapter in any case), the endangerment sensibility arguably infiltrates mass culture more thoroughly with each extreme heat wave, record-setting hurricane, and devastating wildfire. At the time of this writing, the United Nations–sponsored Intergovernmental Panel on Climate Change (IPCC) 2018 report has just been released, and the news is full of the study's key findings. Headlines have focused on the report's claim that we have only twelve years to curb carbon emissions, after which time, if nothing is done, the planet will pass 1.5 degrees Celsius of warming, which will trigger a planetary catastrophe.[14] While news of climate change appears with growing frequency, this report takes a notably alarmist tone, and it has garnered more of a popular response than usual; even *Saturday Night Live* riffed on it for two minutes at the top of its news parody "Weekend Update" in its October 13 episode. By the time this chapter is published, more alarming scientific studies will have appeared. Against this backdrop, endangerment becomes a key sensibility for this moment of dawning mass awareness. The endangerment sensibility implies a perspective of scanning across different moments of history, incorporating a sense of what was, what is, and what might be. In this sense of multiple time frames, it shares some of the temporal disjunction of the concept of the Anthropocene itself.

Although the term is increasingly well-known in the humanities disciplines, here is a brief review. The term *Anthropocene* was introduced in 2000 by biologist Eugene Stoermer and Nobel Prize–winning chemist Paul Crutzen, who proposed that the human species' rapid expansion has transformed the earth's systems so radically that it has entered a new epoch.[15] There is continuing debate about when the Anthropocene began, but each proposed date is tied to a measurable indexical trace left on the planet, known as a golden spike, such as carbon dioxide, nitrogen, or radionuclides measurable in ice and rock cores. The leading contenders for the onset of the Anthropocene are 1610, when the colonization of the Americas can be traced by a dip in planetary carbon dioxide levels; 1782, when the steam engine was invented by James Watt, resulting in worldwide carbon deposits by new coal-powered industries; or 1945, with the Trinity atomic bomb test, which heralded the onset of the nuclear age and its subsequent plutonium fallout. According to one working group, sixty-five golden spikes of the geological time scale are currently being considered (others include plastic traces found in ocean and lake floor sediment). Scientific consensus on the Anthropocene's onset will come from the International Commission on Stratigraphy, which has yet to officially adopt the term as it continues to study it.[16]

Despite the official hesitation of geological science, many other academic disciplines have taken up the term *Anthropocene*.[17] A consensus has clearly formed around the idea that we have entered a new geological epoch in which human actions have irrevocably altered the course of the planet's life cycle. The arts and humanities have been particularly enthusiastic in adopting the term, though its ethical valence is the subject of fierce debate. The conflict over the term *Anthropocene* centers on whether it privileges or decenters the *anthropos,* or humans. Some have argued that the term reinscribes an anthropocentric view of human dominance, and alternative terms, such as *Capitalocene* and *Chthulucene,* have been suggested. There is no doubt that the resource-burning capitalists of the United States and Europe bear most of the responsibility for this crisis, which disproportionately harms people with less wealth and fewer resources. However, I do not see the term as masking this uneven culpability. Moreover, the Anthropocene idea would seem to announce precisely the opposite of a triumphant reign of humanity. From this perspective, the Anthropocene displaces humans from the center of the universe by redefining them as merely one actant among many in a geological history in which the earth will, of course, outlast humans. From this perspective, global warming is earth systems' response to the blundering, selfish actions of (some) humans, all of whom it will eventually expel.

Regardless of what we call the era, the material traces of humanity are now embedded in the earth's soil, trees, and ice cores and are manifest in the millions of tons of plastic microfibers in the ocean. It is no far stretch to recognize that the Anthropocene has also left different kinds of traces in human culture. While some film historians have begun studying cinema as an industrial product that leaves a measurable footprint of waste, I am interested in cinema's ability to trace cultural forces.[18] I contend that film, with its celebrated ability as a medium of capture, allows us to trace the visualization of what we call "nature" and that these traces are particularly revealing before the rise of the mainstream environmental movement at mid-century. The endangerment sensibility that emerged with popular environmentalism changes the meaning of earlier cinematic visualizations.

The Anthropocene upsets traditional historical methodologies. As Dipesh Chakrabarty has written, "the discussion about the crisis of climate change can thus produce affect and knowledge about collective human pasts and futures that work at the limits of historical understanding. We experience specific effects of the crisis but not the whole phenomenon."[19] I suggest that the urgency of the current moment requires a new form of strategic ahistoricism. The reverse zoom of Anthropocene history (akin to the famous reverse zoom camera technique used in Alfred Hitchcock's *Vertigo* [1958]) involves a dizzying confluence of human and nonhuman perspectives. Situating media history in its relation to geological history entails bridging incommensurate time scales, but it is precisely the disorienting perspective of the Anthropocene, where previously slow-paced geological and climatological transformations appear accelerated to the scale of human action, that makes these connections apparent.

Archival Films and the Nature Study Tradition

Film historians and archivists are creatures who dwell in a paradoxical habitat of love and death, attached both intellectually and affectively to the materials we study and preserve. As scholars such as Carolyn Steedman and Lorraine Daston have pointed out, the history of the archive is a history of loss, and the archive can be seen as a space of melancholy.[20] The fragments that remain are signs of everything that has not survived. These fragments are themselves fragile and in danger of disappearance. Jacques Derrida famously dubbed the impossible desire to preserve the past "archive fever" and linked it to the Freudian death drive. Observing the impossible dream of knowing the past through fragments, along with the impossible dream of understanding what these fragments will mean in the future, he wrote, "The archive: if we want to know what this will have meant, we will only know in the times to come. Perhaps. Not tomorrow but in the times to come, later on or perhaps never."[21] Latent in the archival impulse is a utopian fantasy of understanding experience through fragments. Archival nature films present us with tantalizing fragments of nature's past.

Educational cinema was becoming institutionalized in the years before World War II thanks to the development of a nontheatrical distribution network in the 1920s, along with the introduction of 16mm film in 1923.[22] Like other early educational genres, nature films were shown nontheatrically in classrooms and other venues, such as public halls and museums, and they were also shown theatrically as shorts before the feature film. Paralleling these two different exhibition contexts, these films were often released in 16mm for nontheatrical use and 35mm for theatrical exhibition. Generations of children and adults watched these simple films about animal and plant species, seasons, and ecosystems, which attempted to visualize natural history and foster a love of nature. Unlike narrative films, which quickly became outdated due to their use of the stars and styles of a particular cultural moment, these nature films had a longer shelf life and were often shown decades after they were made. Watching these pre–World War II films today, we see what nature looked like in an earlier era, which allows us to see how much "nature" has changed.

Early nature films used the modern form of cinema to present what was by this time an old paradigm of nature study involving a simple visual display of information.[23] The nature study movement that emerged as part of the progressive school reforms of the late nineteenth century aimed to cultivate direct observation of nature. The nature study method involved showing and (when possible) touching specimens and organisms, rather than learning complex facts about their biology. As Oliver Gaycken has written, "instead of objectivity's restraint, nineteenth century popular science retained ties to previous traditions of display and their engagement with the senses and the affective states of curiosity and wonder."[24] The nature study tradition was a form of popular science, and while it was discredited by modern science by the time these films were made, it has remained one of the predominant styles of nature documentaries to this day, and it proved influential for the nature literature tradition as well. These were popular films, not scientific tools, and they did not model up-to-date laboratory methods. Instead, these films present nature as an ideal domain: separate from the human realm, eternal, static.

The three 1920s nature films I discuss herein come from USC's HMIA, which holds a collection of 16mm educational films from the pre–World War II era donated by the late David Shepard. The 550-reel collection originated with Akin and Bagshaw, a Denver-based distributor of educational films whose territory ranged over ten states in the western United States. The collection contains many gems, including science films, travel films, and a number of Eastman Teaching films, and it is particularly rich in nature films. The thousand-foot reels came to the archive with titles written on the cans but nothing more. Searching through the collection is an act of discovery. Many of the films in the collection were previously unidentified or incorrectly labeled, including those I discuss in this chapter, two out of three of which I have been able to positively identify.

Films such as *Nature's Handiwork* (F. Percy Smith, 1921), *The Four Seasons* (Raymond Ditmars, 1921), and *Alaska's Eighth Wonder* (director unknown, circa 1925) presented popularized versions of scientific ideas about the life cycle of organisms, evolution, and earth systems. (All three of these films have been digitized and are available for online viewing at the URLs listed in the endnotes.) Early nature films exploited photochemical cinema's technological capacities to the limit, using slow motion, fast motion, microscopic photography, and an array of staging techniques, such as terrariums, aquariums, purpose-built sets, and careful lighting design, all in the service of offering visually striking perspectives on nature to the film spectator. Each of the three examples I analyze pushes on an aspect of cinema's potential to awaken an ecological awareness in the viewers of the past, and in viewers today.

Nature's Handiwork

Nature's Handiwork was part of the Kineto Review series of nonfiction shorts released in the United States by British-based distributor Charles Urban, starting in February 1921.[25] There were several such "screen magazines" in the 1910s and 1920s, and they were closely allied with the emergent form of the newsreel; these single-reel films emphasized a variety of general interest items and were shown theatrically before feature films. A 1922 advertisement for Urban's Kineto films lists *Nature's Handiwork* as one of fifty-two available titles ranging across a wide variety of subjects, including films such as *Abraham Lincoln, Seeds and Seed Dispersal, Beasts of Prey,* and *Modern Banking.*[26] The Kineto Review series was part of Urban's ambitious project to film what he called a "Living Book of Knowledge." Film historian Luke McKernan explains that this series included a mixture of new material and footage "plundered" from pre–World War I films in the Urban back library.[27] *Nature's Handiwork,* however, was most likely filmed entirely after World War I.[28]

As the title card of *Nature's Handiwork* informs us, the film is about the "Wondrous phases of life and transformation of caterpillars, moths, butterflies" (Figure 3.1). Made by F. Percy Smith, one of the first great auteurs of natural history in popular cinema, in collaboration with camera operator Charles D. Head, the film visualizes basic information in a striking way, presenting extreme close-ups of butterfly faces and showing the metamorphosis of moths using time lapse photography. It is an aesthetically accomplished film as well as a fascinating portrayal of what Smith and Head felt would be important to convey about insects to a

Figure 3.1. *Nature's Handiwork* (F. Percy Smith, 1921) presents insects as wondrous and nature as eternal. Frame enlargement courtesy of the University of Southern California Moving Image Archive.

popular audience. In focusing on insects, the film encourages a broadening of the spectator's appreciation for nature beyond the more commonly beloved animal realm of mammals. Indeed, Smith once said, "If I think anything is a pest, I make a film about it; then it becomes beautiful."[29] True to form, the film opens with an intertitle proclaiming, "The eggs of the Lepidoptera (butterfly) are very beautiful objects," followed by a series of shots that highlight the eggs' circle grid patterns. Most of the film's shots feature a pared-down background of black or white, decontextualizing the insects from their habitat (until the last few shots in the garden) in order to closely study their form and movement. The film exhibits a fascination with graphic shapes throughout: not just butterfly eggs but also scales, eyes, and a striking tongue montage make this visualization of information feel distinctly modern.

This single-reel film was imported to the United States and shown in commercial theaters, where it was projected in 35mm alongside various feature films.[30] It was also distributed on 16mm and shown in schools and other nontheatrical venues, where it remained in circulation for many years. The catalog *1000 and One: The Blue Book of Non-theatrical Films* lists both 35mm and 16mm silent prints available for rent from four different distributors as late as 1936, and the film was most likely being shown in classrooms well after World War II.[31] Upon its theatrical release in 1921, reviewers praised *Nature's Handiwork* for its "surprising amount of informative data" and for being "truly remarkable in the photographic treatment of the subject matter and amount of information contained."[32]

Almost one hundred years later, however, this film's meaning has changed. Take the sequence on the tortoiseshell butterfly (Figure 3.2). This footage renders spectacular the life cycle of an ordinary creature, for the tortoiseshell butterfly was one of the most common species in the United Kingdom when this film was made. But tortoiseshell butterfly populations have plummeted by 75 percent since the 1970s, when their numbers began to be monitored, and this stark decline has been all over the British news for the past few years. (The species' population fluctuates slightly year to year—the numbers improved in 2014 but have declined again in subsequent years.)[33] And the news is bad for all invertebrates, which are facing a so-called insect Armageddon in which all populations have declined precipitously in the past twenty-five years (insect biomass has declined between 45 percent and 75 percent, according to different studies).[34] The causes are various but include pesticides, global warming, and habitat loss. This is a catastrophe of epic proportions, not just for the insects (which make up about two-thirds of all life on earth) but for many other species, including the birds who eat them as well as us humans, who depend on insects to pollinate our food. In light of climate change and other forms of environmental collapse, the nature study films of the early twentieth century register today less as films that cultivate a love of nature and more as melancholy chronicles of loss.

In drawing out the different meanings of this image of a tortoiseshell butterfly in different historical moments, I am not intending to naively reassert the original film's referential realism. Rather, the point is that the passage of time has transformed this image from a visual curiosity to a memento mori. Rather than beaming with pleasure and wonderment at the nature film's revelation of the world's creatures, we now shudder with

Figure 3.2. The small tortoiseshell butterfly, once common in the United Kingdom where *Nature's Handiwork* was filmed, now faces a severe population decline; its numbers have fallen by an estimated 75 percent since 1976. Frame enlargement courtesy of the University of Southern California Moving Image Archive.

dread and despair at their shrinking fortunes and, by extension, our own precarious future. Of course, I am exaggerating somewhat, for this response depends on the spectator's relative level of knowledge about the species being shown and environmental problems more generally. Ecological awareness in the face of threatened and collapsing earth systems is a process, and still a relatively new one. We are all at different points in this process, but it seems clear that new forms of mass subjectivity will form around awareness of planetary crisis as it continues to take shape. As yet, it is unclear what shape these new forms of environmental awareness will take. For now, it is an unpredictable process without end.

We are familiar with talking about how old films are threatened: by nitrate degeneration, by a lack of funding for storage and preservation, and by a general undervaluation by the culture at large. And of course, we all know that historical films show us things that are lost: the people have died, the cities have changed, the clothes and cars no longer exist. But natural history films purport to show timeless nature, enduring species, and regular life cycles. The individual animals may be dead, but the life-forms continue. Indeed, the very point of natural history films is to show that change is cyclical but nature is eternal. As it turns out, what we call nature is not as eternal as we had thought.

The Four Seasons

This logic of nature's eternal cycle is the subject of *The Four Seasons,* an ambitious four-reel feature released to great acclaim the same year as *Nature's Handiwork.* The HMIA holds two of the film's four reels, "Spring" and "Summer," on which I shall concentrate here.[35] In its day, *The Four Seasons* struck a chord: the film was a critical and commercial success around the country, often running as part of a double bill with the Harold Lloyd comedy *A Sailor Made Man.*[36] The complete film containing all four seasons was advertised with the tagline "Living a Year in an Hour."[37] Structured around the compression of time, the film offers fragmented images of plants and animals that are visually striking; however, the film presents very little information about each of the species depicted. The nature film's rhetoric of generalization reaches a kind of limit case in this film, but this generalization is itself significant.

The film was directed by Raymond Ditmars, herpetologist at the New York Zoological Park, otherwise known as the Bronx Zoo. Ditmars was already an established natural history lecturer and had published several books on wildlife before he started filming zoo animals around 1908.[38] He began selling footage to Pathé, which used his footage in its newsreels beginning in September 1913.[39] Like Smith, Ditmars is one of the most important directors of early nature films. Although they were based in different countries (Smith in England and Ditmars in the United States), the men shared much in common. Born within four years of each other (Smith in 1880 and Ditmars in 1876), neither man was formally educated, but both were frequently referred to as "professor" in the press. Also like Smith, Ditmars built a filmmaking "studio-laboratory" at his home in Scarsdale, New York, where he made films with his wife, Clara, as pictured

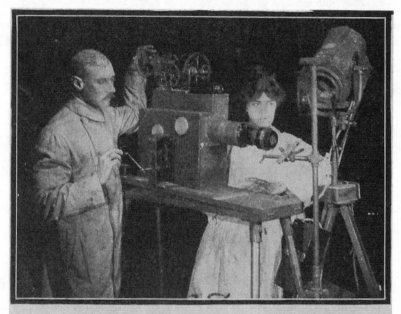

Mr. and Mrs. Ditmars at work in the laboratory with an intricate camera which may be thrown into various ratios of gear in order to photograph and portray types of motion that are too quick for the eye to follow. The camera is fitted with a lens of great magnifying power and records the most intimate close-ups of the smaller creatures.

Figure 3.3. Husband and wife nature filmmaking team, as pictured in *Photoplay*, January 1919.

in an elaborate three-page story in the usually star-obsessed popular film magazine *Photoplay* in 1919 (Figure 3.3). Both Smith and Ditmars were popularizers who did not hesitate to downplay the naturalism of their subject matter in favor of cultivating popular appeal.

Educational film distributor Charles Urban distributed the films of both Smith and Ditmars. To some degree, we can observe that Smith's films prioritize striking visual compositions, whereas Ditmars's films focus more on constructing animal characters, though this distinction is not absolute. Ditmars trained his zoo animals to act for the screen, as he proudly explained in numerous articles for the press. "Monkeys . . . can register every mood that a human can—anger, despair and joy."[40] Ditmars's anthropomorphism runs counter to the (problematic) concept of non-human nature's absolute separation from the human that later came to dominate the nature film in wildlife series such as *Wild Kingdom* (which began in 1963 and has recently been revived on Animal Planet). However, both Smith and Ditmars relied on the camera's ability to produce in humans an anthropomorphic identification with other creatures, a phenomenon that several critics, including André Bazin, discussed some decades later.[41]

In *The Four Seasons,* the natural world is presented as eternal realm, fulfilling the telos of nature as an ideal domain whose organizing principle is the cycle of the seasons. The film shows an array of plant and animal species that perhaps seemed wide ranging at the time, but now seems limited and reliant on what Ditmars had on hand in the Bronx Zoo. We see pussy willows, apple blossoms, pollywogs, woodchucks, peacocks, bears, emus, bats, and deer, among other flora and fauna. Specific details and even species names are omitted; instead, "Spring" focuses on babies, introducing many of the aforementioned animal types in their infant stage. An intertitle tells us, "And all around this big, wide world, Nature entrusts her wild babies to the tenderness of maturing Spring." What this reel lacks in information it makes up for in striking visual imagery; each shot feels designed to elicit wonderment and a kind of sentimental affirmation that all is right with the world.

In "Summer," the natural world becomes a more dangerous domain. While nature is still presented as a nurturing habitat, this reel introduces a fairly long sequence about weather in which dramatic clouds gather over the forest, lightning strikes, and a deluge of rain and hail follows. The emphasis on clouds in this sequence is interesting for its shift away from charismatic fauna to an insistence on the poetic drama of a summer storm. When the storm is over, we are shown "the grandeur of the departing storm from a mountain top, on a level with the boiling cumulous clouds." Subsequent shots portray trees struck by lightning and a girl examining the damage while "standing upon a spot where painless and instant death would have been dealt a moment before." Any threat that creeps into this world, however, is contained by the notion that nature is an ideal domain that admits struggle only within a limited system. Moreover, for the film spectator sitting safely outside the world of the film, the drama of nature depicted feels distant, a visual curiosity but not a bodily threat. In this aspect, the film certainly contributes its share to Francesco Casetti's notion of the theater as a milieu of comfort, safety, and full visibility by providing a contrasting screenscape of nature as a domain of discomfort and danger.[42] That is the properly historical reading.

But watching this film today, we might think how many of the animals shown in the film are now threatened, including bees, bats, frogs, trout, and polar bears (Figure 3.4). Because the film is so general in its categorizations, we cannot know how much this particular kind of frog is endangered, and the same is true for the rest of the species visualized. (The news is not good for amphibians in general, which are one of the most threatened taxonomic groups, and which have come to be known as canaries in the coal mine of climate change.[43]) We can learn something from the lack of specificity in this film, however, for it foreshadows the way that today's viewer might think in a similarly generalized manner about the loss of animal life on the planet. This generalizing effect, present in both the historical nature film and today's emergent popular understanding of climate change, underscores the way in which complex and dynamic scientific topics become generalized into the tropes of mass culture.

Literary scholar Gillian Beer writes about how the visual technologies of modernity increase the appreciation of nature because they "enforce a stark recognition of how much is lost each time a species fails. Whereas in Darwin's time, specimens ... were mainly seen dead and static in museums, now we respond to movement and flight. Instead of taxidermy we have film."[44] Gradually across the twentieth century, the

Figure 3.4. *The Four Seasons* (Raymond Ditmars, 1921) pays particular attention to the life cycle of frogs (without naming any specific species); amphibians are one of the most threatened taxonomic groups today. Frame enlargement courtesy of the University of Southern California Moving Image Archive.

popular conception of the environment shifted from viewing nature as robust, eternally engaged in a battle for survival, toward viewing nature as something vulnerable. Nature films such as these capture in amber a sense of what nature meant in the 1920s, showing the movement of organisms long dead. But like taxidermy, these nature films now constitute an outmoded form of display. Like stuffed specimens, the films have become aesthetic relics, conveying a sense of pastness when seen in the present.

The endangerment sensibility brings about a kind of ecological viewing condition that we might call Anthropocene film reception. Now that climate change is taught to elementary school children (and despite the efforts of numerous corporations and politicians to deny it), it would seem difficult to view these films today outside the endangerment sensibility. But this kind of reception context is relatively new, tracking alongside the increasingly apocalyptic news stories about the environment, and it is relative to the spectator's own level of knowledge about environmental problems. I am well aware that this kind of interpretation is a form of presentism, one of the classic historian's fallacies that we are supposed to avoid. This reading is a deliberate projection of a contemporary idea onto media from the past. But the Anthropocene epoch has created such a singular situation that it challenges established historical methods and requires moving back and forth between thinking across the incommensurate time scales of the human and the planetary.[45]

Alaska's Eighth Wonder

My final example is from a reel labeled simply "An Alaskan Glacier." For more than eleven minutes, this film shows us dramatic images of glacier ice breaking off, crashing down, and floating off in a roiling flood of icy water (Figure 3.5).[46] When I first encountered this reel in the archive, its stunning footage of melting glacier ice read to me as a film about climate change. But this was clearly the second reel of a longer film, and once I identified reel 1 (among the several other Alaska reels in the HMIA collection), I was able to learn more about the history of this specific glacier. Reel 1 gives the film its official title, *Alaska's Eighth Wonder,* and places the footage at Lake George, located about fifty miles north of Anchorage, which means the glacier shown is Knik Glacier (which is never named in the film). Lake George used to be known as the Self-Emptying Lake because it drained suddenly and regularly each year, flooding the nearby area. As it turns out, this film depicts an unusual natural phenomenon, a glacier lake outburst flood (also known by the Icelandic term *jökulhlaup*).[47] What this film recorded is the Knik Glacier's annual glacial outburst flood taking place sometime in the 1920s. The ice is crashing down in this film not because of climate change (which was not happening in the 1920s like it is now) but because of a regular natural phenomenon. In fact, the annual emptying of Lake George ceased in 1967, due to glacial recession caused by a range of factors, including climate change.

In its time, this film showed audiences a remarkable seasonal event in a faraway location. Unlike other Alaska films in the HMIA collection, which focus on local cultures and traditions in addition to the natural scenery, this film concentrates entirely on landscapes and glaciers. In its

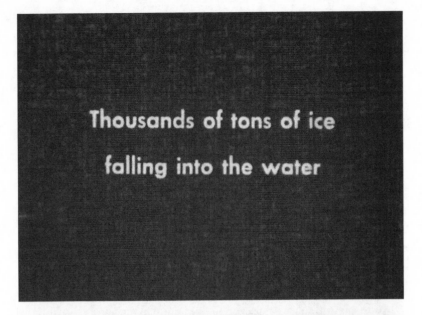

Figure 3.5. *Alaska's Eighth Wonder* (circa 1925) features dramatic images of a melting glacier. While this reads today as a film about climate change, in fact the film shows a naturally occurring glacier lake outburst flood at Knik Glacier on Lake George. This formerly annual phenomenon ceased in 1967 due to factors including climate change. Frame enlargements courtesy of the University of Southern California Moving Image Archive.

original context, this film fit into the popular science logic of natural won-
ders and amazing phenomena; it functioned as a curiosity. Today, however, even when we are told that this is not a film about climate change,
the footage of melting glaciers and dramatic ice shears still makes us
think of climate change.[48] Melting glaciers have of course become one
of the most important symbolic images of global warming, and in the
popular imagination, this is what such images signify. The passage of time
has changed the meaning of this film. Our knowledge of the Anthropocene has created a new reception context in which it is impossible to view
melting glacier images as anything other than harbingers of a warming world.

Ecological Awakening for a Limited Future

Because environmental catastrophe does not happen suddenly, with the
flash of an atom bomb, we have trouble seeing it. Because its point of
no return is not clearly marked, we have trouble understanding just how
bad things are at any given time. Because ecological collapse (and, indeed, the environment itself) is massively distributed in time and space,
we have trouble grasping its scope and scale. Nonetheless, an environmental awareness did develop across the long twentieth century, and film
history, as glimpsed in archival nature films, provides us with an un-
paralleled opportunity to explore the forms this awareness took. Moreover, when viewed today, these films possess an uncanny visual power. As
now-threatened species come to us visualized through the outmoded
technology and styles of silent cinema, these films crystallize a temporal discontinuity. As these long-dead moths and frogs creep through a
rupture in time, they bring a potential to spark new forms of ecological
awakening.

Public consciousness is clearly lagging behind actual developments in
the environmental crisis. Not just a melancholy sense of endangerment
but a kind of shock to the senses or a startling awake is needed to galva-
nize public opinion and action. One consistent thread of environmental
humanities scholarship argues that, while the scientists are collecting and
interpreting the data needed to understand the calamitous deforestation,
defaunation, and global warming afflicting the planet, it is the artists,

writers, and humanities scholars who are needed to produce stories about what is going on so that the public will listen, understand, and act. I contend that these modest archival nature films can contribute to this project of ecological awakening.

According to Timothy Morton, global warming is a "hyperobject" so colossal that it is nearly imperceptible to humans.[49] What Chakrabarty discusses in terms of incommensurable scales of time Morton conceives of as incommensurable scales of space; in both cases, new forms of awareness are needed to awaken humanity to this crisis, which is vastly larger than itself. *Ecological awareness* is a term that Morton uses across his body of work, where it signifies not just knowledge of the crisis but a sense of its uncanny nature.[50] Not everyone may be capable of ecological awareness, given the resistances our culture has already developed in response to it, but there is arguably a sizable section of the public that would be receptive to the uncanny lessons of such films. Today, these films can function as a kind of collective memory. As they circulate in academic conferences and classrooms, on YouTube and the Internet Archive, and as they serve as source material for contemporary found footage films, perhaps these films can awaken us from our complacency and spark new ideas about the history and future of the environment.

In a recent book, film scholar Catherine Russell discusses a contemporary filmmaking practice she calls "archiveology," by which she means the current "practice of remixing, recycling, and reconfiguring the image bank."[51] Focusing on the experimental tradition of filmmakers such as Gustav Deutsch, Bill Morrison, Matthias Müller, and Nicole Védrès, Russell analyzes the trend in which archival footage is recycled and appropriated in new films. Reading this work through the critical lens of Walter Benjamin, Russell argues that archival footage functions as a form of memory in which, following Benjamin's lead, "the 'richest prize' is the correspondence between present and past."[52] I concur with Russell but would take her point further to argue that archival footage itself, whether or not it has been reactivated by an experimental filmmaker, harbors this power of uncanny discontinuity.

Writing in the years before World War II, during the time these archival nature films were made, Benjamin, along with Siegfried Kracauer and several other critics associated with the Frankfurt School, criticized mass culture as a mode of distraction symptomatic of a society headed toward catastrophe. Their arguments were varied, yet they shared a consistent thread that the means to overcome this distraction were to be found within mass culture itself. One of Benjamin's favored (and much-quoted) means of initiating a process of awakening from the dream-world of mass culture was a surrealist practice he called "profane illumination." In this method, what is required is not so much an artwork but *a way of seeing* that reveals "the revolutionary energies that appear in the outmoded."[53] Benjamin was writing in a moment that Miriam Hansen has described as defined by "ongoing crisis—the triumph of fascism in Germany and the threat of its expansion in France, the collapse of an existing socialist regime with the reign of Stalinism—and the challenge to imagine an all-but-impossible future."[54] This moment of urgent crisis bears resemblance to our own moment almost a century later, in which it is becoming ever more difficult to imagine the future. As such, the utopian and even messianic strain of Benjamin's and Kracauer's writings has taken on new appeal in the current moment. This is not the place to work through the ways in which these theorists' work can be applied to the environmental humanities, but suffice it to say for now that Benjamin's commitment to a project of "awakening" is germane to our current need for ecological awakening.

The twentieth-century experience of cinema may have lost its former vitality, but perhaps a better way to conceptualize this is as a metamorphosis into digital formats. Films such as these, preserved in the archive and finding a new digital life online, can help us see what used to seem eternal and thereby shock us into seeing what is on the verge of being lost. There are thousands of these orphaned nature films in archives around the world, whose images wait to be adopted. We can hope that as scholars, curators, and filmmakers study, recycle, and remix these films, and as viewers become more adept at our digital culture's peculiar way of sampling historical images, these films' naive insistence on nature's timelessness can be reconfigured to help us radically rethink our sense of historical time on a planetary scale. Coming to terms with ecological loss is just one of several urgent tasks that face us today. Perhaps, out of the ruins of what we have lost, we might discover the engine for a utopian reimagining of our limited future.

Notes

My thanks to Dino Everett, archivist at the Hugh M. Hefner Moving Image Archive at the University of Southern California. Thanks also to Dan Streible and to audiences who heard earlier versions of this chapter at the eleventh Orphan Film Symposium at the Museum of the Moving Image in New York and at the 2018 Ends of Cinema conference at the Center for 21st Century Studies at the University of Wisconsin–Milwaukee.

1. Motion Picture Association of America, *Theatrical Market Statistics 2016* (Washington, D.C.: MPAA, 2016), 8, https://www.mpaa.org/wp-content/uploads/2017/03/MPAA-Theatrical-Market-Statistics-2016_Final.pdf.

2. See Paul Flaig and Katherine Groo, eds., *New Silent Cinema* (New York: Routledge, 2016).

3. Elizabeth Kolbert, *The Sixth Extinction: An Unnatural History* (New York: Henry Holt, 2014).

4. Daniel Rosenberg and Susan Harding, "Introduction: Histories of the Future," in *Histories of the Future*, ed. Daniel Rosenberg and Susan Harding (Durham, N.C.: Duke University Press, 2005), 3.

5. Jay David Bolter and Richard Grusin, *Remediation: Understanding New Media* (Cambridge, Mass.: MIT Press, 2000).

6. Fernando Vidal and Nélia Dias, "Introduction: The Endangerment Sensibility," in *Endangerment, Biodiversity, and Culture*, ed. Fernando Vidal and Nélia Dias (New York: Routledge, 2016), 2.

7. Vidal and Dias, 1.

8. Vidal and Dias, 2.

9. Vidal and Dias, 3.

10. Vidal and Dias, 5.

11. Bruno Latour, *Facing Gaia: Eight Lectures on the New Climactic Regime* (Cambridge, U.K.: Polity, 2017), 9, emphasis original.

12. J. R. McNeill and Peter Engelke, *The Great Acceleration: An Environmental History of the Anthropocene since 1945* (Cambridge, Mass.: Harvard University Press, 2016).

13. Donna J. Haraway, *Staying with the Trouble: Making Kin in the Chthulucene* (Durham, N.C.: Duke University Press, 2016), 10.

14. Jonathan Watts, "We Have 12 Years to Limit Climate Change Catastrophe, Warns UN," *Guardian*, October 8, 2018, https://www.theguardian.com/environment/2018/oct/08/global-warming-must-not-exceed-15c-warns-landmark-un-report.

15. Paul Crutzen and Eugene Stoermer, "'The Anthropocene,'" *Global Change Newsletter*, no. 41 (May 2000): 17–18, http://www.igbp.net/download/18.316f18321 32347017758000140l/1376383088452/NL41.pdf. Stoermer had been using the term *Anthropocene* informally since the 1980s, but it did not gain traction until he and Crutzen joined forces to launch it.

16. University of Leicester, "Scientists Home in on a Potential Anthropocene 'Golden Spike,'" *ScienceDaily,* http://www.sciencedaily.com/releases/2018/01/18 0115095158.htm.

17. For a useful overview of the Anthropocene's dissemination as an idea, see Rob Nixon, "The Anthropocene: The Promise and Pitfalls of an Epochal Idea," in *Future Remains: A Cabinet of Curiosities for the Anthropocene,* ed. Gregg Mitman, Marco Armiero, and Robert S. Emmett, 1–18 (Chicago: University of Chicago Press, 2018).

18. Hunter Vaughan, *Hollywood's Dirtiest Secret: The Hidden Environmental Costs of the Movies* (New York: Columbia University Press, 2019).

19. Dipesh Chakrabarty, "The Climate of History: Four Theses," *Critical Inquiry* 35, no. 2 (2009): 221.

20. Antoinette Burton, "Thinking beyond the Boundaries: Empire, Feminism and the Domains of History," *Social History* 26, no. 1 (2001): 66, quoted in Carolyn Steedman, *Dust: The Archive and Cultural History* (New Brunswick, N.J.: Rutgers University Press 2002), 5; Lorraine Daston, "The Immortal Archive: Nineteenth Century Science Imagines the Future," in *Science in the Archives: Pasts, Presents, Futures,* ed. Lorraine Daston (Chicago: University of Chicago Press, 2017), 175.

21. Jacques Derrida, "Archive Fever," *Diacritics,* Summer 1995, 27.

22. See Charles R. Acland and Haidee Wasson, *Useful Cinema* (Durham, N.C.: Duke University Press, 2011), and Devin Orgeron, Marsha Orgeron, and Dan Streible, eds., *Learning with the Lights Off: Educational Film in the United States* (London: Oxford University Press, 2012).

23. See Jennifer Peterson, "Glimpses of Animal Life: Nature Films and the Emergence of Classroom Cinema," in Orgeron et al., *Learning with the Lights Off,* 145–67.

24. Oliver Gaycken, *Devices of Curiosity: Early Cinema and Popular Science* (New York: Oxford University Press, 2015), 4.

25. The HMIA's print of *Nature's Handiwork* is available for viewing at https://vimeo.com/237481574.

26. Ad for Urban's Kineto Company films in *Exhibitor's Herald,* August 5, 1922, 18.

27. Luke McKernan, *Charles Urban: Pioneering the Non-fiction Film in Britain and America, 1897–1925* (Exeter, U.K.: University of Exeter Press, 2013), 176–77.

28. Several reviews in the trade press credit Charles D. Head as a co-creator of the film, which indicates that this was a post–World War I production, for Smith worked with Head on the *Secrets of Nature* series beginning in 1922. McKernan observes that the smoothness of the animation looks like a more advanced postwar technique, and he writes, "I'd say from what we see of him at the end of the film that it is a post-war Smith." Email from Luke McKernan to the author, October 9, 2018.

29. Quoted in Gaycken, *Devices of Curiosity,* 87–88.

30. "The Screen," *New York Times,* February 21, 1921, n.p.

31. *1000 and One: The Blue Book of Non-theatrical Films,* 11th ed. (Chicago: Educational Screen, 1935), 84. *Mogull's 16mm Silent Picture Film Library* (New York, 1940) lists the film in distribution as late as 1940.

32. Lillian Gale, review of *Nature's Handiwork, Motion Picture News,* February 12, 1921, 1392; "Short Subjects of Importance," *Moving Picture World,* February 12, 1921, 852.

33. For an update on the small tortoiseshell butterfly's population decline, see Patrick Barkham, "Fears Grow for Small Tortoiseshell Butterfly as Decline Continues," *Guardian,* September 24, 2018, https://www.theguardian.com/environ ment/2018/sep/24/small-tortoiseshell-butterfly-as-decline-continues.

34. New York Times Editorial Board, "Insect Armageddon," *New York Times,* October 29, 2017, https://www.nytimes.com/2017/10/29/opinion/insect-armaged don-ecosystem-.html. See also Ben Guarino, "'Hyperalarming' Study Shows Massive Insect Loss," *Washington Post,* October 15, 2018, https://www.washington post.com/science/2018/10/15/hyperalarming-study-shows-massive-insect-loss/.

35. The HMIA's print of *The Four Seasons,* "Spring" can be viewed at https://vimeo.com/237764828; *The Four Seasons,* "Summer" can be viewed at https://vimeo.com/237461338. While the HMIA apparently holds only two of the feature's four reels, the EYE Filmmuseum Netherlands holds a print of the complete film (with Dutch intertitles and color tinting), which can be viewed at https://www .openimages.eu/media/685757/Four_seasons_The. Reels 1 and 2 of the EYE print are somewhat longer than those held by the HMIA.

36. Dan Eatherley, *Bushmaster: Raymond Ditmars and the Hunt for the World's Largest Viper* (New York: Arcade, 2015), 405.

37. Ad for *The Four Seasons, Motion Picture News,* November 29, 2921, 2258.

38. Eatherley, *Bushmaster,* 389.

39. Eatherley, 393; W. Stephen Bush, "A New Star," *Moving Picture World,* February 28, 1914, 1095.

40. "Ditmars School of Dramatic Arts for Inhuman Beings," *Film Fun,* April 1916, unnumbered page [11].

41. For an account of Bazin's zoophilia, see Jennifer Fay, "Seeing/Loving Animals: André Bazin's Posthumanism," *Journal of Visual Culture* 7, no. 1 (2008): 41–64.

42. Cf. Francesco Casetti's chapter in this volume.

43. U.S. Department of Agriculture, "Amphibians and Climate Change," https://www.fs.usda.gov/ccrc/topics/amphibians-and-climate-change.

44. Gillian Beer, "Darwin and the Uses of Extinction," *Victorian Studies* 51, no. 2 (2009): 326.

45. Dipesh Chakrabarty, "Climate and Capital: On Conjoined Histories," *Critical Inquiry* 41, no. 1 (2014): 9.

46. *Alaska's Eighth Wonder* reel 2 (with the dramatic melting ice footage) can be viewed at https://vimeo.com/237461251. *Alaska's Eighth Wonder* reel 1 can be viewed at https://vimeo.com/259759564. A title card on reel 1 lists the following credits: "Photography by Tom Jackson, Edited by J. Maze." Despite conducting an extensive search in the trade press, I have not yet been able to trace any further information about this film. There was a National Geographic film called *Alaska's Eighth Wonder* released in 1919, also released under the title *Valley of 10,000 Smokes,* but the date of the camera, as well as a very different description of the footage, confirms that this is a different film.

47. See "Jökulhlaups," U.S. National Park Service, https://www.nps.gov/articles/jokulhlaups.htm.

48. Indeed, when I showed this reel at the Orphan Film Symposium in April 2018, several people later told me they had been moved to tears watching it. This was certainly due to the skilled live piano accompaniment by musician Stephen Horne, but it is also because, I contend, such images of glacier ice crashing today cannot mean anything else besides global warming.

49. Timothy Morton, *Hyperobjects: Philosophy and Ecology after the End of the World* (Minneapolis: University of Minnesota Press, 2013).

50. Timothy Morton, *The Ecological Thought* (Cambridge, Mass.: Harvard University Press, 2012), 54.

51. Catherine Russell, *Archiveology: Walter Benjamin and Archival Film Practices* (Durham, N.C.: Duke University Press, 2018), 11.

52. Russell, 13.

53. Walter Benjamin, "Surrealism," trans. Edmund Jephcott, in *Reflections,* ed. Peter Demetz (New York: Schocken Books, 1978), 181.

54. Miriam Hansen, *Cinema and Experience: Siegfried Kracauer, Walter Benjamin, and Theodor W. Adorno* (Berkeley: University of California Press, 2012), 76.

4

When Celluloid Looks Back to You

Mark Paul Meyer

For over a century, celluloid was the basis of film production. Making films was a complex and laborious endeavor that involved dealing with heavy apparatus, careful handling of light-sensitive film stock, and a lengthy photochemical laboratory process that did not allow you to see the results instantly. When the film was finally developed, a labor-intensive process of editing and postproduction followed.

With the disappearance of material carriers, for both image and sound, specific characteristics of analog filmmaking are definitively lost. The history of analog film is a long one of technical inventions and continuous innovation. Color techniques, emulsions, different gauges, frame ratios, editing practices, and so on changed regularly over the years. The fascinating thing about analog film is that almost all these differentiations can be deduced from the film materials: they are manifest in the film strip and can be directly grasped by the human eye. Digital technology caused a radical change because these physical characteristics can no longer be "read" from the object itself with the naked eye. In the case of digital-born films, we deal with an entirely digital environment, and in the case of a scanned analog film, references to the analog source are often lost in the process of transfer or are consciously removed, often under the flag of "restoration" or "remastering."

It is generally agreed that the paradigm of the apparatus has not changed essentially with the advent of digital technology. Film is still a series of recorded images projected on a screen and perceived by a spectator. The regular cinema visitor hardly notices the difference between analog and digital film projection, since her appreciation of film has nothing to do with the carrier of the images. The typical cinema visitor is mainly interested in the narrative, and a certain disinterest in the material aspects of film is normal. After all, throughout the history of cinema, the materiality and the technology that enabled the moving images to appear on the screen was not supposed to be noticed. The history of film is a history of concealing the technology behind it to concentrate on narrative, performance, representation, and so on. Essentially, film is a system of illusions that tries to eliminate all references to its material origins.

Consequently, academic film history and film studies generally have had a secondary interest in the materiality and technology of film and instead focus on what is perceived on the screen. In a dominant ideology of film as illusion, film history is restricted to audiovisual perception, which is essentially a continuation of art history traditions. However, anyone who works in a film archive cannot ignore the fact that analog film is a material both haptic and tactile. Thousands of films are stored in special vaults, and every activity in working with these films means a confrontation with the weight and the robustness of the objects. Working with historical film makes you aware of the fact that the history of filmmaking is largely material and that manual, physical labor was a fundamental aspect of filmmaking. It is this that is lost in the digital era and that gives a distinctive meaning to analog film.

It is now with the disappearance of analog film that an awareness of the relevance of film's materiality seems to grow—not out of nostalgia but because film material reveals a lot about the process of making and thinking behind it. Filmmaking goes hand in hand with thinking because it has to be translated into material in correlation with its characteristics and its properties. This "translation" is a continuous play with both the possibilities and the limitations of the available technology, and this interaction between the mind of the maker and film material is one of the fascinating aspects of analog film for the artist, but also for the archivist.

The material object shows you a story that is not seen on the screen. You can read the object almost as a text, and even if there is much that you cannot explain, you are still aware of the intellectual dynamics that were at play in the realization of the object. The material object contains

Plate 1. The film about filmmaking and the materiality of film par excellence is *The Man with a Movie Camera* (1929) by Dziga Vertov. In this film, we see the editor of the film, Elizaveta Svilova, at work in the editing room. Celluloid goes through her hands and is physically cut into separate fragments and carefully inventoried before being assembled again in a rhythmic and special order. Her eyes are integrated into the film to emphasize the process of editing as a manual, visual, and intellectual activity.

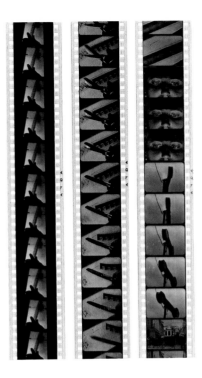

Plate 2. The invention of new dyes in the nineteenth century resulted in all kinds of applications of colors, from clothing to postcards. These new dyes were also applied onto film, first by hand painting and later by immersing entire strips of film in a dye to obtain a monochrome color. The variation of colors was enormous. With tinting, the black silver particles remained black, while the transparent parts obtained a color. With toning, it was the other way around: silver was transformed into a different color, often blue or brown, while the transparent parts remained untouched.

Plate 3. Three-strip Technicolor is based on three negatives for yellow, cyan, and magenta. A picture in the positive print is first colored with one negative, followed by the second and the third. The miracle of the full-color image is demonstrated in the trailer for *Becky Sharp* (1935), with its transition from black and white to color. *Aladdin and the Magic Lamp* (1939) is made with a so-called successive frame negative: each frame in the positive has three frames in the negative, again one for yellow, one for cyan, and one for magenta. Films: *Aladdin and the Magic Lamp* (NL 1939, George Pàl), *Becky Sharp* (US 1935, Rouben Mamoulian).

Plate 4. Numerous techniques were invented to achieve natural colors, but only a few were really successful. From left to right: a Prizma two-color film, a time lapse registration of the development of crystals using Gaspar color, and an experiment with Hérault Trichrome. Films: *From Indians to Tourists: A Journey through America's Grand Canyon* (US 1922), *Crystals in Color* (NL ca. 1934, J. C. Mol), Hérault three-color system demonstration film (FR ca. 1927).

Plate 5. Hand-colored films explicitly show the activity of the painting process. The imperfection of the technique, as in the *Danse des Ouled-Naïd* (1902), is fascinating, but the techniques quickly became more sophisticated. Hand painting was replaced by a semi-mechanical stencil technique, and companies like Pathé and Gaumont achieved incredible results and applied the technique for at least two decades. Films from left to right: *Danse des Ouled-Naïd* (FR 1902), *La peine du talion* (FR 1906, Gaston Velle, Pathé Frères), *L'orgie romaine* (FR 1911, Louis Feuillade, Gaumont).

Plate 6. The colorist of the 68mm British Mutoscope and Biograph film *Conway Castle* (1898) skipped two frames. The images were clearly damaged, and that may have been the reason for him or her to omit these images. Interestingly enough, it gives us insight into how the black-and-white images were "translated" into a color image. The same is true for a stencil-colored Pathé film that survived in its unassembled version: the frames that were supposed to be cut out allow us to look into the process of making. Films: *Conway Castle—Panoramic View of Conway on the L. & N.W. Railway* (GB 1898, William Kennedy-Laurie Dickson), *Au pays des fleurs d'Ajonc* (FR 1915, Pathé Frères).

Plate 7. On the left is a standard 35mm negative. This is a home movie, and it is not edited, because we can see where the camera stopped and then continued with a medium shot. The negative on the right is a 68mm negative from the Dutch branch of the Biograph and Mutoscope company. It is remarkable for its perforation and broad frame line, because the positive prints have no perforation and almost no frame line. As well, the semi-opaqueness of the carrier is remarkable. This must have functioned as a mask to control contrast and achieve a better positive image. Films: *Back Yard* (NL ca. 1930, home movie), *Student Celebrations, Leyden* (NL 1900, Nederlandsche Biograaf- en Mutoscope Maatschappij).

Plate 8. These are examples of films that explicitly experiment with the materiality of film and the characteristics of photographic emulsion. Films from left to right: *Pneuma* (US 1983, Nathaniel Dorsky), *After the Colors* (NL 1972, Mattijn Seip), *Hans in balans* (NL 1970, Frans Zwartjes), *Murder Psalm* (US 1981, Stan Brakhage), *L'arrivée* (AT 1998, Peter Tscherkassky).

Plate 9. These are material experiments with film as substratum for modification and manipulation through editing, applying colors, or attaching pieces from the garbage bin. Films from left to right: *Satisfaction* (NL 1966, Henri Roesems), *Rubbish* (NL 1972, Mattijn Seip), *Swinging the Lambeth Walk* (GB 1939, Len Lye), *Charlot présente le ballet mécanique* (FR 1923, Fernand Leger, Dudley Murphy).

Plate 10. Films can be valued as the documentation of their making, but an inherent agency is also often attributed to the material. In particular, the decomposition of celluloid, emulsion, or dyes can create fascinating results. The two examples on the left are unidentified. The film on the right has been identified as *Mein Name ist Spiesecke* (DE 1914, Emil Albes).

Plate 11. In the silent era, films were edited as positives. Sequences that were tinted in a specific color were tinted in one go and had to be cut loose to be edited. Intertitles were printed separately, often in different languages, and had to be inserted into the film. Films have sometimes survived as half-finished products and therefore disclose information that is normally not seen, such as places and numbers for the intertitles, numbers and lengths of shots, and indications for the colors. Films: *Âmes de fous* (FR 1918, Germaine Dulac), *Kaiserin Elisabeth von Österreich* (DE 1920, Rolf Raffé), and *Meyer aus Berlin* (DE 1919, Ernst Lubitsch).

Plate 12. Celluloid allows inspection with the naked eye. In a fiction film about filmmaking, Asta Nielsen checks the film to judge the results of her acting and the skills of the director and his crew. Elizaveta Svilova checks the film fragments, which she systematically ordered for the final editing. Films: *The Man with a Movie Camera* (SU 1929, Dziga Vertov), *Die Filmprimadonna* (DE 1913, Urban Gad).

Plate 13. Although 35mm was the standard format for cinema projection, many other formats were available over the years, including larger ones, such as 68mm, 70mm, or IMAX, or smaller ones, such as 8mm or 16mm. Smaller formats were often used domestically to make home movies or to make cinema features available for the home market, as, for instance, the 17.5mm and 28mm prints shown here. For reasons of cost and availability, 8mm and 16mm were not only used by amateur filmmakers but also have been used by experimental filmmakers from the 1960s until today. Films from left to right: *Finger Exercises* (Normal 8mm; NL 1966, Henri Plaat), *The Trolley Man* (Super 8mm; NL 1991, Jaap Pieters), *Le Papillon Macaon* (9.5mm; FR 1922), *Povest' o kommuniste* (16mm; SU 1976, Igor Bessarabov, Aleksandr Kochetkov), *Éclat* (Super16; NL 1993, Frank Scheffer), *Visages d'enfants* (17.5mm; FR/CH 1923, Jacques Feyder), *Little Moritz épouse Rosalie* (28mm; FR 1911, Roméo Bosetti).

Plate 14. *Les Parisiennes* (US 1897), a hand-colored film from the American Mutoscope Company.

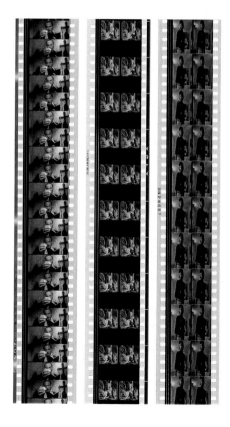

Plate 15. The basic idea of 3D films is that each eye of the spectator gets slightly different information, and the brain merges these two images, yielding one perceived image. Numerous systems achieve a 3D image based on this principle. These three filmstrips show examples. Films from left to right: *Comin' at Ya!* (US 1983, Ferdinando Baldi), *Robinzon Kruzo* (SU 1946, Aleksandr Andriyevski), *Starlets* (US 1976, David Summers).

a complex of artistic, industrial, intellectual, and material "thinking." It is an object that discloses to you its history, meanings, and intentions. The film object looks back at you and speaks through its manifestations of technical and creative ingenuity, through the traces and signs of production and use, and through the inherent properties of the material, the celluloid, and the emulsion.

Film as a material object can be appreciated as the manifestation of a way of thinking, as a result of the struggle between the maker and the physical elements of film material, as the manual film handling in time and space, and as the relation between the human body and the material with the maker's hands and eyes as crucial instruments. Working with film inspires an awareness that you work with objects made out of specific materials that are "molded" by human mental and physical activity. The handling of the physical elements is essential for analog filmmaking, both in the production of the film, as in the use, for instance, in projection, but also when an archivist is confronted with film reels. A number of things can be read or understood from a film print. Most prominent clues are usually given by film editing and by the use and application of colors.

In the case of film editing, the difference between analog and digital editing is enormous. It is often said that the relation between the editor, her body and touch, and the material changed fundamentally, and with it, the way of thinking. In the 1990s, many film editors experienced the difference between working in a traditional editing room and working on a timeline in a computer application. It is perhaps comparable with the observation Friedrich Nietzsche made after the introduction of a typewriting machine when he stated that "our writing tools are also working on our thoughts."[1] In analog film prints, you often can "read" the underlying editing: you can see the splices (even the negative splices), and you can analyze which splices are intended and which are the result of the use of the print or other manipulations, such as censorship.

In the case of the application of colors to early films, you can feel the hand, and with it the mind, of the worker. When a film is hand-colored with a brush, you can see exactly what was done, and the imperfectness of it revives the moment that those films were colored, and with it moments of doubt and decision-making. With later techniques like stenciling and separate two- and three-color systems, of which many were produced only for a short period of time, the history of film became much richer and various than a basic history of cinema would suggest. The fact that you can "read" so many characteristics of analog filmmaking demonstrates that film prints are also a documentation of their making. This is one of the remarkable things about analog films: they contain information that is transmittable to the reader like a book. It is physically present, and many details can be understood immediately, but there is also much that needs further clarification as questions are raised and new paths for research and investigation unfold.

Film prints are also a documentation of their biography and of the life of a film: patina, wear and tear, damage and deterioration, and eventually the signs of duplication and reproduction. This is another captivating aspect of working with film. These "deficiencies" can be fascinating aspects of a film, not necessarily things that need to be corrected in film restoration. They serve as indications for an archivist/film detective to detect the story behind the print and can also serve as a motive for aesthetic appreciation. These physical deficiencies are lost in digital-born films and also often lost in digital restorations that are sometimes so "perfect" that these references to the original films no longer appear.

It is fascinating to see that with analog film, you can achieve results unachievable with digital means. This potential has been rediscovered today by artists and filmmakers. A filmmaker like Quentin Tarantino acknowledges the special characteristics of analog film when he decides to shoot his films on celluloid. Among the many projects of analog film that young filmmakers and students of art currently initiate, it is worth mentioning here a recent project at the University of Applied Arts in Vienna, Austria, with the title *Reset the Apparatus!*, recently concluded with the publication of a book.[2] This project emphasized the making and production of works based on analog technology, extending apparatus theory from a mainly perception-oriented model to a more production-oriented model. Its goals included understanding the technologies of the past and offering a critical reflection on the loss of the material and its haptic qualities and the uniformization of film technology and consequent uniform appearance. Furthermore, *Reset the Apparatus!* is illustrative of a tendency that wants to investigate old techniques not for historical and retrospective reasons but for reasons oriented toward the future. "We live in the ruins of modernity," as Svetlana Boym explained, and we can consider analog film technology as an instance of these ruins par excellence.[3] Boym developed the idea of the *off-modern* as a "detour into the unexplored potentials of the modern project," and for her, off-modern nostalgia is not retrospective but prospective.[4] She pleads for a "prospective nostalgia" that preserves, but also reanimates, the materials and techniques of the past to create new orientations toward the future. The potential and the success of this practice are demonstrated by renowned artists like Tacita Dean and William Kentridge and will continue to inspire generations of filmmakers and artists who want to let their works of art speak through analog film technology. Archive films are often industrial productions, but the ways they look at us and speak to us through their material properties are often as fascinating as looking at a work of art.

Notes

1. Cited in Edgar Lissel, Gabriele Jutz, and Nina Jukić, eds., *Reset the Apparatus! A Survey of the Photographic and the Filmic in Contemporary Art* (Vienna, Austria: De Gruyter, 2019), 22.

2. Lissel et al.

3. Svetlana Boym, *The Off-Modern* (New York: Bloomsbury, 2017).

4. Boym, 3, 39.

5

What Remains, What Returns

Garbage, Ghosts, and Two Ends of Cinema

James Leo Cahill

When—and where—does one begin to think about the end or ends of cinema? What here-and-now does one occupy, or what then-and-there and future-tense-where does one conjure and conjugate in identifying an end—an expiration, limit, or death—or elaborating the ends—the teleology, aims, or anticipated destinations—of cinema? Beyond any cinephilic panic about the death of cinema, such reflections pose generative questions about the medium's ontology and ontogeny, its nature and processes of transformation, that have historiographic and theoretical implications. How one contemplates the ends of cinema inflects the conceptualization of the very object(s) of inquiry: each notion of cinema has its ends, and each end summarizes a particular notion of cinema. This chapter focuses on two ends of cinema in particular, not as terminal points, but more as what remains and what returns in cinematic media across a number of its iterations: its remnants and revenants. Garbage and ghosts provide generative figures—in Eric Auerbach's sense of a mode of historical interpretation that thinks two distinct, temporally separated historical phenomena through each other—for attending to cinema's stubborn materiality (garbage) and haunting ephemerality (ghosts).[1] Garbage and ghosts manifest the negative surplus of cinema: the excessive forms of material and ideational absence constitutive of the medium that it must refuse or exorcise to function but from which it cannot be wholly separated. Garbage entails all the forms of exhausted use-value in the economies of cinema, from the supposedly extraneous materials in an image to unusable footage to the by-products of each stage of production, distribution, exhibition, and even archiving. Ghosts encompass cinema's forms of absent presence, temporal disjunctions and anachronisms, and uncanny effects produced by and fostered in cinema, as well as a mode of address and spectatorial experience.

In an intellectual milieu informed by the emergence of new materialisms as well as a broad "spectral (re)turn," cinema reminds us that there is no garbage without its ghosts and no ghosts without its garbage.[2] Siegfried Kracauer and Georges Bataille, two thinkers not typically associated with the discourse on the ends of cinema or with each other, but whose parallel thinking about the catastrophes of history through photographic and cinematic media makes an untimely address to these two ends of cinema today, offer a particularly cogent approach to this question when read with each other. This chapter proceeds in two parts. The first part develops an exegetical analysis of Kracauer's and Bataille's late 1920s work on the historiographical dimensions of photographic and cinematic media in terms of its finitudes, remnants, and returns. The second part looks to recent works by the Japanese cinéaste Momoko Seto, who explores our roughly contemporaneous moment and speculative futures in which questions of the end(s) of cinema converge with a heightened attunement to climate chaos surrealism. In a context determined by what Dipesh Chakrabarty has referred to as a "negative universal history" of anthropogenic climate destruction—a concern that remains only half-thought if it does not entail a rethinking of ecozoological and biopolitical-racial dimensions—garbage and ghosts provide generative figures for historical inquiry.[3] Garbage and ghosts are the emblems of our times.

Cinema's Negative Surplus: Kracauer with Bataille

At the close of the 1920s, as synchronous sound film production was making industrial headway around the globe, inspiring many obituaries for cinema's death as a silent art and universal language, both Kracauer and Bataille published articles on the historiographic dimensions of photographic media that each considered obsolescence, detritus, and haunting as essential to their theorization. With curious symmetry, Kracauer's October 1927 essay "Die Photographie" and Bataille's April 1929 essay

"Figure humaine" each contrasted photographic portraits and film stills from previous generations with an unprinted photograph of an unnamed film starlet at the beach.[4] Together, the essays draft a research program for thinking through the ends and afterwards of photographic and cinematographic media at the levels of individual example and the cumulative effects. They theorize the capture, storage, and reception of photographic and cinematographic media by means of their affinities with garbage and ghosts. The stakes of Kracauer's project involved nothing less than what he called the "go-for-broke game of history," in which photographic and cinematic images might train us to apprehend the material base and contingent nature of capitalist modernity and to imagine alternative possibilities.[5] Bataille saw in photographic media an opportunity to critique the disastrous consequences of an overinvestment in "human nature," in the form of what Georges Didi-Huberman has called a withering critique of anthropomorphism and Linda Steer analyzes as a vision of history as monstrous.[6] Kracauer and Bataille wrote from obverse sides of a Hegelian philosophy of history, an orientation that distinguishes the two but also interlaces their perspectives. Their thought intersects in a critical conception of natural history that dialectically considers human and more-than-human temporalities and histories as necessary for a nonanthropocentric critical theory.[7] By returning to these two thinkers and putting their work into direct conversation, this chapter illuminates what they offer for thinking through cinema's ends as a historiographic project.

Kracauer's model historian studies garbage from a ghostly perspective. She works with detritus as a way to access material conditions and haunts her subjects from the vantage of a stranger, an exile, a "homeless" wanderer, or a phantom.[8] In his 1928 review of Walter Benjamin's *Origin of the German Tragic Drama* and *One-Way Street,* Kracauer added to this methodological profile the image of the historian as a species of violent conceptual cubist: "he who faces the world in its immediacy is presented with a figure that he must smash in order to reach the essentialities."[9] What Kracauer imagined, Bataille coincidentally realized. With surprising force, he used photography and film to smash the historical inheritance of the "human figure," seeing in these new media an "end of man." Bataille's materialist approach (which, unlike Kracauer's, was absent any redemptive horizon) models a manner of historical reflection that invites ghosts, monsters, cast-off materials, and intense affects as necessary to thought.

When photography initially appeared, according to Kracauer, it was received as a technical manifestation of historicist fantasies of a total preservation of the past in service of its full reconstitution, in the spirit of Leopold von Ranke's founding objective for modern historiography as showing "how it really was" *(wie es eigentlich gewesen).*[10] The use-value of photographs dramatically changed as they accumulated into a "general archive" that overwhelmed individual memory and meaning. Kracauer likened the proliferation of photographs to a natural disaster—a "flood" and a "blizzard"—that washes away individual memory and blinds the observer through its sheer magnitude of particular data.[11] Miriam Hansen notes that in Kracauer's account, photographic media ironically make for an overwhelming and unstable archive, but in one of the great dialectical turns of his essay, this instability also harbors one of the medium's most radical promises as a historical materialist retort to positivist historiography.[12]

Kracauer's essay opens with an experiment in temporal stereography, in which he compares a contemporary photograph of a twenty-four-year-old "demonic diva" taken on the beach at Venice Lido with a photographic portrait taken more than sixty years earlier of a grandmother as a twenty-four-year-old woman in a crinoline dress and chignon bun.[13] The cultural logic that maintains the apparent unity of the image and what it depicts begins to erode and becomes increasingly opaque as the passage of time or the rapid global circulation separates a photograph from its initial contexts of production and reception. Aging photographs (and films, as he later adds) appear as what he calls in his 1931 essay on the destruction of Berlin's Linder Arcade a species of "homeless image" *(obdachlose Bilder).*[14] Temporal and cultural decontextualization disintegrates the coherence of the image, which becomes perceptible as mere spatial contiguity. Thanks to the anthropological indifference of the camera's impassive lens and sensitive substrate, the contents of the image are now perceived as contingent and fragmentary. In its afterlife, the legibility and content of a photographic document may become radically different from that which its initial users saw in it. The grandmother outfitted in a heavy crinoline dress fades from the picture as a distinct individual and, over time, resembles less a person than a mannequin for the display of the curious fashions of yesteryear. "The truth content of the original is left behind in its history; the photograph captures only the residuum that history has discharged." Of this "discharge," Kracauer notes, "photography appears as a jumble that consists partly of garbage [*Abfällen*]" and what he elsewhere in the essay calls "a stockpile of elements" and "remnants of nature."[15] In their dotage or decontextualization, photographs take on the appearance of a junkyard, a shipwreck, a ruin, or a haunted house, in which disintegration of its structures produces the space for new forms to emerge.

Kracauer's essay—which Olivier Agard reads as a meditation on death, time, and emancipation—imagines photographic media to be suffused by a negativity—its negative surplus—that swallows the grandmother from her portrait.[16] This negativity produces what Jennifer Fay, in an innovative reading of Kracauer's "cold love" in *Inhospitable World*, provocatively calls a "significant hole" from which a productively alienated—and even alien and extraterrestrial—mode of vision and historical analysis may be practiced.[17] For Kracauer, "what appears in the photograph is not the person but the sum of what can be subtracted from him or her."[18] What we see in old photographs is negativity made visibly manifest as a "disintegrated unity," in which the various elements held together by a combination of familiarity and ideology in the original context become estranged from each other and us. These elements take on appearances of an "unredeemed ghostly reality" that causes a shudder. Like any good ghost story, Kracauer's essay marks the invisible appearance of something phantomatic with three shudders, causing both laughter and disquiet. The aging image "wanders ghost-like through the present, like the lady of the haunted castle. Spooky apparitions occur only in places where a terrible deed has been committed. The photograph becomes a ghost because the costumed mannequin was once alive."[19] Aging photographic media bear traces of something dead insisting upon the present and making enigmatic demands of us but also mark the unsettling experience of knowing that we too will be swallowed whole, unredeemed, by and in the black hole of time's passage.

Kracauer saw the capacities of photography potentially intensified and radicalized by film and cinema—an insight performatively theorized in the photography essay, which, as Unfried Pfeifer-Duwe argues, uses the techniques of cinematography as a way of interpolating the reader into the argument and, as Hansen notes, provides eight "takes" as if from different camera positions.[20] Kracauer continues: "The disorder of the detritus reflected in photography cannot be elucidated more clearly than through the suspension [*Aufhebung*] of every habitual relationship among the elements of nature. The capacity to stir up the elements of nature is one of the possibilities of film. This possibility is realized whenever film combines parts and segments to create strange constructs."[21] It is not just costume and fashion that photography can reveal to be contingent but also our perceptions of inhuman nature, which no longer appear as a transhistorical given. Alluding to the ghostly effects of photographs and old newsreels, such as those collected at flea markets and projected in the context of avant-garde film programs at the Studio des Ursulines and other cinemas in Paris, Kracauer emphasizes the power of film to animate and actualize the productive negativity and alienation of photographic images. Photographs *suspend*. Kracauer's use of the Hegelian term *Aufhebung* to describe photography's treatment of the relations of detritus and milieu suggests an abolishing negation, an overcoming that is at once the preservation and transformation of what the camera captures. Films *agitate*. Moving images potentially "stir up" and set in motion new relations among nature's heterogeneous elements, particularly through the "strange constructs"—the creative anatomies, geographies, and historiographies—made possible by juxtaposition, montage, and spatial and temporal dislocations and rearticulations.

A year prior to publishing his 1927 photography essay, as Hansen and Fay note, Kracauer was already rehearsing this line of thinking about cinema's capacity to produce strange constructs in his report on the Universum Film AG (Ufa) film studios in Neubabelsberg. He described the studio as a "calico world" *(Kalikowelt)* where all possible aspects of nature and the built world—"the ruins of the universe"—have been "cut to pieces" and "ripped out of time and jumbled" in service of the production of modern spectacles.[22] The film studio instantiates a production process—both highly rational and expressive of a "regime of arbitrariness"—whereby the world is collected and archived in order to be reassembled in a made-to-order fashion.[23] "This dismantling of the world's contents is radical;

and even if it is undertaken only for the sake of illusion, the illusion is by no means insignificant."[24] Kracauer's significant insight was that even prior to the assembly involved in montage, energy-intensive studio production subjects the profilmic world to a form of aesthetic disassembly and reassembly that teaches curious onlookers not to accept "reality as a finished product."[25] The *by no means insignificant illusions* produced by the studios required incredible technical proficiency and resources, which artificially produce an image of a unified world by bathing the heterogeneous "things and people" in a surfeit of energy-consuming electric lighting that "melts them together."[26] Kracauer notes that much of what is collected and created is done so as to be destroyed in a resource- and energy-intensive manner.

Kracauer continued to think film and cinema through garbage and ghosts, as is apparent in Miriam Hansen's examination of his 1940 notes written in Marseille for what would become *Theory of Film*. Kracauer mused, "[Film] does not aim upward, toward intention, but pushes toward the bottom, to gather and carry along even the dregs. It is interested in the refuse, in what is just there—both in and outside the human being. The face counts for nothing in film unless it includes the death's-head beneath."[27] The co-constitutive relationship of face and skull, animating spirit and dead matter, forms the dialectical component of Kracauer's media theory. Kracauer's understandings of the historiographic potential of photographic media and modern film production helps one perceive the present in manners that reveal the contingency of what might otherwise be mistaken for necessary and the fragility of what otherwise might be taken for durable and solid. He believed one could train one's perception to recognize in all images the historical contingency of the spatial continuum captured by photographic media and to regard with critical eyes the garbage and ghosts latent in every image. From such an attuned perspective, *every film* takes on the appearance of Georges Lacombe's 1928 *La Zone: Au Pays des Chiffonniers,* a documentary following the rag-pickers in Paris and its unincorporated periphery, who, shrouded by clouds of hazardous dust, collect and organize the refuse and detritus of the city of light (Figure 5.1).

It is unlikely that Bataille had direct familiarity with Kracauer's account of photographic media, but his 1929 essay "Figure humaine"—which

Figure 5.1. Screen capture of ragpickers from *La Zone* (Georges Lacombe, France, 1928).

translates as "Human Face" or "Human Figure" (the polyvalence of *figure* is important)—also reflects on the historiographic dimensions of photographic media through remnants and revenants. Like Kracauer, Bataille's text is framed by considerations of photographs of previous generations compared with a moving picture of "the planet earth trampled underfoot by a dazzling American film star in a bathing suit"—an image of modern eroticism that, he concludes the essay by noting, will also appear absurd in due time.[28] Bataille's essay stages a conversation with two dozen found photographs, including a fin de siècle photograph of a provincial wedding party solemnly posed in front of a hardware store in Seine-et-Marne and numerous portraits of performers taken at the Atelier Nadar in Paris. That the bodies of the archival imagery that bear the brunt of this conceptual labor are nearly all female in both Kracauer's and Bataille's essays is not coincidental, both in terms of the erotic investments of the authors and the fetishistic fantasies of woman, archive, and photograph as *matrixes* of historical significance.[29]

Bataille also saw in aging photographs and films something both com-ical and disturbing. "The mere sight (in photography) of our predeces-sors in the occupation of this country now produces, for varying reasons, a burst of loud and raucous laughter; that sight, however, is nonethe-less hideous."[30] If the strange fashions and affectations of the previous generation of humans cause laughter, the purported hideousness of such aging photographic images, to Bataille's eyes, was not just the fact that they constituted a haunting of the living by the dead but that they did so in such a diminished and lamentably banal manner. Their hideous-ness lay in that they were not monstrous enough. They produced rather pale ghosts when compared with the manifestations of souls of the dead in "other places," where phantoms assume "the wretched appearance of a half-decomposed cadaver" and even threaten to cannibalize the living.[31] The images set into conversation with this part of Bataille's text include a full-page spread of Nadar portraits of the belle epoque performers Mlle. de Rigny, Cécile Sorel, Mlle. Langoix, and Mlle. Boroni, the last of whom was a member of the Châtelet *corps de ballet* who appeared in the 1877 production of Jacques Offenbach's *Voyage dans la lune* (see Figure 5.2). The models appear outfitted in wasp-waisted corsets, adorned with wings and other animal talismans, and posed in exotic locales, such as the polar/lunar landscape from *Voyage dans la lune.*[32] Such effigies are more likely to cause embarrassment than terror for Bataille (who was, perhaps, un-familiar with the grip of a corset or the flammability of crinoline—such as Maggie Hennefeld chronicles in the context of early cinematic come-dies of female catastrophe—even as he appreciated the anthropological excesses of fashion).[33] They hardly lived up to the tasks of marking either the radical irrecoverability of the past or the disturbances of its purchase upon the present.

Even as he found something shabby and depressing in the accumula-tion of ancestral effigies in the forms of portrait photography and the cast-off accoutrements of fashion growing moldy in attics, these abandoned articles and absurd ghosts did have a potential heuristic value. Bataille saw in the photographs of predecessors the negation of claims to an eter-nal human nature and any principle of harmony that implied an ideal order to the universe.[34] In a rather unconventional reading of the provin-cial wedding photograph, he invites readers to *not* see stable documents

Figure 5.2. Portrait of Mlle. Boroni in the Théâtre du Châtelet production of *Voyage dans la lune* taken at the Atelier Nadar in Paris, circa 1877. Courtesy of the Bibliothèque Nationale de France.

functioning by means of the principle of identity but rather records of "nonrelation," "disproportion," and an "absence of common measure" revealing discontinuity: among humans, between humans and nature, between present and past, and within the present.[35] Bataille imagined the newlyweds as "parents of a wild and apocalyptic rebellion" in which "a juxtaposition of monsters breeding incompatibles would replace the supposed continuity of *our* nature."[36] Didi-Huberman reads in such lines the anti-anthropomorphic dimension of Bataille's thought, stressing that his reading of the wedding photograph aimed to lacerate the concept of stable resemblances conforming to and confirming the human being.[37] As Steer notes, Bataille's photohistoriography solicited "recoil and negation" rather than identification.[38] In "Human Face," photography produces and reproduces ruptures in the supposed continuity of history and fosters a nonanthropomorphic—and potentially nonanthropocentric—historiographic gaze. In Bataille's unorthodox view, photographic media might be intended for the preservation of the human countenance, but their most promising effects, *via negativa*, relate to the fractures they introduce into the human face and figure.

The ambivalence of the *figure* in the article's title demonstrates the difficulties of translating Bataille. In French, *figure* signifies an "exterior form," such as a body, a representation, but it also refers to the human face.[39] The development of photography, in Bataille's account, coincided with—and seems to drive—two relatively recent historical phenomena: the impoverishment of ghosts, whereby our dead ancestors appear to us in the highly domesticated form of the family photo, and the rise of "the most obstinate efforts pursued by white men and women to finally regain a *human face [figure humaine]*."[40] *Figure humaine* here conjures not just the face but the human form, and beyond that the very figure of the human. Portrait photography appears as a totemic attempt to capture, preserve, and reanimate what has been lost: a sense of the human face and form (body) as givens. What photography generates instead is new forms of monstrosity. The radical particularity of photographs presents new levels and layers of difference that tend toward the ruination of any tidy synecdoche passing smoothly from the white face (*figure*) to body (*figure*) to the figure (ideal concept) of the human species. The harmonious proportion of part to whole exemplified by the geometry of Leonardo da Vinci's *Vitruvian Man* is countered by the "concrete expression" of this assembly of monsters breeding disproportionate incompatibles.[41] The collection of the winged women in the full-page spread of the article suggests that the eroticism of the images relies on a nonhuman surplus or prop that registers the mournful separation of humans from animal life while also expressing, as he notes in another text from 1929, on metamorphoses, an uneasy envy for the perceived freedom of animals—"the only real outlaws"—that "lurks in comic disguise within our grandmothers' feathered hats."[42] Bataille follows up on his assertion that Caucasian men and women have been trying to regain the human face by linking photography with fashion in noting its rapid passage from use-value into material ruins and natural history: "Those wasp-waisted corsets scattered throughout provincial attics are now the prey of moths and flies, the hunting grounds of spiders."[43] The essay concludes with the surprising admission of implication. Bataille avers that the "strange, half-monstrous characters" of the photographs hold an inescapable lure. Even contemptuous youth, who find the erotic iconography of previous generations so absurd as to spoil their own onanistic impulses, will eventually find themselves "running absurdly towards some provincial haunted house, nastier than flies, and more vicious and rank than a hairdresser's salon."[44] Bataille's key historical insight, prosecuted with the fervor of a fanatic, was to recognize the material heterogeneity in any asserted unity.

Bataille's materialist insistence reverberates with a key insight of Kracauer's. The opening of his 1927 essay brings our attention to the two ways of looking at any photographic image. Our gaze may pivot between "the millions of little dots" or the verisimilar figure of a particular demonic diva at a particular beach.[45] As Hansen summarizes, the photograph for Kracauer is both "material object that can be perceived in its sensory texture and a symbolic representation whose referent is elsewhere."[46] If we learn to see through the dot matrix such that it becomes invisible to us, Kracauer retrains our perception to hold both the material substance and immaterial presence of the garbage and ghosts of photographic media in view. We only see one clearly at the expense of the other, but Kracauer's intellectual stereoscopy helps envision them together in their differences and extends their scope by attending to the dynamic temporal dimension of photographic media. Kracauer and Bataille each developed experimental protocols of perception attuned by and to the medium's residues and surpluses. Where Kracauer saw a possibility of a "redemption of physical reality" (as he would later name it) and the development of historical insight in a critical regard trained by photographic media, Bataille learned from photographs and films to view the present as absolutely heterogeneous and the past as monstrous, shifting attention from a model of history concerned with origins and identification to one focused on difference and disproportion, or the nonsymmetrical relationship between past and present, as well as ideal and particular phenomena. Remnants—in the form of superannuated photographs and the cast-off fashions of a previous generation—become revenants that, at first blush, strike Bataille as desultory. One might recall that in 1925, Bataille's analyst Adrian Borel furnished him with the photographic images of Fou Tchou-Li, a young Chinese man who in 1905 was subjected to *lingchi*, or torture of a hundred pieces, a profoundly disturbing series of images of carnal disassembly and ecstatic suffering that haunted and obsessed him, and likely provided the unnamed standard by which he so harshly judged the other photographic documents of human figures surrounding him.[47] Bataille's critique in "Human Face/Figure" pushes against the limits of its own terms in not recognizing the sheer terror that the accumulating material remnants present in the form of a nonanthropomorphic, suprahuman revenant haunting not just the parlors and attics of provincial homes but the entire planet. So what cinematic or postcinematic forms might materialize ghosts adequate to our age?

Ghost Planet, or Cinema's Accursed Share

If Kracauer and Bataille belong to a long tradition of thinkers who understand photography and cinema as ghostly media that reconfigure a particularly modern relation to absence and presence, the stakes of their attention to remnants and revenants have only become heightened in a present quite alien to their own.[48] Cinema, in its variant forms, is an excessively material medium whose industrial production, distribution, exhibition, and conservation require incredible resource expenditures. Garbage and ghosts are not just the privileged content of photographic and cinematic images; they are also a significant by-product of their production.

Garbage, detritus, and industrial by-products have a way of haunting, of sticking around as a disturbing reminder of the presence of the past and the limits of the future. With the life span of plastics estimated to be more than four hundred years, to give but one example, they too challenge, to paraphrase Bliss Cua Lim's account of fantastic cinema, the traditional calendars and clocks of historiographical practice rooted in secular, anthropometric scales.[49] The by-products and waste of the collective creative endeavors of cinema production—and not merely photographic and cinematic images that are their most visible manifestation— may be the ur-form of modern ghosts. But cinema in its plurality of forms still remains a vital medium for visualizing and thinking about this problem in which it is intimately implicated. It is another way that cinema materially haunts.

What is a ghost if not a medium of haunting, of an unsettling recurrence, producing a mode of address that troubles one's relations to the present, past, and future? A ghost is an actualization of seemingly impossible configurations of time and space. Ghostly apparitions help focalize and even reorient the attention of the living to consider alternative configurations of space-time, presence, and being. Folklore traditions across the globe have conceived of ghosts as figures for enduring but repressed or unattended-to injustices or as harbingers of present or future dangers. Ghosts call for the haunted to bear witness, to take account, and even to become responsible to an untimely call for justice. In this respect, ghosts occasion a particular spectatorial experience whose historical specificity may be characterized by a mixture of astonishment and ethical appeal.

Does the era of postcinema call for a posthuman account of ghosts? A chorus of ghosts might reply here "we have always already been posthuman," for it is one of the conditions of possibility of ghosts to be a form of afterlife to the finitude of human being. Reformulating this question with further nuance, or at least more humility toward specters in their many forms, one might ask, have scholarly conceptions of ghosts—as modes of address—been themselves haunted by a limiting anthropomorphism?[50] The silence of the chorus of ghosts is deafening here, and far more frightening. How and to what purpose might one pursue a de- or nonanthropomorphized and maybe even nonanthropocentric vision of ghosts? How, for example, might one rethink haunting at a planetary

level (a question haunted as much by Marx as his specters) or instanti-
ate a geo- and ecopolitics of spectrality, which is to say, an account of the
ghost planets that haunt our present and future?[51] In the vernacular of
astronomy, ghost planets refer to hypothetical or empirically unproven
planets that are indirectly suggested by data or fleeting observation. In an
era marked by ecological precarity, anthropogenic climate destabilization,
widespread extinctions, and environmental degradation, how might the
question of the ghostliness of our own planet come to matter and become
perceptible? Cinematic media illuminated by cinema and media studies
suggest one manner, for if it was ever possible to think cinema inno-
cently of its relationship to milieu and futurity, this is no longer a viable
luxury.

Nadia Bozak's, Nicole Starosielski's, and Hunter Vaughan's provocative
analyses of cinema and media's ecological footprint are exponentially—
and disproportionately—amplified by the infrastructural and resource
demands as well as the caloric intake and expenditure supporting the
many recent forms of digital and postcinema.[52] Cinema, as Kracauer had
already noted in his account of the UFA studios, is an energy-intensive
endeavor that builds and destroys environments. The material substrate
of analog film, particularly in its first half-century, when nitrate was a
primary ingredient, was highly flammable. Hot and even incendiary at
the moment of projection, even the safety stocks that emerged in the
1950s require cold storage as part of their preservation, though in these
conditions it is a stable and durable storage format. The shift to digital
capture, storage, distribution, and exhibition formats heralded over the
last decade as an end of cinema and the emergence of postcinema also
comes with considerable caloric expenditures, exemplified by the incredible thermal output of server farms that provide the infrastructural support for digital media. While exhibition via digital formats is far cooler
than its analog predecessors, the storage and distribution of digital materials (not to mention the mineral resources used to produce all of the
hardware) are incredibly hot and energy horny. Recent studies collated
by Greenpeace in 2015 and updated in 2017 on the carbon footprint and
energy demands of data storage and video streaming cite a total draw
of about 12 percent of the global electricity demand, though this figure
was expected to rise by as much as 7 percent annually over the following

decade.[53] One of the lead researchers on this problem, Anders Andrae, estimates that without considerable efficiency strides, world data consumption (which includes but is not limited to storage and streaming of media) could claim as much as 20 percent of global electricity by 2025 and account for 14 percent of carbon emissions.[54] What these data make clear is that certain end(s) of cinema and the end of the world as we have known it are becoming synchronous. Cinematic media, as Jennifer Fay eloquently argues, provide the exemplary aesthetic practice and experience of the Anthropocene but also, it is worth adding, increasingly act as substantial agents of acceleration in their forms of destruction and displacement of precarious environments and biodiversity.[55]

Can cinema "envision" its own ends? The remarkable work of the filmmaker Momoko Seto offers an alluring approach to these problems in a manner that suggests a contemporary animation of the critical insights of Kracauer and Bataille in a context of ecological crisis. Her series of short, speculative, experimental documentaries *Planet A* (2008), *Planet Z* (2011), *Planet Σ* (2014), and *Planet ∞* (2017), the latter of which was produced with the Franco-German cultural television channel ARTE as a VR movie, combines rigorous documentation, anime aesthetics, and surreal composites in service of a strange cinematic natural history (Figures 5.3 and 5.4). In the context of cinema's ends and new means, as well as the context of increasing planetary precarity, Seto's work conjures the kinds of ghosts Bataille called for to be adequate to the scale of the terrors of our times. Her movies activate the refuse-fueled perceptual pedagogy of Kracauer's account of photographic media.

Seto's *Planets* series presents landscapes that configure the primeval and postcatastrophic, before and after the end, in which humans appear to have no place. These movies resonate with the avant-garde aspirations of both Giorgio de Chirico and Max Ernst to somehow envision landscapes in which humans have no part—an almost impossible task, but a productive and necessary thought experiment all the same.[56] In such a scenario, we spectators are the ghosts, exiled from a proper place in these worlds. Seto's movies, which have no commentary save ambient music and clever Foley effects, seem to ask us to try to imagine worlds—perhaps this world—apart from ourselves and our ends if only to better understand our implications in and with them. Each of her ghost

Figure 5.3. Frame from *Planet Z* (Momoko Seto, France, 2011). Copyright Momoko Seto. Courtesy of the artist.

Figure 5.4. Frame from *Planet Σ* (Momoko Seto, France, 2014). Copyright Momoko Seto. Courtesy of the artist.

planets—as hypotheticals, to return to the idiom of astronomy—potentially holds a relation to the one we inhabit and collectively destroy
(though not with equal culpability). Her planets are uncanny laboratories of decay and exuberant proliferation. They establish experimental
milieux and second-nature environments from organic materials and
various forms of mold and plant life, and then allow entropy to take its
uncharted course. In *Planet Z* elegant tracking shots follow the paths
of slime molds traveling across landscapes of desiccating organic matter
and blizzards of digital spores snow down on the surface of rotting fruit
(see Figure 5.3). She produces strange constructs that composite hetero-
temporal processes of high-speed photography (such as bees flying in slow
motion) and time-lapse photography (showing the accelerated growth of
mushrooms and molds) into a single visual field, giving concrete forms
to the disjointed temporalities and surreal nature of climate chaos, but
also to a historiographic gaze stereographically attuned to human and
nonhuman temporalities (see Figure 5.4). Each of her films presents the
emergence, growth, and mysterious destruction of a planet—which is
often revealed to be common organic matter, such as salt crystals, a rot-
ten orange, or moldy berries filmed with extreme magnification and temporal manipulation.

Seto's movies invite us to see our own troubled present with eyes atten-
tive to remnants and revenants, to what goes, comes back, sticks around,
and disappears in and as cinema. The accelerated processes of proliferation and decay suggest what goes on without us but that we haunt, and
are in turn haunted by, be it the colony collapse of bees or the multiplica-
tion of species that overtake an ecosystem and devour its resources in a
manner that can only be suicidal. The movies combine the wonder and
beauty of nature with the horror appropriate to struggles over limited
resources, ecological collapse, and mass extinction. Their brilliance lies
in part in their imaginative use of scale, which finds entire worlds in salt
crystals and the surfaces of fruit skins. Seto and her collaborators produce spectacles matching any Michael Bay film, displaying the glorious
and catastrophic forms of expenditure Bataille imagined as the "accursed
share," the excess wealth (of energy, resources, etc.) irrecuperable to any
economic system (be it organic or cultural), and do so with a few modest elements in terrariums.[57] With scraps of waste products, her movies

produce haunting visions of worlds made and unmade, of the persistence of life, of dying, and of the strange forms of after- or postlife. The planet movies are at once elegies for lost worlds and inventions of new ones, set at the end of cinema but setting new ends for it.

From Kracauer, Bataille, and Seto, across a century of extinctions, metamorphoses, and reinventions, one may hazard a response to the vital question *what is cinema?* in the face of its many ends. The answer is double, at least.

Cinema is what remains.

Cinema is what returns.

Notes

Thanks to Richard Grusin, Jocelyn Szczepaniak-Gillece, Maureen Ryan, Nicholas Baer, the participants of the Ends of Cinema symposium at the Center for 21st Century Studies, and Momoko Seto.

1. Erich Auerbach, "Figura," in *Scenes from the Drama of European Literature,* trans. Paolo Valesio, 11–76 (Minneapolis: University of Minnesota Press, 1984).

2. For an overview of new materialisms, see Diana Coole and Samatha Frost, eds., *New Materialisms: Ontology, Agency, and Politics* (Durham, N.C.: Duke University Press, 2010). For an overview of the spectral turn and its cinematic iterations, see Avery F. Gordon, *Ghostly Matters: The Haunting and the Sociological Imagination* (Minneapolis: University of Minnesota Press, 2008); Maria del Pilar Blanco and Esther Peeren, eds., *The Spectralities Reader: Ghosts and Haunting in Contemporary Cultural Theory* (New York: Bloomsbury, 2013); Murray Leeder, ed., *Cinematic Ghosts: Haunting and Spectrality from Silent Cinema to the Digital Era* (New York: Bloomsbury, 2015); James Leo Cahill and Timothy Holland, eds., "Derrida and Cinema," special issue, *Discourse* 37, no. 1–2 (2015); and Elain Gan, Anna Tsing, Heather Swanson, and Nils Bubandt, *Arts of Living on a Damaged Planet: Ghosts and Monsters of the Anthropocene* (Minneapolis: University of Minnesota Press, 2017).

3. Dipesh Chakrabarty, "The Climate of History: Four Theses," *Critical Inquiry* 35, no. 2 (2009): 201, 222, and Kathryn Yusoff, *A Billion Black Anthropocenes or None* (Minneapolis: University of Minnesota Press, 2018). Chakrabarty adapts the term "*negative universal history*" from Antonio Y. Vázquez-Arroyo's reading of Adorno in "Universal History Disavowed: On Critical Theory and Postcolonialism," *Postcolonial Studies* 11, no. 4 (2008): 451–73.

4. Siegfried Kracauer, "Photography," in *Mass Ornament: Weimar Essays,* trans. and ed. Thomas Y. Levin, 47–63 (Cambridge, Mass.: Harvard University Press, 1995); Kracauer, "Die Photographie," in *Das Ornament der Masse: Essays,* 21–39

(Frankfurt am Main, Germany: Surhkamp, 1977); Georges Bataille, "Human Face," in *Encyclopedia Acephalica,* ed. Robert Lebel and Isabelle Waldberg, trans. Iain White, Dominic Faccini, Annette Michaelson, John Harman, and Alexis Lykiard, 99–106 (London: Atlas Press, 1995); and Bataille, "Figure humaine," *Documents* 4 (1929): 194–201.

5. Kracauer, "Photography," 62, and "Die Photographie," 38.

6. Georges Didi-Huberman, *La ressemblance informe* (Paris: Macula, 1995), and Linda Steer, *Appropriated Photographs in French Surrealist Periodicals, 1924–1939* (New York: Routledge, 2017).

7. For considerations of Kracauer's and Bataille's relationship to a critical practice of natural history, see James Leo Cahill, "Cinema's Natural History," *Journal of Cinema and Media Studies* 58, no. 2 (2019): 152–57, and Cahill, "Absolute Dismemberment: Georges Bataille's Burlesque Natural History," in *Abjection Incorporated: Mediating the Politics of Pleasure and Violence,* ed. Maggie Hennefeld and Nic Sammond, 185–207 (Durham, N.C.: Duke University Press, 2020). Passages from pages 154–55 of "Cinema's Natural History" appear here in revised form.

8. Siegfried Kracauer, *History: The Last Things before the Last,* ed. Paul Oskar Kristeller (1969; repr., Princeton, N.J.: Markus Weiner, 1995), 83–84, and Gertrude Koch, *Siegfried Kracauer: An Introduction,* trans. Jeremy Gaines (Princeton, N.J.: Princeton University Press, 2000), 114–20.

9. Kracauer, "On the Writings of Walter Benjamin," in Levin, *Mass Ornament,* 260, and "Zu den Schriften Walter Benjamins," in *Das Ornament der Masse,* 250.

10. For a précis of Ranke's historiography, see Kracauer, *History,* 48–49, 81.

11. Kracauer, "Photography," 58, and "Die Photographie," 34.

12. Miriam Bratu Hansen, *Cinema and Experience: Siegfried Kracauer, Walter Benjamin, and Theodor W. Adorno* (Berkeley: University of California Press, 2011), 36.

13. On the demonic diva and speculations about her possible identity, see Unfried Pfeifer-Duwe, "Jenseits des fotografischen Einzelbildes. Siegfried Kracauer und das Foto der dämonischem Diva," in *Das ABC des Kinos,* vol. 3, ed. Sabine Hartung (Frankfurt am Main, Germany: Stroemfeld, 2009).

14. Siegfried Kracauer, "Farewell to the Linden Arcade," in *Mass Ornament,* 340, "Abschied von der Lindenpassage," in *Das Ornament der Masse,* 330.

15. Kracauer, "Photography," 55, 51, 52, 53, and "Die Photographie," 30, 25.

16. Olivier Agard, *Kracauer: Le chiffonnier mélancholique* (Paris: CNRS, 2010), 264.

17. Jennifer Fay, *Inhospitable World: Cinema in the Time of the Anthropocene* (New York: Oxford University Press, 2018), 176.

18. Kracauer, "Photography," 56–57.

19. Kracauer.

20. Pfeifer-Duwe, "Jenseits des fotografischen Einzelbildes," and Hansen, *Cinema and Experience,* 27.

21. Kracauer, "Photography," 62–63, "Die Photographie," 39.

22. Kracauer, "Calico-World: The UFA City in Neubabelsberg," in *Mass Ornament,* 281–82; "Kalikowelt," in *Das Ornament der Masse,* 271–78; Hansen, *Cinema and Experience,* 14; Fay, *Inhospitable World,* 8.

23. Kracauer, "Calico-World," 283.

24. Kracauer, 281–82.

25. Kracauer, 283.

26. Kracauer, 286.

27. Hansen, introduction to *Theory of Film: The Redemption of Physical Reality* (Princeton, N.J.: Princeton University Press, 1997), vii.

28. Bataille, "Human Face," 106 (trans. modified), and "Figure humaine," 200.

29. For examinations of the sexual politics of archival imagery, see Paul Flaig, "Supposing That the Archive Is a Woman," in *New Silent Cinema,* ed. Paul Flaig and Katherine Groo, 180–99 (New York: Routledge, 2015), and Catherine Russell, *Archiveology: Walter Benjamin and Archival Film Practices* (Durham, N.C.: Duke University Press, 2018), 184–217.

30. Bataille, "Human Face," 100, and "Figure humaine," 194.

31. Bataille, "Human Face," 100, and "Figure humaine," 194.

32. Bataille, "Figure humaine," 195.

33. Maggie Hennefeld, *Specters of Slapstick and Silent Film Comediennes* (New York: Columbia University Press, 2018), 31–82.

34. Bataille, "Human Face," 101, and "Figure humaine," 196.

35. Bataille, "Human Face," 101, and "Figure humaine," 196.

36. Bataille, "Human Face," 101, and "Figure humaine," 196.

37. Didi-Huberman, *La ressemblance informe,* 36–37.

38. Steer, *Appropriated Photographs,* 142.

39. See *Le Grand Robert de le langue française,* n.v. "figure." On the view that only human beings have a face, see Hegel, *Aesthetics: Lectures on Fine Art,* trans. T. M. Knox (New York: Oxford University Press, 1975), 2:728.

40. Bataille, "Human Face," 104 (translation modified), and "Figure humaine," 200.

41. Bataille, "Human Face," 102, and "Figure humaine," 196.

42. Bataille, "Metamorphosis: Wild Animals," trans. Annette Michelson, *October* 36 (1986): 22, and "Métamorphoses: Animaux sauvages," *Documents* 6 (1929): 333.

43. Bataille, "Human Face," 104, and "Figure humaine," 200.

44. Bataille, "Human Face," 106 (translation slightly modified), and "Figure humaine," 200.

45. Kracauer, "Photography," 47, "Die Photographie," 21.

46. Hansen, *Cinema and Experience,* 28.

47. Bataille, *The Tears of Eros,* trans. Peter Connor (San Francisco: City Lights, 1989), 205, and Bataille, *Oeuvres completes* (Paris: Gallimard, 1987), 10:627.

48. For a brilliant consideration of cinema's ghosts in deconstructive thought, see Timothy Holland, "Ses Fantômes: The Traces of Derrida's Cinema," *Discourse* 37, no. 1–2 (2015): 40–62.

49. Bliss Cua Lim, *Translating Time: Cinema, the Fantastic, and Temporal Critique* (Durham, N.C.: Duke University Press, 2009).

50. An important exception to the anthropomorphism of specters occurs in Rudolph Otto, *The Idea of the Holy: An Inquiry into the Non-rational Factor in the Idea of the Devine and Its Relation to the Rational,* trans. John W. Harvey (1923; repr., London: Oxford University Press, 1936), esp. 27–29, where he considers ghosts as a weak symptomatic displacement of the shattering experience of the "wholly other" with which no possible form of identification or categorization is possible.

51. The talk from which this chapter was developed was given on May 5, 2018—Karl Marx's two-hundredth birthday. The specters emerge from Jacques Derrida, *Specters of Marx: The State of Debt, the Work of Mourning, and the New International,* trans. Peggy Kamuf, introduction by Bernd Magnus and Stephen Cullenberg (New York: Routledge, 1994).

52. Nadia Bozak, *The Cinematic Footprint: Lights, Camera, Natural Resources* (New Brunswick, N.J.: Rutgers University Press, 2012); Nicole Starosielski, "The Materiality of Media Heat," *International Journal of Communication* 8 (2014): 2504–8; and Hunter Vaughan, *Hollywood's Dirtiest Secret: The Hidden Environmental Cost of Movies* (New York: Columbia University Press, 2019).

53. Peter Corcoran and Anders Andrae, "Emerging Trends in Electricity Consumption for Consumer ICT," http://vmserver14.nuigalway.ie/xmlui/handle/10 379/3563, and David Pomerantz et al., *Click Clean Scorecard: Key Findings and Sources Explained* (Washington, D.C.: Greenpeace, 2015), 5. I thank Gabrielle Dupuis for bringing this research to my attention in "The Afterlife of Digital Images" (MA thesis, University of Toronto, 2017).

54. Andrae, cited in John Vidal, "'Tsunami of Data' Could Consume One Fifth of Global Electricity by 2025," *Climate Home News,* December 11, 2017, http://www.climatechangenews.com/2017/12/11/tsunami-data-consume-one-fifth-glo bal-electricity-2025/.

55. Fay, *Inhospitable World,* 4.

56. Giorgio de Chirico, "On Metaphysical Art" [1919], in *Metaphysical Art* 14–16 (2016): 39, and Max Ernst, *Histoire naturelle* (Paris: Galerie Jeanne Bucher, 1926).

57. Georges Bataille, *The Accursed Share: An Essay on General Economy: Vol. 1. Consumption,* trans. Robert Hurley (New York: Zone, 1988), 21, and *La Part Maudite* in *Oeuvres Complètes,* vol. 7 (Paris: Gallimard, 1976), 29.

6

Shot in Black and White

The Racialized History of Cinema Violence

Caetlin Benson-Allott

When contemplating the "ends" of cinema, one naturally considers the death of cinema. Often foretold but never forthcoming, the death of cinema can incite panic in cinéastes and scholars. Based on personal yet abstract idealizations of moviegoing, these responses belie the long history of death *at* the cinema. Investigating violent assaults at movie theaters reveals much about the racist, neoliberal fantasy undergirding popular conceptions of cinema, however. Since the early 1920s, trade organizations for motion picture producers, distributors, and exhibitors have promoted movie theaters as safe, family-friendly entertainment centers. Such image management is a means to an "end" of cinema, namely, greater ticket sales and corporate profits. But marketing cinemas as safe means denying their real history. Cinema violence has been a documented component of U.S. film culture since at least 1915, when antiracist audiences rioted at screenings of D. W. Griffith's *The Birth of a Nation.* Violence in cinemas is a particular subcategory of *spectator violence,* a term coined in 1951 by Albert D. Kirwin to describe riots, assaults, and murders at public events, including political debates, sporting matches, concerts, and plays.[1] Such incidents occasionally inspire moral panics, but not invariably. For although cinema violence is always tragic, not all cinema violence gets treated as tragic, due to racialized fantasies undergirding past and present notions about who does and does not belong in movie theaters.

Since the 1970s, anti-Black racism and white privilege have shaped public responses to cinema violence, turning it into a crucial discursive site for discriminating among moviegoers. When and how moral panics over cinema violence develop depends—I argue—on racialized perceptions of the individuals allegedly involved. Stanley Cohen coined the term *moral panic* in 1973 to describe the widespread fear of a relatively minor or rare threat to the social order.[2] Sociologists Erich Goode and Nachman Ben-Yehuda have since observed that "moral panics are not 'about' specific activities."[3] Rather, they synthesize long-simmering fears around a specific event. Thus one of the major differences between a moral panic and a social problem is the discrepancy between the anxiety a situation generates and the actual danger involved. For that reason, moral panics tend to arise not from common hazards, such as traffic accidents, but from prejudice and fear.

Cinema shootings and stabbings provide particularly powerful stimuli for moral panics because they are rare—although not as rare as we think. Nevertheless, they trigger many prejudices about violence in the United States, particularly the fantasy that affluent white Americans ought to be—indeed, deserve to be—insulated from social violence. That fantasy emerges from U.S. histories of slavery, institutionalized racism, and de facto segregation that include the cinema. Moral panics about cinema violence help enforce such mind-sets. For instance, after James Eagan Holmes fired on a mostly white audience in Aurora, Colorado, in 2012, he was accused of violating the "sanctuary" of movie theaters.[4] This seemingly benign claim obscures the long history of cinema violence in the United States to perpetuate a white fantasy about the multiplex as a safe space. Historicizing moral panics about cinema violence exposes the cultural supposition that white Americans ought to be exempt from social violence while other groups are plagued by it. Hence public responses to cinema violence panics change from anger to grief when the victims and assailants are white instead of Black or Latinx.

Historicizing moral panics about cinema violence is different from historicizing actual violence, and this chapter does the former at the expense of the latter. It also explores how the movies themselves come to play a role in these panics. Certain movies' subjects, genres, and compositions inform the discourse of related moral panics, not through any fault of their own, but because their fictions inadvertently provide scripts for interpreting cinema violence. Individual acts of cinema violence may have a coincidental or causal relationship to the screenings they accompany. Either way, the incidents' social impact inheres in the media's representation of them, as both journalists and their interviewees frequently reference and borrow reasoning from afflicted films, especially from their discourses around race. The media have variably represented cinema violence as predictable or random, contemptible or tragic, depending on

1. the racial identity of the shooter(s),
2. the racial identity of the victim(s),
3. the racial identity of the audience targeted by the film's distributor,
4. the racial identity of the film's protagonists, and
5. the racial discourse of prior moral panics about cinema violence.

Critiquing moral panics about cinema violence thus requires one to read these incidents in the context of film reception, for indeed, moral panics are a mode of film reception. Textual analysis then provides further opportunity for ideology critique—and this ideology needs to be critiqued. Hence this chapter analyzes three moral panics about death at the cinema to argue that because cinema violence only gets to be "random" and "tragic" when it happens to white people, it remains an expedient of anti-Black prejudice.

The first of these panics began after three young men died in conjunction with screenings of Walter Hill's *The Warriors* (1979). Their deaths led reviewers, pundits, politicians, parents, and even one pediatrician to call for the film's censure. They blamed *The Warriors* for attracting gangs—specifically gangs of African American young men—to the cinema, a rhetorical trope that would shape anticipation of and reporting on cinema violence for decades. Its critics used Hill's antiracist movie to blame young men of color for the very violence and disenfranchisement that the film shows them enduring. Not all of the assailants at *The Warriors* incidents were African American, nor were most of its characters. Yet Blackness remained a key figure in collective fantasies of theater violence for the next thirty-odd years, until mental illness provided the media with exculpatory discourse for the increasing number of non-Black shooters.

When *The Warriors* premiered on February 9, 1979, no one took it very seriously. The first in a cycle of urban gang films, its cast was virtually unknown, and its director had barely begun to make a name for himself. Yet Paramount opened *The Warriors* wide with a provocative newspaper ad campaign hailing "the armies of the night." Above an image of men in leather vests and women in tight jeans, many brandishing baseball bats, the film's poster warned, "They are 100,000 strong. They outnumber the cops five to one. They could run New York City. Tonight they're all out to get the Warriors." Paramount coupled this provocative placard—which conjures a future in which law is threatened by a new order—with an equally exploitative television spot. Both promised that *The Warriors* would be an extravaganza of teen violence, so it should come as no surprise that reviews were tepid, although some critics reserved modest praise for Hill's mannerist approach to the material. Nevertheless, *The Warriors* was popular at the box office. Within three weeks, it was the highest grossing film in theaters and stood at the center of a nationwide controversy.

Word was spreading that *The Warriors* did not just depict gang violence but provoked it. On Monday, February 12, two young Californians died at screenings of *The Warriors*. The first, Marvin Kenneth Eller, was shot in the head at a drive-in theater in Palm Springs. Who shot him and why remains unclear. One article claims that Eller "argued with a youth who blocked the way to the bathroom."[5] Another suggests that Eller's death was part of a racially motivated face-off between two local gangs, the African American Blue Coats and the white Family.[6] Other reports assert that Eller "was fatally stabbed . . . in a reenactment of the film's savage bathroom battle."[7] Here Eller's assault seems to have been confused with that of Timothy Gitchel, who died at another *Warriors* show in Oxnard, California. Authorities never figured out what led to the conflict between Gitchel, his friends (two of whom were also stabbed), and the other young men involved. Lieutenant Dan Hanline of the Oxnard Police Department suggested that "the dispute started when a black youth asked for a quarter from Timothy Gitchel and then bloodied Gitchel's nose when the money was not given."[8] Every single report on Gitchel's death notes that he was white and his assailants were Black, although the number of alleged assailants varies between one and twenty. *People* magazine painted a particularly inflammatory picture, contending that "just as *The Warriors* came on, the four youths suddenly found themselves battling at least fifteen blacks who were suspected of drinking and smoking grass during the previous show."[9] No one questioned why these young Black men suddenly assaulted Gitchel's crew. Watching *The Warriors* was considered impetus enough.

The *Warriors* panic gained momentum after Martin Yakubowicz was fatally stabbed outside a Boston subway station on February 15, 1979, by another teenager who had just been to *The Warriors* and allegedly paraphrased a key line of dialogue while attacking Yakubowicz.[10] Over the next few weeks, gangs of *Warriors* fans were reported marauding the New York City subway system, and a Boston hitchhiker was attacked and nearly killed by three men who purportedly called themselves the Warriors.[11] On March 23, a fourth young man was stabbed at a drive-in in San Juan Capistrano, California, also while watching *The Warriors.*[12]

News of "Murder in the Cinema" spread across the globe.[13] Yakubowicz's family filed suit against Paramount and the Saxon Theater of Boston, Massachusetts, where their son's assailant saw the movie. Massachusetts state senator Michael LoPresti asked that the film be banned in Boston.[14] Protestors picketed screenings of *The Warriors* in New York and Los Angeles, alleging that it glorified gang violence. Newspaper columnists condemned Hill's film as irresponsible and irredeemable. Indeed, the *Christian Science Monitor* denounced it as nothing more than "one long tracking shot of the gangs battling—with knives, guns, bicycle chains, clubs, switchblades, Molotov cocktails, and baseball bats."[15]

That sounds like a great movie, but it isn't *The Warriors,* which contains almost no on-screen bloodshed. Based on Xenophon's *Anabasis, The Warriors* follows an interracial Coney Island street gang as they travel to a citywide gang summit led by messianic leader Cyrus (Roger Hill). Cyrus's congress recalls an actual truce negotiated between Black and Latinx gangs in the Bronx in 1971. Hill's vision is more radical than mere armistice, however, as Cyrus hails an integrated future for all crews. "Can you count, suckers?" he asks his assembled audience:

You're standing right now with nine delegates from a hundred gangs, and there's over a hundred more. That's 20,000 hard core members—40,000 counting affiliates—and 20,000 more not organized but ready to fight.... The problem in the past has been the man turning us against one another. We have been unable to see the truth because we have been fighting for ten square feet of ground: our turf, our little piece of turf. That's crap, brothers. The turf is ours by right, because it's our turn.

Cyrus's thesis—"the future is ours"—earns wild applause from the assembly, a generation of disenfranchised kids coming of age in a collapsing city and in the wake of multiple failed social movements. When Cyrus is then killed by the leader of the only all-white gang in the film and the Warriors are blamed, they must fight their way home past an eclectic series of wildly dressed Gotham gangs, including the Turnbull ACs, an integrated group of skinheads who maraud the Bronx from a desecrated school bus (Figure 6.1). The gangs' costuming advances the fluorescently bright color palette of Hill's slightly surreal gangland epic, which further emphasizes its stylization with mannered choreography, a synthesized score, and flashy wipes between scenes.

As unlikely as it may seem, though, Hill's film offers both a phantasmagoria of crazy costumes and artistically choreographed fight scenes *and* a well-researched representation of 1970s New York City and its gang scene. During the 1960s and 1970s, the city suffered immensely from the

Figure 6.1. The Turnbull ACs in Walter Hill's *The Warriors.*

emigration of middle-class residents, a decreasing tax base, and national economic stagflation. These factors brought the city to the brink of bankruptcy in 1975, leading it to cut many of the social programs that reduced gang operation during the 1960s. In the mid-1970s, experts estimated there to be twenty thousand active gang members in New York City—the same number Cyrus cites in his speech.[16] Such historical accuracy bespeaks the great respect that *The Warriors* shows gang members, including their frustration with the American Dream. "This is what we fought all night to get back to?" one Warrior asks when his group finally gets home to Coney Island. The so-called People's Playground is nearly derelict. It has no future to offer its youth, only a horizon of crushed hopes. In this manner, Hill's movie calls out the conditions of disenfranchisement that breed gang violence.

Yet just as the Warriors were falsely accused of killing Cyrus, *The Warriors* was unfairly blamed for the murders of Marvin Eller, Timothy Gitchel, and Martin Yakubowicz. Critics denounced the film for sparking interracial violence, even though the Warriors are a multiracial gang. Indeed, one of the few ways that *The Warriors* misrepresents gang culture is in its emphasis on integration. Furthermore, the film models its only all-Black gang—Cyrus's Riffs—on social justice gangs like the Blackstone Rangers, thereby associating the Riffs with leadership, hope, and community activism.[17] Nevertheless, one Los Angeles antigang activist called *The Warriors* "a mind control picture," arguing that it induced violent uprising among young viewers.[18] Other commentators indicted the film's viewers directly, contending, "If you bring that sort of crowd into the moviehouse, you will have the same trouble with *The Sound of Music* [Robert Wise, 1965]."[19]

Such an apology absolves the film, but only by suggesting that "that sort of crowd" does not belong in movie theaters in the first place. In the context of the article and the era, "that sort" clearly refers to gang members. The alleged *Warriors* killings all happened in places where gang violence was already a concern, where a movie about gang violence would seem not exotic but ominous. In 1979, Harvard sociologist Walter Miller noted that Boston "rank[ed] third, behind Los Angeles and Philadelphia, as the most lethal gang city in America."[20] Palm Springs is only a little more than one hundred miles from Los Angeles, Oxnard barely sixty. In cities with minority gangs, *Warriors*-related incidents were blamed on African American crews even when no evidence existed to support that rush to judgment. Only in Boston, where the gangs were mostly white, did white reporters blame white assailants for a white victim's death. That being said, Boston papers also published the most (and the most vitriolic) attacks on *The Warriors*. Here it is important to recall that Boston experienced violent desegregation protests between 1974 and 1977, which may have fueled local antipathy for *The Warriors*. At root, the moral panic over *The Warriors* was a panic over desegregation, over heterogeneity within cinema audiences. Alarmists feared that "that sort of crowd" would take the wrong message away from Hill's film and into the community. Such fear rests on the supposition that only some kinds of people should go to the cinema at all.

Hence many called for the film's censure. *Boston Globe* film reviewer Bruce McCabe recommended that it be banned, noting that "the sophisticated reaction to this film is that the film mustn't be censored. . . . If we want the risk of this violence to be avoided, [however] the film must be taken out of circulation."[21] Over the next three weeks, the *Globe* would publish two editorials condemning "a motion picture whose after-effects seem to be civil disorder, mayhem and murder," as well as nine letters from readers debating the relative merits of censorship.[22] The *Washington Post* chimed in too, opining, "It's not fascism to publicly disapprove of those who use the First Amendment to mislead and miseducate."[23] Maybe not, but in that case, disapproval should be directed at the *Post* for misrepresenting *The Warrior*'s call for social justice and not at the film itself.

To be clear, *The Warriors* was not to blame for the violence that occurred during or after its screenings. The film's surreal aesthetic and social realist themes confused its detractors, however, and thereby contributed to the media's transformation of a few isolated incidents into a nationwide moral panic. That panic established a rhetoric that others would use to predict and denounce cinema violence a decade later. Between 1979 and 1988, the U.S. media largely forgot their fear of cinema violence, or rather, it was eclipsed by a larger moral panic over gang violence. Gang activity did increase in the United States during this period, but media coverage exaggerated and sensationalized the problem, vilifying all African American youth by association. As a result, reporters, and even some reviewers, began predicting cinema violence at films by and about African American men, most notably Spike Lee's *Do the Right Thing* (1989).[24] In essence, such urban dramas stood accused of soliciting violence by soliciting Black viewers. An entire audience group was both courted and criminalized in advance, so that when violent incidents did occur, as they did at *Boyz n the Hood* (John Singleton, 1991), they provided confirmation bias for further prejudice and disenfranchisement.

Although critics predicted riots at *Do the Right Thing*, there were none, and the film's critical and financial success helped launch a cycle of low-budget films by African American men about the problems facing African American urban communities. Beginning with Mario Van Peebles's *New Jack City* in March 1991 and Singleton's *Boyz n the Hood* in July 1991, the films of the so-called "ghetto action cycle" continued Lee's politicized violation of what Salim Muwakkil dubs the "once-sacrosanct taboo against the portrayal of 'negative' images of African-Americans by African-Americans."[25] These movies were blamed for inciting violence despite their antiviolence messages of personal responsibility—messages that, ironically, downplay the larger social forces undergirding gang activity in the United States. Perhaps for this reason, the media never described cinema violence at ghetto action films as "random." That label would be reserved for future incidents where white victims were attacked at movies aimed at white audiences.

The perceived cycle of cinema violence at ghetto action films began with a riot outside one Los Angeles theater's screening of *New Jack City*. Although the riot was in fact unrelated to the film, journalists were thereafter "lying in wait," as Singleton put it, to find and report on any violence when *Boyz n the Hood* premiered four months later.[26] *Boyz n the Hood* did not induce violence any more than any other film at which an altercation occurred. However, cinema violence shaped *Boyz*'s reception and legacy more than it did those of any other film—including *The Dark Knight Rises* (Christopher Nolan, 2012), which currently has the dubious distinction of accompanying the biggest mass shooting at any U.S. cinema. *Boyz n the Hood* and its representation of Black masculinity in South Central Los Angeles have been understood almost entirely in terms of violence. This includes Singleton's message of personal responsibility, which helped the film court a white crossover audience but also encouraged that audience's fear of Black men. The result was that when violent incidents did occur, they provided confirmation bias for further racist prejudice.

Like many other ghetto action films, *Boyz n the Hood* was preceded by a deceptive and exploitative marketing campaign. In her book on American film cycles, Amanda Ann Klein shows how the campaign for *Boyz n the Hood* "sought to confirm an image of authentic or realistic 'blackness'... synonymous with aggressive masculinity, random violence, and gang culture in general."[27] While the film itself denounces gang violence and challenges the racist assumption that all young Black men must be gang members, its trailers and posters belie such intentions. Instead, Columbia Pictures sold *Boyz n the Hood* by underscoring the film's ethic of personal responsibility and its social realism with images of violence. Thus the film's cinematic trailer introduces its three young protagonists—Tre (Cuba Gooding Jr.), Doughboy (Ice Cube), and Ricky (Morris Chestnut)—through their contrasting responses to the dire underdevelopment of their community. The trailer acknowledges that "In South Central LA, it's tough to beat the streets," as Doughboy pulls out his gun and loads the chamber, but such phrasing notably imports an individual's responsibility to rise above rather than, say, demanding that state agencies intervene. Individualism absolves the spectator of doing anything about the world they see on-screen, while social realism rewards them for taking an interest at all. Columbia exploited the latter strategy in its home video trailer for *Boyz n the Hood,* which begins with footage from the Vietnam War and a narrator intoning that "five minutes away from your nice, safe neighborhood, there's a war going on. And the news isn't covering it. *Boyz n the Hood*: it's the kind of news that usually gets buried."[28] This trailer presumes a "safe" audience physically and psychically distant from the inner city and uses that distance to sell Singleton's film as a realistic exploration of an underreported crisis. In so doing, it counters the cynicism of *Boyz n the Hood*'s first poster, where the taglines "Once upon a time in South Central LA" and "It ain't no fairy tale" suggest that Singleton's film will serve as a wake-up call to apathetic or ignorant audiences. Columbia later replaced these taglines with the imperative slogan of the film's closing title card, "Increase the Peace." As important as that message is, it too emphasizes individual responsibility without specifying

how different individuals (and social institutions) are variously responsible for preventing social violence.

Columbia's advertising strategies inadvertently provided fodder for the
moral panic that took off after people started getting hurt at screenings
of *Boyz*. When *Boyz n the Hood* opened in 829 theaters on July 12, 1991,
shots were fired at theaters in sixteen cities. More than thirty people were
injured, and two died: Michael Booth and Jitu Jones.[29] Booth saw the
film at the Halstead Twin Drive-In in Riverdale, Illinois, with his girl-
friend and young son. As they waited in line to leave, Timothy Turner
walked up to their car and asked for a light.[30] Booth refused, and Turner
shot him. Jones was shot outside the Skyway 6 cinema in downtown Minneapolis, Minnesota, after fleeing a gun battle inside the theater. Police
noted that Jones was not involved in the fracas and that the bullet "apparently was intended for someone else."[31]

Reporters did little to commemorate Booth or Jones. Instead their
articles brought together unrelated incidents to suggest that *Boyz n the
Hood* was causing mayhem from coast to coast. These included non-
lethal shootings in Los Angeles, Las Vegas, Detroit, Tuscaloosa, Miami, and
Brooklyn, among other cities.[32] People were also stabbed at or outside
four other screenings, while riots were reported in Tukwila, Washington,
and Orlando, Florida.[33] Newspapers sensationalized all of these events
with headlines like "Trail of Trouble for *Boyz*" and "Film Opens with Wave
of Violence."[34] One *Washington Post* reporter had the audacity to contend that "there has never been anything like the kind of trouble now
being associated with black movies," a patently ridiculous claim.[35] Such
contentions depend on a fantasy of the cinema as a safe, racially homog-
enous space, a fantasy only made possible by ignorance of actual cinema
history and presumptions of de facto segregation in movie theaters.

Racist fears of cinema violence fueled a backlash against African
American films throughout the 1990s, a backlash that compromised the
careers of many promising Black filmmakers. Within two weeks of *Boyz n
the Hood*'s premiere, General Cinema began intentionally extending the
time between its shows to prevent crowds gathering outside theaters.[36] As
Variety reporter Mark Becker observed, other industry executives started
"pre-screening films for their off-screen violence potential," a move Charles
Acland compares to racial profiling.[37] At the same time, some exhibitors

began releasing "urban" films on Wednesdays rather than Fridays.[38] Such "preventative measures" averted big opening weekends for those movies, reducing their ticket sales and, by extension, their filmmakers' career prospects.

It is ironic that U.S. film exhibitors were so frightened of a film cycle overtly committed to a politics of personal responsibility. The movies' antiviolence messages should have absolved them of suspicion, but in fact they aided the agents of moral panic in blaming Black men for the degradation of their communities. Espousing personal responsibility helped *Boyz n the Hood* court a white crossover audience, but it also encouraged that same audience to fear Black men when cinema violence did occur. *Boyz n the Hood* embeds this philosophy in its ideal of Black masculinity, Furious Styles (Lawrence Fishburne). Early in the film, Furious sets out to teach his son Tre how to be a man, which amounts to lessons in individual accountability. When Tre resists, Furious explains, "You may think I am being hard on you now, but I'm not. I'm trying to teach you how to be responsible. Your friends across the street, they don't have anybody to show them. You're gonna see how they end up too." This seemingly idle threat in fact portends the film's outcome. Before Tre graduates from high school, his friend Ricky will be shot by members of the Crips for being in the wrong place at the wrong time. Ricky's brother Doughboy will be killed two weeks later. Furious does not literally foresee their deaths, but he surmises that young Black men need a philosophy of personal accountability to avoid becoming the one out of twenty-one Black men who "will be murdered in their lifetime," per the film's opening title card.

Boyz n the Hood juxtaposes Furious with other Black male authority figures to emphasize the singular righteousness of his vision. After Furious misses a shot at a burglar in his house, Tre laments that the man escaped with his life. "Don't say that," Furious reprimands him. "Just would have been contributing to killing another brother." When the police show up to take Furious's statement, it quickly becomes clear that Furious and Officer Coffey (Jesse Ferguson) have opposite opinions with regard to the criminalization of Black men. The film cuts to a close-up of Coffey, who is African American, as he mutters to Furious, "You know it's too bad you didn't get him. Be one less nigger out here in the streets we have to worry about." Coffey raises his eyebrows while speaking through gritted teeth, subtly but purposefully appealing to Furious for validation. Ferguson's delivery makes it clear that the "we" to whom Coffey refers are not the police but Black men not affiliated with gangs. But Furious, mindful of the model he must set for Tre, refuses to be drawn into an us-versus-them critique of other African Americans. When the film cuts to Furious for a reaction shot, he is looking down at Tre, who stares at Coffey, his face blank. Coffey greets Tre with cheerful menace, but Furious sends his son away. "Something wrong?" the cop asks Furious. "Something wrong?" he replies. "Yeah. It's just too bad that you don't know what it is." Furious lifts his eyebrows on "you" to convey that his critique of Coffey is personal, not professional. In this film, personal responsibility means not just protecting one's self, home, and family but also showing respect and compassion for African Americans, something Coffey fails to do.

Throughout the rest of the film, Furious remains an idol and sage for his entire community. Nowhere is Singleton's veneration for the character clearer than in Furious's lecture on gentrification, which is formally presented as a Sermon on the Mount (Figure 6.2). In it, Furious stands on a hill above a local audience, explaining, "What we need to do is keep everything in our neighborhood, everything, Black: Black-owned with Black money." "They want us to kill ourselves," he reminds his listeners,

Figure 6.2. Furious Styles, played by Laurence Fishburne, delivering his Sermon on the Mount in *Boyz n the Hood*.

to which one replies, "What am I supposed to do? Fool roll up and try to smoke me, I'm going to shoot the motherfucker if he don't kill me first." "You're doing exactly what they want you to do," Furious retorts. "You have to think, young brother, about your future."

Furious's serious tone is neither condescending nor demeaning, but it suggests that every man is responsible for how he responds to institutionalized racism and social violence—precisely the attitude journalists would take toward cinema violence at *Boyz n the Hood*.[39] Furious is not indifferent to the effects of deterritorialization and disenfranchisement, but he nevertheless espouses an individualist philosophy of social uplift reminiscent of Booker T. Washington and W. E. B. Du Bois.[40] With Furious lionized by his own community and by the film itself—in glamor shots that routinely emphasize Fishburne's strong jaw and muscular physique—he serves as the mouthpiece of the film's philosophy. The solution to Black suffering will not come from schools, the police, or social services but from Black men assuming the middle-class individualist morality of U.S. capitalism. Anyone who doesn't assimilate can be held responsible for failing himself, be he a drug dealer like Doughboy or a teenager shooting another teenager in a movie theater.

Boyz n the Hood advocates this logic of personal responsibility to discourage violence against and among Black men, but the 1990s moral panic about cinema violence deployed it as a means of victim-blaming. One position was antiracist and the other deeply racist, yet both implicitly held that the violence happening in Black communities and among Black audiences was not random. Of the dozens of filmmakers, exhibitors, policemen, and journalists who commented on cinema violence in the 1990s, only two ever describe it as *random*. These exceptions comprise a short statement from Columbia Pictures in July 1991 acknowledging that "random violence exists not only in Los Angeles but all over the country . . . It predated the opening of *Boyz N the Hood* and sadly it almost certainly will continue well into the future," and a September 1997 article in the *Ottawa Citizen* satirizing the film industry's investment in cinema violence.[41] Notably, Columbia uses the term "random" to minimize the bloodshed and dispel fear, while the *Ottawa Citizen* columnist employs it as part of a cavalier and thoughtless attempt at humor. In all other press about *Boyz n the Hood*, cinema violence is presented—implicitly or explicitly—

as the specific, even logical outcome of exhibiting films by and about African American men.[42] Not one single journalist acknowledges that the violence at *Boyz n the Hood*—or any other ghetto action film—might have been random, meaning arbitrary, senseless, and heartbreaking.

The press would only subsequently use such language in the twenty-first century for white victims of white assailants at movies aimed at white audiences. In the twentieth century, cinema violence was so closely associated with African American gang violence that reporters treated cinema shootings and stabbings by non-Black assailants as anomalies rather than a troubling trend. Cinema violence was *never* limited to Black audiences or movies aimed at Black audiences, but that was the only kind of violence recognized as cinema violence from the 1970s into the 2000s. Despite incidents at *Cocktail* (Roger Donaldson, 1989), *Schindler's List* (Steven Spielberg, 1994), *King Kong* (Peter Jackson, 2005), and *X-Men: The Last Stand* (Brett Ratner, 2006), the media did not represent cinema violence as a white problem. The category had been constructed around Blackness, so shootings among other races failed to garner national attention. How else can one explain the national media's lack of interest in James Michael Kirby shooting Ellen Campbell at a screening of *Schindler's List* "to test God"?[43] It was a shocking assault, committed, as the *Los Angeles Times* notes, "at a time when Congress is debating the effect of television and movie violence on real violence."[44] Yet it received none of the sensational press coverage bestowed on the ghetto action cycle incidents. Like other white-on-white assaults in movie theaters, the Kirby shooting only became recognizable as cinema violence retroactively, really after James Eagan Holmes killed twelve people and injured seventy more at a midnight screening of *The Dark Knight Rises* in Aurora, Colorado.

Holmes opened fire on approximately four hundred viewers at 12:38 A.M. on Friday, July 20, 2012. Within hours, commentators on Reddit and CNN had begun to refer to the event as *the Aurora massacre*. This epithet distinguished the incident among mass shootings and also among incidents of cinema violence, as it divorced the attack from the film it accompanied by localizing it instead. The Aurora massacre was further distinguished by its victims. At the time of his arrest—minutes after the shooting—Holmes asked the police, "There weren't any children hurt, were there?"[45] There were four, the youngest of whom died of her wounds at the scene. As Holmes's question anticipates, juvenile victims would contribute significantly to the construction of this incident as horrifying, although whiteness played an even more important role.

In the wake of Holmes's assault, journalists and celebrities repeatedly venerated the movie theater as a safe, even "innocent" space despite all evidence to the contrary.[46] No one explicitly compared Holmes's attack with ghetto action cycle cinema violence. However, differences in the tenor and quantity of their respective media coverage show how deeply race and class are imbricated in U.S. cinema culture and American ideas about violence and victimhood. Not only did the media recognize the Aurora massacre as "random," they also lamented it as "tragic."[47] This rhetoric retroactively reveals popular distress over cinema violence as limited to middle-class white victims, given that only their deaths—and not the previous deaths of working-class people or people of color— were hailed as tragedies. For of the many articles on *The Warriors* murders, only one—the write-up in *People* magazine—deems them "tragic."[48] A few journalists called the plot of *Boyz n the Hood* tragic, but only one considered the violence at its screenings to be so.[49] From the 1970s through the 2010s, the media almost exclusively invoked tragedy for middle-class white victims of cinema violence. Black and working-class victims were never mourned in the same way, especially if their murders were associated with gang activity, as in the cases of Eller and Yakubowicz. Because affluent white Americans presume themselves insulated from social violence, its "random" appearance disrupts the social order, making its victims "tragic."

This is why mental illness provides such a convenient scapegoat for moral panics about white-on-white cinema violence: it explains the event without challenging the system. While James Eagan Holmes was most definitely mentally ill, what was at stake in the moral panic around his theater shooting was the sensational threat of mental illness. Focusing on Holmes's mental illness allowed the press to ask and answer the question "why?"—a question no one bothered to ask about cinema violence involving Black assailants. Not one journalist investigated why men of color were shooting, stabbing, and assaulting movie theater patrons, no doubt due to the centuries-old stereotypes of Black men as violent. White people do not typically racialize their history of public violence, however, and so Holmes's race was never linked, even euphemistically, to his murders. Thus reporters had an opportunity and a social responsibility to explain why Holmes attacked. Their accounts focus on madness and related, fantastical concepts such as "evil" and monstrosity.[50] The crazier Holmes seemed, the more random his crime seemed—and the more innocent his victims, who were of course no more or less innocent than any others affected by cinema violence.

Madness marked the Aurora massacre as anomalous, while anti-Black racism led reporters to characterize the *Warriors* and *Boyz n the Hood* incidents as inevitable, yet none of these tragedies produced widespread demands for social intervention. The earlier panics did not generate calls for change because they presumed the certitude of violence and death for the individuals involved. By contrast, the Aurora massacre did not produce calls for change—beyond facile appeals for greater gun control—because an insane gunman is outside the system, beyond the system's capacity to regulate. Holmes's madness could not be predicted or prevented, only isolated and contained—or so the story goes. Indeed, an uncanny precedent for this narrative came from Nolan's previous Batman movie, *The Dark Knight* (2008). The film suggests that anarchist villains like the Joker—and Holmes—complete the logic of, and are thus an unfortunate yet inevitable result of, the conservative rhetoric of law and order.

The Dark Knight follows Bruce Wayne (Christian Bale), a member of the American corporate aristocracy, as he disciplines his fellow citizens under the name and mask of Batman. The movie begins with the arrival of "a better class of criminal," namely, the Joker (Heath Ledger), a self-proclaimed "agent of chaos" who wants to show Batman and Police Commissioner Gordon (Gary Oldman) "how pathetic their attempts to control things really are." After making his debut by stealing the collected savings of every gang in the city, the Joker announces that he wants to end Batman's reign of righteousness. He publicly vows to kill one Gothamite every day until Batman reveals his true identity. Batman and his fellow agents of justice try to but cannot derail the Joker's plans, because—as Wayne's butler, Alfred Pennyworth (Michael Caine), explains—they cannot recognize that "some men just want to watch the world burn." Alfred comes the closest to understanding the Joker's antiphilosophy, but he still assumes that the Joker wants something, that he wants *for* something. In fact, he lacks nothing, for as he tells Batman, "you complete me." From another perspective, however, the Joker completes Batman; he is the unstoppable—because unmotivated—engine of destruction that gives Batman a reason for existing. Just as Gotham produced Batman—the elite white vigilante enforcing law and order where the state cannot— Batman produced the Joker, an anarchist who exists for no reason except to threaten conservative social values. Without the Joker, Batman might eventually be able to defeat Gotham's crime syndicates and retire to his house in the country with the ostensible love of his life, Assistant District Attorney Rachel Dawes (Maggie Gyllenhaal). The Joker keeps Batman relevant, which is why, as he so lovingly reminds his caped crusader, "you have nothing to threaten me with."

Of course, Batman roundly rejects the Joker's observations, just as the U.S. media refused to consider that James Eagan Holmes might be a foreseeable product of America's social order and a necessary component of its economy of fear. However, *The Dark Knight* does its best to convey the Joker's integral role as the apotheosis and the scourge of its white world. All of Nolan's Batman films construct bastions of whiteness—via their casting and their commitment to law and order at any price—but *The Dark Knight* epitomizes this trend.[51] Although it includes a few supporting characters played by actors of color—namely, Bruce Wayne's technical consultant, Lucius Fox (Morgan Freeman); the corrupt Detective Ramirez (Monique Gabriela Curnen); and the gangster Gambol (Michael Jai White)—all the agents of power, both good and bad, are white, as they are in all Nolan's Batman films. To that end, the Joker represents the horror of whiteness turning on itself. In his white make-up and bespoke three-piece suit, he is a caricature of Wayne's corporate cronies. He also understands white privilege far better than any other character; as he patiently explains to Batman, "no one panics when the expected people get killed. . . . If I tell the press that tomorrow a gang banger will get shot, or a truckload of soldiers will be blown up, nobody panics. . . . But when I say that one little old mayor will die, everyone loses their minds!" The Joker terrifies because he exploits white privilege to torment its enforcers (albeit without naming it as such). He even drives Gotham's "white knight," District Attorney Harvey Dent (Aaron

Eckhart), insane by reminding him of the arbitrary nature of the universe. Randomness is fair, they agree, but it is also fundamentally incompatible with U.S. (racialized) ideals of justice, so Dent abandons the latter forthwith.

Radicalized to the point of psychosis, Dent ultimately attempts to kill Commissioner Gordon's young son, thereby invoking the trilogy's superlative icon of innocence: the threatened white boy, always a stand-in for Bruce Wayne himself.[52] This white boy metonymizes—and racializes—victimhood during the climactic face-off between Dent, now Two-Face, and Batman. His death would be the most tragic, exceeding even that of Batman's childhood sweetheart, since the boy might be the next Batman, the next enforcer of law and order. Hence Nolan deploys images of terrorized white boys throughout his Batman trilogy to convey the immorality of Batman's nemeses (Figure 6.3). These youngsters bestow innocence on all the villains' victims, absolving them—and whiteness more broadly—of instituting and perpetuating the system of violence to which they have become suddenly, unexpectedly vulnerable. In a culture organized around the veneration of whiteness, unmotivated attacks on white children represent the ultimate random tragedy. Indeed, it took children dying at *The Dark Knight Rises* for the American media to acknowledge that white people do kill white people at the movies—even as they also invented a new exculpatory rhetoric for white cinema assailants.

After *The Warriors*, people feared "them," a social group, specifically African American young men. After *The Dark Knight Rises*, people feared "him," the single shooter whose threat was not socially legible because of his race. The movies played a role in this transition. White audiences felt able and willing to blame movies about disenfranchised Black youth for bringing disenfranchised Black youth—that is, violence—to the movie theater. But fantasy blockbusters assure viewers of safety—that is, of racial and economic homogeneity, which cinemas tacitly promise and too often provide. Movies are rarely shot in black and white these days, but shootings in movie theaters still happen in Black and white. This, sadly, appears to be one of the "ends" of cinema. Race determines which assailants get reduced to stereotypes and which get profiled as individuals, which deaths are sensationalized and which mourned as "tragic." These patterns will continue until media consumers

Figure 6.3. Director Christopher Nolan deploys images of terrorized white boys to convey the immorality of Batman's nemeses.

insist on a full and accurate history of the racialization of cinema violence in the United States.

Notes

1. Albert D. Kirwin, *Revolt of the Rednecks: Mississippi Politics 1876–1925* (Lexington: University of Kentucky Press, 1951), 222.

2. Stanley Cohen, quoted in Richard C. McCorkle and Terance D. Miethe, *Panic: The Social Constructions of the Street Gang Problem* (Upper Saddle River, N.J.: Prentice Hall, 2002), 15.

3. Erich Goode and Nachman Ben-Yehuda, *Moral Panics: The Social Construction of Deviance,* 2nd ed. (Malden, Mass.: Wiley Blackwell, 2009), 17.

4. Dan Frosch and Kirk Johnson, "Gunman Kills 12 in Colorado, Reviving Gun Debate," *New York Times,* July 20, 2012, https://www.nytimes.com/2012/07/21/us/shooting-at-colorado-theater-showing-batman-movie.html.

5. "The Flick of Violence," *Time* 113, no. 12 (1979): 39.

6. Specifically, *People* magazine suggests that "during an intermission a white girl drew comment from blacks belonging to a youth gang called the Blue Coats. Their white counterparts, the Family, came to her rescue." "A Street-Gang Movie Called *The Warriors* Triggers a Puzzling, Tragic Wave of Audience Violence and Death," *People,* March 12, 1979, https://people.com/archive/a-street-gang-movie-called-the-warriors-triggers-a-puzzling-tragic-wave-of-audience-violence-and-death-vol-11-no-10/.

7. Louise Sweeney, "Does Violence on the Screen Mean Violence on the Street?," *Christian Science Monitor,* April 3, 1979, B26.

8. "Youth Fatally Stabbed, 2 Injured in Theater Fracas," *Los Angeles Times,* February 13, 1979, A1.

9. Ed Trielberg, quoted in "A Street-Gang Movie Called *The Warriors.*"

10. Yakubowicz's assailant could not have quoted *The Warriors,* in fact, because he slept through the screening he attended after getting drunk on beer, whiskey, and wine. Megan Rosenfeld, "Violence in the Wake of *Warriors,*" *Washington Post,* February 22, 1979, C1; Douglas Crocket, "Death Ends a Gentle Kid's Dream," *Boston Globe,* February 18, 1979, 25; Alan Sheehan, "'Warrior Case' Defendant Guilty," *Boston Globe,* October 26, 1979, 21.

11. Rosenfeld, "Violence in the Wake of *Warriors*"; "Hitchhiker Says 3 Youths Tortured Him," *Boston Globe,* March 5, 1979, 16.

12. The *Los Angeles Times* reports that "Rosenbaum was walking to the rest room at the theater when he encountered a group of eight to ten Mexican-Americans ready for a fight." "San Juan Hits Screening of *The Warriors,*" *Los Angeles Times,* April 8, 1979, B10.

13. William Scobie, "Murder in the Cinema," *Observer,* March 4, 1979, 12.

14. William V. Yakubowicz, administrator v. Paramount Pictures Corp., 404 Mass. 624 (December 8, 1988–April 18, 1989); "Rite Held for Slain Boy; DA Aides View Movie," *Boston Globe*, February 21, 1979, 31.

15. Sweeney, "Does Violence on the Screen Mean Violence on the Street?"

16. James C. Howell, *The History of Street Gangs in the United States: Their Origins and Transformations* (Lanham, Md.: Lexington Books, 2015), 10.

17. Notably, the Riffs' costumes and discipline resemble and may well have been modeled on the militant black empowerment gangs of the 1960s, including the Black Panthers, the Blackstone Rangers, and the Devil's Disciples. For more on gangs and community empowerment in the 1960s and 1970s, see Walter B. Miller, "American Youth Gangs: Fact and Fantasy," in *Deviance and Liberty: Social Problems and Public Policy*, ed. Lee Rainwater (Piscataway, N.J.: Transaction, 1974), 267.

18. "Gang Film Draws Community Protest," *Los Angeles Sentinel*, February 22, 1979, A2.

19. "Flick of Violence."

20. Marguerite Guidice, "Tough Luck: Playing to Lose in the Game of Violence," *Boston Globe*, July 29, 1979, D9.

21. Bruce McCabe, "There's No Debate on *Warriors*," *Boston Globe*, February 25, 1979, D1.

22. David Wilson, "1st Amendment Not a License to Profit," *Boston Globe*, March 11, 1979, A7. See also "Letters to the Editor: Should *The Warriors* Be Banned?," *Boston Globe*, March 7, 1979, 18; "Letters to the Editor: *Warriors*, Violence, the First Amendment," *Boston Globe*, March 21, 1979, 16; "Letters to the Editor: Good *Warriors* Reaction," *Boston Globe*, April 3, 1979, 18.

23. Nicholas von Hoffman, "Assault by Film: A Commentary," *Washington Post*, April 13, 1979, D4.

24. See David Denby, "He's Gotta Have It," review of *Do the Right Thing* (Universal film), *New York Magazine*, June 26, 1989, 53, 54; Joe Klein, "The City Politic: Spiked?," *New York Magazine*, June 26, 1989, 14; Jack Kroll, "How Hot Is Too Hot; the Fuse Has Been Lit," review of *Do the Right Thing* (Universal film), *Newsweek*, July 3, 1989, 64.

25. S. Craig Watkins, "Ghetto Reelness: Hollywood Film Production, Black Popular Culture, and the Ghetto Action Film Cycle," in *Genre and Contemporary Hollywood*, ed. Steve Neale, 236–50 (London: British Film Institute, 2002); Salim Muwakkil, "Spike Lee and the Image Police," *Cinéaste*, 14, no. 4 (1990): 35.

26. *New Jack City* opened on March 8, 1991, only four days after KTLA broadcast George Holliday's video of Rodney King being beaten by Los Angeles Police Department (LAPD) officers. To call the Holliday video incendiary is, of course, insufficient; it provided documentation of the LAPD's long-term, systemic brutality toward African Americans. Yet most journalists failed to appreciate the significance of Holliday's video when reporting on a riot outside of one *New Jack*

City screening, even though rioters were heard chanting King's name as well as "Black Power" and "Fight the Power!" Elaine Woo and Irene Chang, "Rampage in Westwood," *Los Angeles Times*, March 10, 1991, http://articles.latimes.com/1991 -03-10/news/mn-388_1_police-department; Robert Reinhold, "Near Gang Turf, Theater Features Peace," *New York Times*, July 15, 1991, A13.

27. Amanda Ann Klein, *American Film Cycles: Reframing Genres, Screening Social Problems, and Defining Subcultures* (Austin: University of Texas Press, 2011), 142.

28. "*Boyz n the Hood* VHS Trailer," August 29, 2018, YouTube video, 0:28, https://www.youtube.com/watch?v=ESFCdoJ29fM.

29. John Lancaster, "Film Opens with Wave of Violence," *Washington Post*, July 14, 1991, A1; "Minneapolis Youth Second Victim of Violence at Film Showing," *New York Times*, July 19, 1991.

30. Cheryl W. Thompson, "Man Guilty in Killing at Drive-In," *Chicago Tribune*, May 14, 1993, http://www.chicagotribune.com/news/ct-xpm-1993-05-14 -9305140315-story.html; Jerry Thomas and Andrew Gottesman, "Violence Distorting Message in *Boyz*," *Chicago Tribune*, July 17, 1991, http://www.chicago tribune.com/news/ct-xpm-1991-07-17-9103200457-story.html.

31. "Minneapolis Teen Shot at *Boyz* Debut Dies," AP News Archive, July 18, 1991, http://www.apnewsarchive.com/; "Minneapolis Youth Second Victim."

32. "Trail of Trouble for *Boyz* Screenings across the Nation," *Hollywood Reporter*, July 15, 1991, 6; "Gunfire Mars Opening of *Boyz*," *St. Louis Post-Dispatch*, July 14, 1991, 4A; "*Boyz n the Hood* Violence Ebbs," *United Press International*, July 15, 1991, http://www.upi.com/.

33. "Trail of Trouble for *Boyz* Screenings."

34. "Trail of Trouble for *Boyz* Screenings"; Lancaster, "Film Opens with Wave of Violence."

35. Courtland Milloy, "Screening Out Violence," *Washington Post*, July 16, 1991, D3.

36. Charles R. Acland, *Screen Traffic: Movies, Multiplexes, and Global Culture* (Durham, N.C.: Duke University Press, 2003), 147.

37. Mark Becker, "Stepping Up Cinema Security," *Variety*, July 22, 1991, 13, quoted in Acland, *Screen Traffic*, 147.

38. Linda Lee, "A Midweek Opening Pattern in Urban Black Films," *New York Times*, March 10, 1997, https://www.nytimes.com/1997/03/10/business/a-mid week-opening-pattern-in-urban-black-films.html.

39. As the film's title suggests, *Boyz n the Hood* is narrowly interested in how Black men cope with Black oppression and intraracial violence. Women play a marginal role in its narrative and philosophy. See Michael Eric Dyson, "Between Apocalypse and Redemption: John Singleton's *Boyz n the Hood*," *Cultural Critique* 21 (Spring 1992): 121–41.

40. See Thomas Doherty, "Two Takes on *Boyz n the Hood*," *Cinéaste* 18, no. 4 (1991): 18.

41. David Landis, "Is the Message Lost?," *USA Today*, July 15, 1991, 1D; James Surowiecki, "Shooting Film," *Ottawa Citizen*, September 14, 1997, M6.

42. It may go without saying, but not one single article referred to any of the violence at screenings of *The Warriors* as "random." Rather, the popular interpretation held that "gang movies will inevitably attract gang members as an audience," which will inevitably lead to violence. Aljean Harmetz, "Gang Film Is Cancelled in Some Areas," *New York Times*, April 8, 1979, 45.

43. Michael Granberry, "Prosecutors Cite Film's Theme in Theater Shooting," *Los Angeles Times*, February 8, 1994, http://articles.latimes.com/1994-02-08/news/mn-20485_1_movie-violence.

44. Granberry, "Prosecutors Cite Film's Theme in Theater Shooting."

45. Jack Healy, "Colorado Killer James Holmes's Notes: Detailed Plan vs. 'a Whole Lot of Crazy,'" *New York Times*, May 28, 2015, https://www.nytimes.com /2015/05/29/us/james-holmess-notebook-and-insanity-debate-at-aurora-shoot ing-trial.html.

46. Gregg Kilday, "*Dark Knight Rises* Director Christopher Nolan: Colorado Shooting 'Devastating,'" *Hollywood Reporter*, July 20, 2012, https://www.holly woodreporter.com/news/colorado-shooting-dark-knight-rises-christopher -nolan-352628.

47. See, e.g., David Carr, "In Aurora, a Sadly Familiar Template Kicks in for the News Media," *New York Times*, July 23, 2012, https://mediadecoder.blogs.nytimes .com/2012/07/23/in-aurora-a-sadly-familiar-template-kicks-in-for-the-news -media.

48. "A Street-Gang Movie Called *The Warriors*."

49. Jerry Thomas and Andrew Gottesman, writing for the *Chicago Tribune*, note that Michael Booth's trip to see *Boyz n the Hood* "brought tragedy" to his family after he was shot exiting the Halstead Twin Outdoor Theater, and Dan McDonnell, writing for the Brisbane *Courier-Mail* and the Melbourne *Herald Sun*, called the violence "routine if tragic" in both of his articles, a formula that all but disavows the devastation and injustice implied by the term *tragic*. Jerry Thomas and Andrew Gottesman, "Violence Distorting Message in *Boyz*"; Dan McDonnell, "Blood on the Screen Sparks More Blood on the Streets," *Courier-Mail*, July 17, 1991; Dan McDonnell, "Lights, Action . . . War," *Herald Sun*, September 4, 1991. For examples of reporters calling the events of, but not the loss of life associated with, *Boyz n the Hood* tragic, see Milloy, "Screening Out Violence"; Danny R. Cooks, "*Boyz* Is a Crying Shame Not Worthy of a Tear," *Michigan Citizen*, August 10, 1991.

50. Frosch and Johnson, "Gunman Kills 12 in Colorado"; Kilday, "*Dark Knight Rises* Director Christopher Nolan."

51. See Martin Fradley, "What Do You Believe In? Film Scholarship and the Cultural Politics of the *Dark Knight* Franchise," *Film Quarterly* 66, no. 3 (2013): 15–27.

52. In *Batman Begins* (Christopher Nolan, 2005), one learns that both of young Bruce Wayne's parents were murdered in front of him during a mugging gone awry. Their deaths set Wayne on the path to cleaning up Gotham, making it the kind of haven his father wanted it to be.

7

Pieces of a Dream

Film Blackness and Black Death

Michael Boyce Gillespie

I'm interested in ways of seeing and imagining responses to terror in the varied and various ways that our Black lives are lived under occupation; ways that attest to the modalities of Black life lived in, as, under, and despite Black death.

—Christina Sharpe, *In the Wake: On Blackness and Being*

Christina Sharpe's conception of "wake work" concentrates on how visual and expressive culture renders and contemplates death and the afterlives of slavery in black life.[1] Her assessment of existence "in the wake" attends to the structural and the affective with reference to a range of connotations, including "keeping watch with the dead, the path of a ship, a consequence of something, in the line of flight and/or sight, awakening, and consciousness."[2] Consequently, she mobilizes new investments for the study of black death and the art of blackness with particular attention to how the arts "mediate this un/survival."[3] This chapter responds to Sharpe's claim of art's mediating capacity with the notion of film blackness and a focus on the critical tendencies and consequence of black film along with matters of affect, narrativity, visual historiography, and genre/modalities.[4] With contemporary black film and video in mind, Sharpe emphasizes a shift from the portrayal of horror to a concentration on how film and video enact a critical and aesthetic resistance to the horror of antiblackness. This is a formal and political proposition that this piece will channel toward an examination of black death in contemporary black film and video.

133

Black death in contemporary cinema requires understanding how the idea of black film always means provoking new measures of the aesthetic, political, social, and cultural capacities of black visual and expressive culture. Black death in this context signifies both antiblack violence and the rendering of death in cinema. This chapter focuses on an ever-growing archive of recent works that merit greater attention as they advance cinematic practices that point to new political philosophies and circuits of knowledge related to blackness, death, and film form. This examination of black death and its rendering will be considered through an analysis of four short films by black women filmmakers as a *cinema in the wake*: Leila Weefur's *Dead Nigga BLVD* (2015), Nuotama Frances Bodomo's *Everybody Dies!* (2016), Ja'Tovia Gary's *An Ecstatic Experience* (2015), and A. Sayeeda Clarke's *White* (2011). An organizational principle and an analytic, cinema in the wake provides a way to consider how these films pose a range of formal propositions and critical interventions about black death that include animation, the racial grotesque, experimental cinema, and speculative fiction. These films do more than merely depict or reflect; they devise.

Shuffle Along

> These representations are mediated by screens, filtered through estranged voices, and processed by infinite amounts of digital data. . . . I grappled with how to communicate the ways in which Black bodies are constantly confronted with and negotiating the liminal space between life and death. I wanted to build this fictional place as though it existed. But, like heaven and hell, [this place] had no specific location or associations to a tangible geography. . . . The characters inhabit and function within the space of necrosis, which the natural staccato of stop-motion lends itself to.[5]

From above, a puppet is lowered into the frame by a string and placed in a sparse set of model buildings with bottles and debris strewn on a fabricated ground. Nooses hang from artificial trees. Three cycles and three puppets arrive. The first one wears a dress shirt, slacks, and a fedora; another is in a gray hoodie with jeans. The last one sports a black knit cap with a black hoodie and jeans. These puppets are not anonymous or unknown objects. Each bears an iconic image as its face: Emmett Till, Trayvon Martin, and Oscar Grant. These photograph-faced objects produce an eternal return of the look. Their eyes are the arrested apertures of three absented souls, all figured as threat, judged disposable, and framed ineligible for empathy or protection.[6] A black-and-white film, Leila Weefur's *Dead Nigga BLVD* centers on these solemn puppets (Figure 7.1).[7] Selective grace, three for all the world to see.

Constituted by phantasmagoric force through stop-motion animation, the puppets are "performing objects" and moving pictures incarnate.[8] The inspiration of Jan Švankmajer's early animation practice rouses Weefur's own fabulation of a contemporary hauntology revue. In *Dead Nigga BLVD*, those that were terminally disarticulated become articulated figures in motion through the repetitive stillness and posing of stop-motion. Yet, this formal conceit also infers a crucially mortal sense of calm and stir, as "the dynamic between motion and stillness is the dynamic between life and death that is nowhere more dramatically captured than in stop-motion animation."[9] Not the stumble or stutter of the improperly buried, nor the undead, these moving figures echo a point that Sianne Ngai makes about race, automatization, and animation. She argues how the affect of animatedness thickens around a fusing of "signs of the body's subjection to

Figure 7.1 Still from Leila Weefur's *Dead Nigga BLVD* (2015).

power with signs of its ostensive freedom."[10] In the case of *Dead Nigga BLVD*, its stop-motion dynamism activates a conjuring of black matter and a summoning of active remnants that refuse to be curbed by and subjected to time and execution.

Throughout the film, the voice-over operates less as an omniscient and abstracted narrator and more as a voice of deliberation and dispute. Significantly, it operates with a slippage, an equal division between omniscient narrator and the interior monologues of its embodied figures. "How did we come to exist in this state of nothingness. . . . There is a moment when your senses of the exterior work dissolve and you can feel, touch, see, and taste the end. . . . On Dead Nigga Boulevard, the sum of our existence is almost irretrievable." Unmoored, the voice cycles between deadpan introspection and observation. Across and through these performing objects, the voice recites vernacular precarity.

The face of the Emmett Till puppet bears the photograph of a sharply dressed and smiling boy from Christmas 1957, an image that once was half of a crushing dyad, meant to compel a recognition of and empathy for the life of an ordinary boy, someone's son, someone who was loved.[11] A hoodied selfie, Trayvon Martin's photograph suggests casual self-portraiture and self-valuation that has retroactively circulated as a veneration and foreshadowing.[12] The Oscar Grant puppet shows him smiling with a baby in his lap. This photograph, provided by his family and later cropped and circulated, often has a portion of a baby's head in its lower-left corner. The cropping connotes a grievous shearing, a brutal demarcation of his absence among kin and the living. All three photographs resonate with a distinct identificatory solicitation that attests to an "I am ____" and "I was ____." They are black boys and men executed by institutional (and freelance) social contract killers.

Each of these photographs, recast as a puppet's face, conveys a distinct frequency of memory and grievability, each a singular irreconcilability.[13] Weefur's scripting of postmortem comprehension and distress escalates their indexical sentience. The film's formalization of the photographs as well compounds their use toward what Tina Campt terms a "practicing of refusal," which in this instance means a refusal and disavowal of the postmortem accounting that seeks to justify their murders.[14] These iconic photographs, coupled with their motion process, are propelled by historiographies devoted to the mobilizing of bodies and provocations of resistance. These photographs do not merely function as triggers to reminisce; they incite. As Leigh Raiford vitally asks, "photographs become tools to aid memory. We are invited, expected, even demanded to recount and memorialize. To remember. But what exactly are we being asked to remember? How are we being asked to remember? And to what end?"[15] For *Dead Nigga BLVD*, each photograph registers a distinct measure of invitation and expectation, insurrection and resurrection.[16]

In three recurring sequences, each puppet individually approaches a monitor on a wall of one of the set's model buildings that then projects the circumstances of their respective arrivals in this place. *This Is Your Life. This Is Your Death.* For the Till figure, the monitor features a close-up of his Christmas photo, a coffin carried by pallbearers, and the photo of a boy destroyed—a body that a mother would not let be hushed away by lye and lies. It is this final image of Till in the open casket during his funeral service that always demands bearing witness.[17] The Martin puppet's monitor features the surveillance footage of his purchasing Skittles and an Arizona Iced Tea before walking home and meeting his end. He wears a hoodie and, by the visualizing logic of antiblackness, becomes cast in a lethal profiling scenario in which "the hoodie first signals a possible threat and second renders the potential criminal visible."[18] For the Grant figure, the monitor plays the cell phone footage of his murder at Fruitvale Station. The viral circulation of the Grant video occurred, as is the case in many other instances of digital recordings of unarmed African Americans being murdered by police, in the hope that the sight of the act itself might be an evidentiary truth that would guarantee justice.[19] This mediatic circuit includes print journalism and the social media virality of observational footage. The latter echoes "dark sousveillance" and its resistance to the antiblack, surveillant practices of the state.[20]

The collective narratives of the trio insist and craft the everyday and systemic horrors visited upon black life, not by the Fates or others versed in the craft of strings and destiny, but by random arbiters and executioners. The puppets exhibit sadness, console each other, stir with chatter, and bond as a fellowship of the black dead. This gathering of black dead needs more than coins on their eyelids to find peace (or justice) on the other side. The black dead can cross with the aid of those who have gone before, those stolen away, as Claudia Rankine explains: "because white men can't police their imaginations, black men are dying."[21]

In her comments on black collective memory, legacies of violence, and Pat Ward Williams's *Accused/Blowtorch/Padlock* (1986), Elizabeth Alexander comments, "What do people do with their history of horror? What does it mean to bear witness in the act of watching a retelling? What does it mean to carry cultural memory in the flesh?"[22] *Dead Nigga BLVD* offers an additional proposition: "what does it mean for the dead to bear witness to their own deaths?" Before the start of the credit sequence at the film's close, a note appears: "When Will It End?" The puppet animation of the film, its exercise in black object life, offers an answer to this question through recognizing that what distinguishes a puppet from a person, a thing from a subject, is a matter of power and not just interpretation.[23]

Theme for a Jackal

> I was being asked to make a dream film and I was having a lot of nightmares surrounding police violence and those were the images in my mind.... The emotional center of my film is a woman named Elizabeth Poles. She was an older black woman who got up one day and just started walking. She was walking on the highway in Virginia and had been seen in various states dressed head to toe in black with a black bag and a cane. There was an emotional weight about her in this very frantic moment that stuck with me.[24]

Ruth Wilson Gilmore writes, "Racism is the state-sanctioned and/or extra-legal production and exploitation of group-differentiated vulnerabilities to premature death."[25] She discerns how institutional and noninstitutional forces regulate and construct the lifeworld possibilities of specific groups according to exacting susceptibilities and an acute serialization of death. Antiblackness always provides for the occasion of the racial grotesque, which in cinema fundamentally means a staging of an antinomy between human and nonhuman, person and property.[26] The epistemological verve of the racial grotesque mercilessly disputes the ways and means of America.[27]

Nuotama Frances Bodomo's mobilization of the racial grotesque in *Everybody Dies!* enacts a disquieting impression of violent absurdity (Figure 7.2).[28] The word "PLAY" appears in the upper-right corner of a blue screen. A crackling fuzz on the sound track accompanies the soft, full-frame image. Tracking lines streak across the display as image dropouts settle along the top and bottom of the frame. A permanent wave of missing bits of oxide, this old-school glitch of videotape degradation indicates the stress and friction of repeated viewings. The unstable image acts as a sign of the video's slow disintegration with every mechanized turn of the reels. An abandoned media, the videotape infers analog nostalgia coupled with a point-of-view shot that posits the film spectator as the video viewer.[29] This video viewer is a phantom collector, perhaps an aficionado revisiting a treasured recollection. Be kind, rewind.

The screen cuts to a montage sequence with images of black children playing, varying expressions on their faces; the show's title arranged to resemble a rainbow; and a black woman in a black robe with a large black shawl atop her head. In one shot, she holds a scythe. In another, she stands next to a door labeled "DEATH." An announcer delivers the show's opening line over the canned cheers/screams/squeals of children: "From death's antechamber, welcome to *Everybody Dies!*, your portal to the afterlife, Thursdays at 8:30 A.M., 7:30 Central. Watch as your host Ripa the Reaper

Figure 7.2. Still from Nuotama Frances Bodomo's *Everybody Dies!* (2016).

ushers the newly dead into their new home. And now, the star of *Every-body Dies!*, Ripa the Reaper."

Ripa (Tonya Pinkins) stands on a stage with a DIY proscenium with a wall of gold streamers as a backdrop, a map of the United States and the *Everybody Dies!* rainbow banner hanging on the wall above, and a microphone on a stand connected to an amplifier on the floor. A caption announces her official title: Department of Black Death. The generic stickers on the prop doors stage left and stage right are simply stated: "LIFE" and "DEATH." A mirror ball hangs above. This is death disco.

The low-fi production values of this television show allude to public access programming and its presumed community of *we*, but as the faces of the opening montage illustrate, this is a show devoted to black children. They are the target audience in every sense. The film's public access television conceit entails a show equal parts children's program and game show about dead black children being ushered into the afterlife. *Everybody Dies!* is not simply the revival of an old or dead style. Mastery and convincibility are not its goals. Instead, this absurd staging dramatizes the enduring and casual ways of black death.

Ripa directly addresses the camera throughout the show. "You might not be ready, but I'm ready for you," she warns. She holds her smile too long, it strains and tremors. A xylophone cues her singing of the show's theme song to the strains of "Twinkle, Twinkle, Little Star," a lullaby that now portends a deeper sleep.

> *Kids you know that you all die*
> *No matter how hard you try*
> *You can squeal or whine or pray*
> *Everybody dies one day*
> *I'm your last and only friend*
> *Because this is where your story ends*
> *Take my hand, walk through the door*
> *And you'll live in this world no more*

"You might not be ready, but I'm ready for you," Ripa says as she then lists the unexpected ways one can perish: slipping in the shower, being hit by a car, or succumbing to sudden illness. The film's trafficking in estrangement escalates with the sound of children's screams and gun-shots as the film cuts to the map that the announcer declares to be the "Murder Map." A cartography of black death and American cultural geog-raphy, the map erupts with the flashing of the red bulbs that signal a newly expired somebody. It buzzes like the closed electric circuit thrills of the board game Operation. Yet, this black death-themed variant adapts Adam's apples, butterflies in stomach, wishbone, water on the knee, and a broken heart as Ferguson, Sanford, Beavercreek, Cleveland, and Staten Island. A game for all ages. Ripa pulls out her inner-ear headphone as her tone shifts from formal to frantic. She goes off script: "You might be running from the police. You might be running from a stranger who thinks he's the police. You might be playing with a toy gun. You might be not selling cigarettes." She adds new lyrics to the theme song:

Everybody dies it's true
Him and her and you and you
Kids beware when they attack
Especially if you are black

The screen cuts to color bars and a message: "Please stand by. We are expe-riencing technical difficulties." An executive decision made from the off-screen studio control room?

Michael Brown. Trayvon Martin. John Crawford III. Tamir Rice. Eric Garner. They are the murdered to whom Ripa alludes in her deviation from the script. Her deviation supplements the litany of chance and the accidental with the incongruity of more systemic and fatal acts. There are natural acts and there are ruthless ones that are deeply structured by the social fantasy of justifiable homicide. Ripa's equal opportunity labor—she traffics in inadvertent and systemic victims—is a misequivalence and the crux of the film's racial grotesque festivities.

In a chilling variant of the whack-a-mole carnival game, a WHACK-A-SOUL segment opens with a static shot of a young black boy, captioned "DeShawn Matthews. Juvenile Delinquent." A sharp cut to a scream with a bloody hand darting upward from a trash bag follows as a hunched-over Ripa pummels the bag with a metal frying pan. The strikes produce the nauseating thud of a blunt object striking a fleshy one. The bag finally stills, and she rises. "Now that's how you whack a soul." She strains as she drags the bag through the DEATH door. Ripa's labor is inelegant disposal, not recycling.

In the show's segment titled "Today's Catch," she welcomes a group of seven children who dance in a circle around her. Perplexed by the presence of two white children in the group, Ripa pulls them aside. "You two are lost. You want the third door down the hall on the left," she says, then sends them back through the LIFE door with word of milk and cookies awaiting them. Turning to her properly assigned wards lined up on the stage, Ripa asks, "What's the right answer?" The children respond with forty-eight, periwinkle, New Jersey, 12:30, and basketball. Ripa replies, "Ohhhh, kids. Those were the wrong answers. Death is the right answer because everybody dies!" The children scream while they are pushed, pulled, and dragged through the DEATH portal. The physical comedy and carny theatrics of the "Today's Catch" and WHACK-A-SOUL scenes are especially horrific and emblematic of the film's sharply unhinged enactment of the racial grotesque. Black death occurs as amateur sport and summer stock.

Ripa is having a bad day on the job, a public servant with no more fucks to give. She attempts to break out and escape from her role, but she is as trapped as her wards. She sprints through the DEATH door only to arrive back at the LIFE door. Ripa is, interminably, a mere prop in the Department of Black Death, the institutional face of a larger off-screen bureaucracy. She is just a worker, neither management nor executive, and certainly not a board member.

Ripa's role as a Sisyphean shepherd of the past/present/future invokes a long history of fatal gamesmanship. After all, the vicious cycling of the show's form signifies a ceaselessness, a black death seriality. The show's finale farce offers neither righteousness nor warm serenity on an other side. It insists on black death as a broken narrative of deficient exposition and rising action where cold climaxes abound.[30] Not contests steeped in luck or chance—there is only the systemic predictability of black death. The show must go on. In the end, a fatigued and distressed Ripa attempts to sing the lullaby theme again, but now her smile quivers and tears fall. They shoot horses, don't they? The announcer's voice abruptly directs viewers to the next cycle. "That's all for this week's episode. Tune in next week when we start all over again." With a hard cut to black and a space of nothingness, a sharp inhale is heard. Perhaps the sound of someone awakening from a nightmare or being snatched? Playing as a VHS relic from a hopeless time when black lives didn't matter, *Everybody Dies!* is a children's show for children who are never coded as children. With black disposability as entertainment, the racial grotesque seethes with a cruel anachronism, an incongruity between the analog past and the quotidian horror of the future present. EJECT.

Songs of Experience

> I am simultaneously creating and destroying, remaking and unmaking. My intimate interaction with the archive . . . expresses my desire to be a part of it, to make my presence felt in and on that history while also interrogating it.[31]

That which is beautiful and holy, an entanglement. Ja'Tovia Gary's *An Ecstatic Experience* (2015) derives its title (and arguably its enraptured spur) from Kathleen Collins's *Losing Ground* (1982).[32] Ecstatic experience is the research interest of Collins's philosophy professor protagonist Sara Rogers (Seret Scott). Rogers works to conceive of ecstasy in ways more attendant to the artist's practice than to the strict terms of Christian doctrines. She must also manage the new ecstatic experiences developing in her life. As Rogers states while researching in the library, "if ecstasy is an immediate apprehension of the divine then the divine is energy." The energy of *An Ecstatic Experience* in total is a churning of performativities, affective economies, and temporalities. Black matter, a (w)holy syncretic revolution (Figure 7.3).

The film opens with found footage of Sunday morning people, black folk moving to and through glory. They come for His lesson. As the cross atop the church steeple makes plain, "He is alive again." With the readymade scenes of lost and found parishioners arriving suited and crowned, the rumors of an ethnographic ramble shifts to the metahistorical trace generated by the footage and Gary's manipulation of the stock.[33] The animation and score together recompose these parishioners. This is call and response with an image and the capacity to sketch and conjure. Gary's hand-processing of the film stock, her direct animation process, proffers a range of colors and shapes that regulate the worship beneath the frame.[34] Antibodies in motion. Escalation. Modulation. An anointing gesture, the animation on the film surface recodes the images of folks fanning in the heat, children sleeping, the preacher man preaching. "I'm just a vessel." Holy ordinance. They are folk fighting to keep the Devil from stealing their joy. Yet, as the film proceeds, it becomes clear that evil is not singularly incarnate.

Alice Coltrane's "Journey to Satchidananda" scores this section and compounds the vernacular faith of the previous section with transmogrification and cosmic consciousness-raising. The title cut from the 1971 album of the same name, the song begins with Cecil McBee's bass. A beat. A foundational pulse. A point of origin. And then Tulsi's tambura and Alice Coltrane's harp forge a harmonic counterpoint of strings that build texture and timbre along with the accents of Rashied Ali's drums. This orchestration builds to a synchrony of the concussive and the vibrational—a shaping of resonance and direction as the music settles into the stratospheric melodies of a raga swirl when Pharoah Sanders arrives on soprano sax. A consecration complete, the song settles into what Kara Keeling notes as "Coltrane's creation of a sonic 'world galaxy' . . . in the interest of producing a set of affective . . . conditions for a new humanism."[35] Coltrane's transcendental sounding is an invitation and a sonic mapping. As new gospel boosted by the harmonics of conversion and ascension, it is a praise song in the black experimental idiom of jazz. Our text for today is the Word and jazz collectivity. Satchidananda. Ultimate. Satchidananda. Truth.[36]

Cutting from the rise of the spirit and rapture, the second section of *An Ecstatic Experience* begins with Ruby Dee on a television stage performing

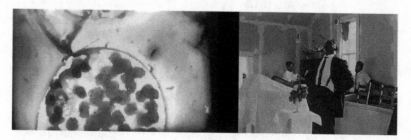

Figure 7.3. Still from Ja'Tovia Gary's *An Ecstatic Experience* (2015).

a slave. This is the "Slavery" episode for the *History of the Negro People* series broadcast on National Educational Television in 1965. Dee is a woman reminiscing about her mother's refusal to be a slave. She remembers her mother working in the field. She remembers her mother stopping and shouting, "Someday we ain't going to be slaves no more... I'm free, I'm free, I'm free." A black body at rest is a conspiratorial act. A woman caught the spirit and for that she caught cowhide lashes. Before suicide by cop, was there suicide by overseer? Ruby Dee is reading an Ossie Davis penned adaptation of an account given by Fannie Moore, a woman born a slave in South Carolina in 1849. Ms. Moore gave this account in 1937 at the age of eighty-eight as part of the WPA's Federal Writers' Slave Narrative Project.[37]

During Dee's monologue, Gary's animating hand on the surface again engineers the diegesis beneath. The love below. Remediation. Again, the animation stipulates process and energy. Trembling. Cellular. Mitochondrial. Animated shape fury. The shape of things to come. Ruby Dee meets mitosis. Her image divides. Framed by cubes and triangles. She is crowned, scarred, erased. She persists. Speckled and haloed. Unbowed and sainted. Transmogrification. Radiation ruling the nation. Black matter. Two trains running. Two freedom circuits. Two temporality scripts. A fusing of a rebel slave and a civil rights celebrity, a memory of resistance and a performative historiography.

From the Fannie Moore/Ruby Dee remembrance and hope for divine intervention, *An Ecstatic Experience* cuts to a video of Assata Shakur speaking in Cuba. A 1987 interview with Gil Noble for his long-running "African American affairs" program, *Like It Is* (1968–2011), Shakur comments. "I decided it was time to escape... and that's what I did. It was a clean escape. No one was hurt. I planned it as well as I could plan it and that's all I have to say about it."[38] At the mention of "escape," there is brief insert of Fannie Moore/Ruby Dee from the previous sequence. In this moment flashes a historical continuum of shared resistance. An activist and revolutionary, Assata Shakur was a member of the Black Liberation Movement and associate of the Black Panther Party. Convicted of the murder of a New Jersey state trooper (1973) during a (disputed) confrontation on the New Jersey Turnpike in 1977, Shakur escaped prison in 1979. Since 1984, she has resided in Cuba since granted political asylum.

"Freedom. I couldn't believe that it had really happened, that the nightmare was over, that finally the dream had come true. I was elated. Ecstatic."[39] The terms of worship that the film first mounted with found footage refabulation and a testimonial memory of slavery now evinces direct action and resistance. There are all kinds of prayer in this world.

From the deliver us ~~from~~ evil revival at the film's start to the Fannie Moore/Ruby Dee lenticular testimony of refusal to the free exile option of Shakur, *An Ecstatic Experience* closes on footage of Baltimore in a state of insurrection following the murder of Freddie Gray. Black lives matter. You think? This protest riot revolution disputes the quotidian shenanigans of black death. Gary's hand continues the treatment of the celluloid as fabric, a material dyed and cast. Her animation continues to stir as an instrument for improvisational and tinting historiographics. Chromopoetics. Haptic texturing. Scalar intimacies. In this the film's final act, a chorale performance by Voices Inc., the group that stood on a riser behind Ruby Dee during the "Slavery" broadcast and performed throughout the show, is intercut with the Baltimore footage. The sequence's rapid intercutting produces a flicker effect as the group begins to sing "The Battle Hymn of the Republic," a song that timelessly calls out for judgment against wickedness. The quickened intermittence of the flashing facilitates the song's even bleed across spatiotemporalities and calls for justice between 1849 and 2015. Neural inscription. Affective acceleration. Escape velocity. "Glory, glory, hallelujah / His truth is marching on." Arcane and prodigious, *An Ecstatic Experience* deregulates the American archive. The film's historiographic circuit deliberates on worship, states of freedom, and resistance. Dead reckoning? Liberation cartography?

What do you call a film compelled by many stains/genealogies/materials/conceits?

~~Worldmaking.~~

Blackmaking.

Be anointed

Be still

Escape

Exile

Resist

Live

Fuck it, get free
A
black woman's hand . . .

Tomorrow People

> You unlock this door with the key of imagination. Beyond it is another dimension—a dimension of sound, a dimension of sight, a dimension of mind. You're moving into a land of both shadow and substance, of things and ideas. You've just crossed over into *The Twilight Zone*.[40]

Rod Serling's brand of speculative critique in *The Twilight Zone* (CBS, 1959–64) consistently operated along a thematic arc that included estrangement, irony, deus ex machina, or merely poetic justice. There's not enough time; we let the Devil free. We don't believe in wishes; we hurtle away from a sun that didn't come. We are dead. Part of the enduring legacy of *The Twilight Zone* lies in the ways that the television series conceived of time.

Speculative fiction often concentrates on measuring the conditions of the present through an excavation of the remains of tomorrow that distends the temporal logics of narrative or historiography. Posing speculative fiction as "a genre of inventing other possibilities," Aimee Bahng compellingly notes, "Speculation is not exclusively interested in predicting the future but is equally compelled to explore different accounts of history. It calls for a disruption of teleological ordering of the past, present, and future and foregrounds the processes of narrating the past (history) and the future (science)."[41] With black speculative fiction in mind, its historical accounting advances prodigious stagings of the political life, cultural memories, and historiographic textures of blackness. Afrofuturism operates as an organizing principle and critical plotting of the black speculative tradition and its "possibilities for intervention within the dimension of the predictive, the projected, the proleptic, the envisioned, the virtual, the anticipatory and the future conditional."[42] This is what Kodwo Eshun terms the *chronopolitical* possibilities of Afrofuturism as an artistic mode of resistance that frames time as the generative crux of cultural and political fabulation:

I tell people that the second that we were put on the slave ships, we were already living in the world of *White*. Anything that could be siphoned from us—our souls, our very being—was taken and commodified.[43]

A. Sayeeda Clarke's (née Moreno) *White* realizes *The Twilight Zone* in a black speculative key. The film was part of the second season of the *Twilight Zone*–inspired *Futurestates* (2010–14), a web series initiative developed by the Independent Television Service to support and fund filmmaking on an alternative platform by independent filmmakers ("prognosticators") selected to "explor[e] possible future scenarios through the lens of today's global realities."[44]

With an aesthetic palette of a distressed urbanscape inspired by films such as *Dog Day Afternoon* (Sidney Lumet, 1975) and *Children of Men* (Alfonso Cuarón, 2006), *White* opens with a scene of a black man riding a rickshaw bicycle through the street (Figure 7.4). His name is Bato (Elvis Nolasco). A community activist, he calls out "Not one drop!" as he peddles through the market-lined city streets. There are no cars. A radio broadcast sends out news and holiday greetings. This is New York City five days before Christmas on a typical 120-degree day.

Bato arrives at the community center where he works. Entering, he tears down flyers that read "NEED CA$H FAST. THERE IS AN EASY

Figure 7.4. Still from A. Sayeeda Clarke's *White* (2011).

ANSWER: EXTRACTION. TURN COLOR INTO CA$H." A cut to the building's interior opens onto a room full of children doing art projects. Emory Douglas illustrations, drawings of James Baldwin and Jean-Michel Basquiat, a Happy Kwanzaa sign, and a painting of a menorah decorate the space. This is a space of artmaking and a zone of black instruction. As the children gather their things to leave, one girl lingers behind at her drawing station. When Bato asks what's wrong, she replies, "My daddy did it." Bato pauses. "It's a blackout," he tells her as he takes her hand, touches her skin, and says, "You always have his inheritance right on you."

Bato is called home. His partner is in the final month of pregnancy, and Bato arrives to find her experiencing prenatal distress. She needs immediate medical attention, but they lack the funds for the clinic's entry fee. Needing money immediately, Bato quickly leaves—but not before his mother-in-law solemnly tells him, "You know what they'll take instead." With the community center safe empty, followed by a failed armed robbery attempt, only one option remains. Everything is revealed.

The final sequence begins with Bato entering a building. A Melanin Extraction Center with a reassuring slogan, "Together We Can Survive the Sun." Cut to a medical office inside the building, with Bato sitting in front of a map of the world in various shades of brown, labeled "Human Skin Color Distribution." Bato mulls over a consent form. When asked his race by a dispassionate technician, Bato replies, "Black. Black Puerto Rican." The technician tells him that after the procedure, his official status will be "melan*out*." The film's final shot is of Bato, arriving home in time for the birth of his daughter. His ashen, melanin-extracted arms hold his newborn, melanin-rich baby girl. New to the world, she cries. Her wailing continues as the screen goes black.

Poised between disaster and conspiracy, the film's scenario of a severely compromised ozone layer resonates as what Selmin Kara terms *Anthropo-cinema*. For Kara, this term refers to a cinema that, "rather than focusing on the causes of our ecological demise . . . brings us face to face with the effects of the so-called Epoch of Man, including the possibility of a total ecosystemic collapse or human self-annihilation."[45] Furthermore, *White* demonstrates particular attention to racial geopolitics, white supremacy, and "white extraction regimes."[46] Thus the film considers an end of the world structured by white supremacy as concurrently an ecological and antiblack event. Science and theories of adaptation contend that dark-pigmented people, with higher levels of melanin, can tolerate sustained and elevated exposure to ultraviolet radiation better than their light-pigmented and low-level-melanin counterparts.[47] Thus, in *White*'s future, melanin circulates as a forestalling remedy for the ecosystemic crisis of increased susceptibility. Melanin is a commodity reaped and bought from people of color at a fixed rate to be graded, refined, and sold for a profit to rich white folks, now known as the melanin-challenged. Black skin, white tears.

The film's dual cast of speculation as historiography and finance capital engineers an eco-Fanonian conceit of climate change adaptation whereby epidermalization becomes reformulated as an industrial process of melanin extraction technology.[48] This skin trade does not quibble about climate policy, sustainability, or greening initiatives. In *White*, the "melanout" are devoid of autobiography, skinned and left as an exhausted resource.[49] As David Marriot writes, "capital feeds on living labor, all become perishable commodities."[50] *White* demonstrates how this feeding mobilizes ferocious terms of expendability and nonhuman commerce.[51] Bato's "Not one drop" slogan speaks to this point, as the slogan revises the Jim Crow rule of "one drop" and its rhetoric of miscegenation fears and purity fantasies. In *White*, these drops are a currency in a climate of antiblack finance and Pantone price points: Black Walnut, Chocolate Mocha, Burnt Almond #9.[52]

If skin functions as a feeling border and affective threshold between interiority (the subject) and exteriority (the other), in *White*, Bato becomes a body without borders or options.[53] Hortense Spillers's analysis of gender and the transatlantic slave trade in which bodies were recast as flesh is crucial for an understanding of *White*. For Spillers, the "profitable 'atomizing' of the captive body provides another angle on the divided flesh. . . . The procedures adopted for the captive flesh demarcate a total objectification, as the entire captive community becomes a living laboratory."[54] The film's living laboratory of race, science, and capital resonates with fungibility and the afterlives of slavery. Fundamentally, the film centers on the transaction of black and brown folks as natural resources.[55] Thus Bato's total commodification at the Melanin Extraction

Center processing center leaves him an empty vessel, a body dispossessed and valueless.[56]

Together We Can Survive the Sun. The ecopolitical horizon envisioned by *White* examines how racial and class exploitation becomes a more amenable and efficient option than any effort at climate change adaptation or mitigation.[57] *We* will not suffer equally. Black and brown are vulnerable to more than the sun when the antiblack climate includes no access to health care, lack of employment, and predatory lenders.[58] This is a climate of market culture as a harvesting process. Bato initially attributes an epigenetic value to skin as an inheritance of culture and history, but the market value of skin annuls any such assurance of heritage. In the end, his depletion, now a sign of his obsolescence, signals erasure and social death.[59] The film narrates a world compromised by ozone depletion and consumed by a biopolitical endgame.

Save the Children (Detroit Mix)

With distinct and compelling conceptions of black death, these four short films are deeply located in their contemporary American moment. Thinking with these films involves thinking through performing objects, the racial grotesque, a black radical avant-garde, and a futurity of social deletion by market forces. Together these films exquisitely suspend, disrupt, and disturb. *Dead Nigga BLVD*, with its stop-motion articulation of the dead, gathers three historical narratives to demonstrate a compounding arc of injustice. *Everybody Dies!* mounts a public access game show for children as an absurdist comedy devoted to black death. *An Ecstatic Experience*'s experimental engagement with the materiality of film and the historiographic operation seditiously maps out an account of struggle and resistance. *White*'s enactment of Afrofuturism sketches a global crisis and the speculative probabilities of ever-more debilitating iterations of racial capital.

As cinema in the wake, these films are an assembly composed of incitements of film form, materiality, temporality, and conceptions of black being. They are a circuit, a cinema of ends, that thinks through black death across the formal experimentation and the capacities of film as art to contend with an enduring urgency: the precarity of black life.

Notes

Thanks to Lisa Uddin, Amber J. Musser, Paula J. Massood, Tess Takahashi, Annie J. Howell, Racquel J. Gates, B. Ruby Rich, Richard Grusin, Charles "Chip" Linscott, Michael Zryd, Tiffany E. Barber, Jocelyn Szczepaniak-Gillece, and Nicholas Sammond for their comments and suggestions. Special thanks to Leila Weefur, Nuotama Frances Bodomo, Ja'Tovia Gary, and A. Sayeeda Moreno for their films and thoughts. Earlier versions of this piece appeared as "Death Grips," *Film Quarterly* 71, no. 2 (2017): 53–60, and "Cinema Notes/American Letters," *ASAP/J*, June 2017, http://asapjournal.com/cinema-notes-american-letters-elizabeth-reich -courtney-r-baker-and-michael-b-gillespie/.

1. Christina Sharpe, *In the Wake: On Blackness and Being* (Durham, N.C.: Duke University Press, 2016), 20.

2. Sharpe, 17–18.

3. Sharpe, 14.

4. See Michael Boyce Gillespie, *Film Blackness: American Cinema and the Idea of Black Film* (Durham, N.C.: Duke University Press, 2016).

5. Leila Weefur, personal communication to the author, June 29, 2017.

6. Robin D. G. Kelley, "Thug Nation: On State Violence and Disposability," in *Policing the Planet: Why the Policing Crisis Led to Black Lives Matter*, ed. Jordan T. Camp and Christina Heatherton (New York: Verso, 2016), 67–68.

7. Following the grand jury decision on December 3, 2014, not to indict Daniel Pantaleo for the July 17, 2014, murder of Eric Garner, Smack Mellon gallery in Brooklyn, New York, postponed a planned exhibition and put out a call for work that responded to "the continued failure of the United States to protect its black citizens from police discrimination and violence." Much of the work gathered from this call became the *Respond* show (January 17–February 22, 2015). *Dead Nigga BLVD*, made during Weefur's first year as an MFA student at Mills College, is one of the pieces that was included in the *Respond* exhibit: http://smackmel lon.org/index.php/exhibitions/past/respond/. For more on Weefur's work, see http://www.leilaweefur.com/. She is a founding member of The Black Aesthetic, an Oakland-based "curatorial collective whose mission is to curate a collective understanding of Black visual culture." The group's community-based film programming operates as an undercommons for the study of black film. To date, they have published three collections as a part of their ongoing series. See https:// www.theblkaesthetic.com.

8. See Frank Proschan, "The Semiotic Study of Puppets, Masks, and Performing Objects," *Semiotica* 47 (1983): 4.

9. Jack Halberstam, *The Queer Art of Failure* (Durham, N.C.: Duke University Press, 2011), 177.

10. Sianne Ngai, *Ugly Feelings* (Cambridge, Mass.: Harvard University Press, 2005), 100.

11. For more on Emmett Till, ethics, and visual culture, see Courtney R. Baker, *Humane Insight: Looking at Images of African American Suffering and Death* (Champaign: University of Illinois Press, 2015).

12. Nicole R. Fleetwood, *Racial Icons: Blackness and the Public Imagination* (New Brunswick, N.J.: Rutgers University Press, 2015), 16–17.

13. See Judith Butler, *Frames of War: When Is Life Grievable?* (New York: Verso, 2009).

14. As Tina M. Campt writes, "practicing refusal means embracing a state of black fugitivity, albeit not as a 'fugitive' on the run or seeking escape. It is not a simple act of opposition or resistance. It is neither a relinquishing of possibility nor a capitulation to negation. It is a fundamental renunciation of the terms imposed upon black subjects that reduce black life to always already suspect by refusing to accept or deny these terms as their truth." Tina M. Campt, *Listening to Images* (Durham, N.C.: Duke University Press, 2017), 109, 113. Also see Campt, "Black Visuality and the Practice of Refusal," *Women and Performance: A Journal of Feminist Theory* 29, no. 1 (2019): 79–87, and Campt, "The Visual Frequency of Black Life: Love, Labor, and the Practice of Refusal," *Social Text* 37, no. 3 (2019): 25–46.

15. Leigh Raiford, *Imprisoned in a Luminous Glare: Photography and the African American Freedom Struggle* (Chapel Hill: University of North Carolina Press, 2011), 4.

16. Commenting on Emmett Till, Fred Moten writes, "Some attribute to Emmett Till—which is to say to his death, which is to say to the famous picturing and display, staging and performance, of his death or of him in death—the agency that set in motion this nation's profoundest political insurrection and resurrection, the resurrection of reconstruction, a second reconstruction like a second coming of the Lord." I am extending Moten's consideration of Till's imaging and resurrectional possibilities manifested through political action as equivalent to the circulation and agential instrumentalizing of Trayvon Martin's selfie and the Oscar Grant with child photograph. Moten, *In the Break: The Aesthetics of the Black Radical Tradition* (Minneapolis: University of Minnesota Press, 2003), 195.

17. See Margaret Schwartz, *Dead Matter: The Meaning of Iconic Corpses* (Minneapolis: University of Minnesota Press, 2015), 56–61.

18. Mimi Thi Nguyen, "The Hoodie as Sign, Screen, Expectation, and Force," *Signs* 40, no. 4 (2015): 799.

19. Jennifer Malkowski, *Dying in Full Detail: Mortality and Digital Documentary* (Durham, N.C.: Duke University Press, 2017), 170; Alexandra Juhasz, "How Do I (Not) Look? Live Feed Video and Viral Black Death," *Jstor Daily,* July 20, 2016, https://daily.jstor.org/how-do-i-not-look/. Also see Caetlin Benson-Abbott, "Learning from Horror," *Film Quarterly* 70, no. 2 (2016): 58–62, and Michael Boyce Gillespie, "Empathy Complicity," in *Unwatchable,* ed. Nicholas Baer, Maggie

Hennefeld, Laura Horak, and Gunnar Iversen, 126–30 (New Brunswick, N.J.: Rutgers University Press, 2019).

20. If *sousveillance* is a term for how people monitor and dispute the ubiquitous presence of surveillance in our everyday lives, then for Simone Browne, *dark sousveillance* names those acts that observe and subvert the antiblack surveillant practices of the state. For Brown, these acts operate as "a critique of racializing surveillance, a critique that takes form in antisurveillance, countersurveillance, and other freedom practices." Brown, *Dark Matters: On the Surveillance of Blackness* (Durham, N.C.: Duke University Press, 2015), 21.

21. Claudia Rankine, *Citizen: An American Lyric* (Minneapolis: Graywolf Press, 2014), 135.

22. Elizabeth Alexander, "'Can You Be Black and Look at This?' Reading the Rodney King Video(s)," *Public Culture* 7, no. 1 (1994): 94.

23. See Mel Chen, *Animacies: Biopolitics, Racial Mattering, and Queer Affect* (Durham, N.C.: Duke University Press, 2012), 210; Uri McMillan, "Objecthood, Avatars, and the Limits of the Human," *GLQ: A Journal of Lesbian and Gay Studies* 21, no. 2/3 (2015): 224–27.

24. Noutama Frances Bodomo, personal communication to the author, July 30, 2017. Living in Alabama at the time, Poles was reported to be grieving over the recent loss of her father. Poles was sighted walking in Georgia, Tennessee, Kentucky, Ohio, and Virginia over the course of several weeks during summer 2014. Lindsey Bever, "The Saga of the 'Woman in Black,'" *Washington Post,* July 31, 2014, https://www.washingtonpost.com/news/morning-mix/wp/2014/07/31/the-social-media-saga-of-the-woman-in-black/.

25. Ruth Wilson Gilmore, "Race and Globalization," in *Geographies of Global Change: Remapping the World,* ed. R. J. Johnston, Peter J. Taylor, and Michael J. Watts (Malden, Mass.: Blackwell, 2002), 26.

26. See Stephen Best, *The Fugitive's Properties: Law and the Poetics of Possession* (Chicago: University of Chicago Press, 2010), and Leonard Cassuto, *The Inhuman Race: The Racial Grotesque in American Literature and Culture* (New York: Columbia University Press, 1997).

27. See Michael Boyce Gillespie, *Film Blackness: American Cinema and the Idea of Black Film* (Durham, N.C.: Duke University Press, 2016), 17–49, and Gillespie, "Dirty Pretty Things: The Racial Grotesque and Contemporary Art," in *Post-Soul Satire: Black Identity after Civil Rights,* ed. Derek Maus and Jim Donahue, 68–84 (Jackson: University Press of Mississippi, 2014). My thinking about the racial grotesque and *Everybody Dies!* is informed by Daphne Brook's conception of "Afro-alienation acts." In *Bodies in Dissent: Spectacular Performances of Race and Freedom, 1850–1910,* Brooks examines late nineteenth- and early twentieth-century black performances, such as song, dance, and theater, as performative acts of resistance that dispute the categorical delimitations of race and being. She states, "In what I call 'Afro-alienation acts,' the condition of alterity

converts into cultural expressiveness and a specific strategy of cultural performance. Afro-alienation recurs as a trope that reflects and characterizes marginal
cultural positions as well as a tactic that the marginalized seized on and reordered
in the self-making process" (4). Furthermore, "Afro-alienation acts invoke largely
anti-realist forms of cultural expression in order to call attention to the hege-
mony of identity categories. This strategy also provides a fruitful terrain for marginalized figures to experiment with culturally innovative ways to critique and
disassemble the condition of oppression" (5). I believe Bodomo is doing something adjacent to Brooks's formulation of Afro-alienation, but I do not wish to
recuperate the film as an act of disassembling or a self-making process.

28. *Everybody Dies!* is one of the five shorts by five different New York–based
filmmakers that compose the anthology film *Collective: Unconscious* (2016). Each
filmmaker (Daniel Patrick Carbone, Lauren Wolkstein, Josephine Decker, Lily
Baldwin, and Bodomo) shared a "dream statement," a very brief description of a
dream they had, which was then assigned to and adapted by one of the other
filmmakers. Bodomo's film was inspired by Josephine Decker's dream statement.
Bodomo was a writer and director for Terence Nance's *Random Acts of Flyness*
series (HBO, 2018). A version of *Everybody Dies!* was featured in episode 1 ("What
Are Your Thoughts Raising Free Black Children?") of the series. In episode 4
("Items Outside the Shelter but Within Reach"), Bodomo revisits the Ripa character as Tanya Pinkins reprises her role with a backstory of her mortal life before
her afterlife duties.

29. Lucas Hilderbrand, *Inherent Vice: Bootleg Histories of Videotape and Copyright* (Durham, N.C.: Duke University Press, 2009), 6, 13.

30. I'm thinking here of the white vengeance role-playing/amusement park
scenario of Nana Kwame Adjei-Brenyah's "Zimmer Land" in *Black Friday* (Boston: Mariner Books, 2018), 85–103.

31. Ja'Tovia Gary, personal communication to the author, March 2, 2017.

32. Gary is a member of the New Negress Film Society with Noutama Frances
Bodomo, Dyani Douze, Chanelle Aponte Pearson, Stefani Saintonge, and Yvonne
Michelle Shirley: https://newnegressfilmsociety.com/. A collective of black women
filmmakers, they "focus primarily on works that break boundaries in film politi-
cally and artistically. Womanist in their content and experimental in form, often
these are some of the most challenging for a marginalized filmmaker to create and
distribute." Gary's nod to Kathleen Collins speaks to the reemergence of Collins's
Losing Ground through festival programs and revival screenings, a DVD release
(2016) of the film that includes some of Collins's other work, and the discovery
and release of her short fiction (*Whatever Happened to Interracial Love?* [2016] and
Notes from a Black Woman's Diary: Selected Works of Kathleen Collins [2019]). All
of this has produced a crucial and generative reappraisal of the history of black
women filmmaking.

33. As Michael Zryd observes, "found footage filmmaking is a metahistorical form commenting on the cultural discourses and narrative patterns behind history. Whether picking through the detritus of the mass mediascape or refinding (through image processing and optical printing) the new in the familiar, the found footage artist critically investigates the history *behind* the image, discursively embedded within its history of production, circulation, and consumption." Zryd, "Found Footage Film as Discursive Metahistory: Craig Baldwin's *Tribulation 99*," *The Moving Image* 3, no. 2 (2003): 41. For more on found footage and ethnographic film, see Catherine Russell, *Experimental Ethnography: The Work of Film in the Age of Video* (Durham, N.C.: Duke University Press, 1999), 239–72.

34. See Tess Takahashi, "'Meticulously, Recklessly Worked-Upon': Materiality in Contemporary Experimental Animation," in *The Sharpest Point: Animation at the End of Cinema,* ed. Chris Gehman and Steve Reinke, 166–78 (Toronto, Ont.: YYZ Press, 2006).

35. Kara Keeling, *Queer Times, Black Futures* (New York: New York University Press, 2019), 204.

36. Alice Coltrane, "Journey in Satchidananda," track on *Journey in Satchidananda,* Impulse Records, 1970. See Tammy Kernodle, "Freedom Is a Constant Struggle: Alice Coltrane and the Redefining of the Jazz Avant-Garde," in *John Coltrane and Black America's Quest for Freedom: Spirituality and the Music,* ed. Leonard Brown, 73–98 (New York: Oxford University Press, 2010); Franya J. Berkaman, *Monumental Eternal: The Music of Alice Coltrane* (Middleton, Conn.: Wesleyan University Press, 2010); and Cauleen Smith's *Pilgrim* (2017). Also, for a basic primer, see Andy Beta, "Transfiguration and Transcendence: The Music of Alice Coltrane," *Pitchfork,* January 12, 2017, https://pitchfork.com/features/from-the-pitchfork-review/10009-transfiguration-and-transcendence-the-music-of-alice-coltrane/.

37. Fannie Moore's account was published in *Federal Writers' Project: Slave Narrative Project: Vol. 11. North Carolina, Part 2, Jackson-Yellerday* (1936), 127–42, https://www.loc.gov/item/mesn112/.

38. For more on black public affairs television, see Devorah Heitner, *Black Power TV* (Durham, N.C.: Duke University Press, 2013).

39. Assata Shakur, *Assata: An Autobiography* (Chicago: Lawrence Hill Books, 1987), 266.

40. Opening narration of *The Twilight Zone.* This introduction was used only for seasons 4 and 5 (1963–64).

41. Aimee Bahng, *Migrant Futures: Decolonizing Speculation in Financial Times* (Durham, N.C.: Duke University Press, 2017), 8.

42. Kodwo Eshun, "Further Considerations on Afrofuturism," *CR: The New Centennial Review* 3, no. 2 (2003): 293.

43. A. Sayeeda Clarke, personal communication to the author, August 4, 2017.

44. http://www.pbs.org/show/future-states/.

45. Selmin Kara, "Anthropocenema: Cinema in the Age of Mass Extinctions," in *Post-cinema: Theorizing 21st Century Film,* ed. Shane Denson and Julia Leyda (Falmer, U.K.: REFRAME Books, 2016), 770.

46. Yusoff, *A Billion Black Anthropocenes or None* (Minneapolis: University of Minnesota Press, 2018), 16–17. For further consideration of the epochal status of the Anthropocene with necessary attention to the transatlantic slave trade, genocide, and white supremacy, see Dana Luciano, "The Inhuman Anthropocene," *Avidly, a Channel of the Los Angeles Review of Books,* March 22, 2015, http://avidly.lareviewofbooks.org/2015/03/22/the-inhuman-anthropocene/; Nicholas Mirzoeff, "Visualizing the Anthropocene," *Public Culture* 26, no. 2 (2014): 213–32; Mirzoeff, "It's Not the Anthropocene, It's the White Supremacy Scene; or, The Geological Color Line," in *After Extinction,* ed. Richard Grusin, 123–49 (Minneapolis: University of Minnesota Press, 2018).

47. Nina G. Jablonski, *Skin: A Natural History* (Berkeley: University of California Press, 2013), 83.

48. For more on epidermalization as the visualizing process whereby skin becomes the overdetermining and delimiting measure of the racial body, see Frantz Fanon, *Black Skin, White Masks,* trans. Charles Lam Markmann (1952; repr., New York: Grove Press, 1967).

49. See Jay Prosser, "Skin Memories," in *Thinking through the Skin,* ed. Sara Ahmed and Jackie Stacey, 52–68 (New York: Routledge, 2001).

50. David Marriott, *Haunted Life: Visual Culture and Black Modernity* (New Brunswick, N.J.: Rutgers University Press, 2007), xviii.

51. I am thinking here especially of the contemporary market of organ trafficking and transplant tourism. See Stephen Frears's *Dirty Pretty Things* (2002) and Nancy Scheper-Hughes, "Commodity Fetishism in Organs Trafficking," *Body and Society* 7, no. 2–3 (2001): 31–62.

52. See Angélica Dass's Humanae project, https://www.angelicadass.com/humanae-project. Thanks to Redd Foxx for the shade titles. See also the material ecology work on skin being done by Neri Oxman at MIT's Media Lab, http://www.materialecology.com/projects, and Neri Oxman's "Material Ecology" in *Theories of the Digital in Architecture,* ed. Rivka Oxman and Robert Oxman, 319–26 (New York: Routledge, 2013). Oxman presciently noted in a *New York Times* profile about being approached by a wealthy fragrance manufacturer, "he said, 'I'll give you this amount of millions of dollars if you can produce perfume diffusers by Christmas,' she recalled. 'I thought, I'll take your money, but you won't see any perfume diffusers. The challenge for me is to scale while maintaining ideological purity. It would be too easy to start a line of melanin makeup. Easy! Vitamin-infused melanin for sun-protection-slash-makeup. Easy! That's a billion-dollar industry. But why not have an architect enter the race to cure cancer?'" Penelope Green, "A Modern-Day da Vinci," *New York Times,* October 7, 2018, ST7.

53. Sara Ahmed, *Strange Encounters: Embodied Others in Post-coloniality* (New York: Routledge, 2000), 44–45.

54. Hortense Spillers, "'Mama's Baby Papa's Maybe': An American Grammar Book," in *Black, White, and in Color: Essays on American Literature and Culture* (Chicago: University of Chicago Press, 2003), 208.

55. My thinking on natural resources in this context is inspired by Britt Russert, "Naturalizing Coercion: The Tuskegee Experiments and the Laboratory Life of the Plantation," in *Captivating Technology: Race, Carceral Technoscience, and Liberatory Imagination in Everyday Life,* ed. Ruha Benjamin, 25–49 (Durham, N.C.: Duke University Press, 2019).

56. Saidiya Hartman, *Scenes of Subjection: Terror, Slavery, and Self-Making in Nineteenth-Century America* (New York: Oxford University Press, 1997), 21.

57. Thanks to Harold Perkins at Ohio University for his thoughts about *White* and the future of climate change adaptation. Personal communication to the author, October 14, 2014.

58. As Christina Sharpe notes, "the weather is the totality of our environments; the weather is the total climate; and that climate is antiblack." Sharpe, *In the Wake,* 104.

59. It's useful to think about *White* in relationship to other speculative and science fiction films devoted to capital and the future utility of black and brown bodies, such as Reginald Hudlin's "The Space Traders," an adaptation of Derrick Bell's short story (1992) of the same name from the HBO series *Cosmic Slop* (1994). Bell's story opens with the arrival of visitors from outer space who offer to bail out the nearly bankrupt nation, clean the environment, and gift the world a safe energy supply in exchange for all African Americans. Other films include Alex Rivera's *Sleep Dealer* (2008), Barry Jenkins's *Remigration* (2011), Damir Lukacevic's *Transfer* (2010), Jennifer Phang's *Advantageous* short (2013) and feature (2015), Jordan Peele's *Get Out* (2017), and *Sorry to Bother You* (Boots Riley, 2018).

8

The Resilience of the Word *Cinema* and the Persistence of the Media

André Gaudreault

Something strange (to my mind at least!) occurred with respect to the English language around 1912 in the marvelous world of what the French would eventually call, following Ricciotto Canudo, the "seventh art":[1] the importation of the word *cinéma* into the language of Shakespeare and Faulkner! This importation took place after the borrowed term was "shorn" of the aigu accent atop the *e*.[2] And so *cinéma* became *cinema*. What seems strange to me about this story is that the creation of a Gallicism (whose origin, it must be pointed out, is Greek: κίνημα, *kínêma* [movement]) to describe the *res cinematografica* came about despite the fact that back then, most English-language speakers appeared to have no actual need of another word, because they already had at their disposal a very substantial vocabulary to describe both cinematic activity as a whole (the *cinéma*, as we say in French) and individual works in particular (a *film*, as we say in French). This vocabulary includes terms like *movie, film, flick, moving picture, motion picture,* and *motography.*

That said, it must be acknowledged that such a borrowing concerns first and foremost the lexical unit itself: once imported into the English language, the word *cinema* certainly looks like a sibling of the term from which it is derived, but this is not necessarily true of the meaning the word ends up taking on.[3] What is more, from 1912 to 2018, in its English-speaking home, the word *cinema* followed a different itinerary from that of the word *cinéma* in the French-speaking world. Each lexical unit has a familiar effect in its respective language, its own avatars, world, vicissitudes, and distortions, such that we find ourselves, a hundred and some odd years later, with two almost identical lexical units (only the accent on the letter *e* distinguishes them) in two different languages, yet each bears a number of resolutely specific connotations, rendering interlanguage communication difficult.[4]

I myself have been able, on a few occasions, to gauge the different meanings that the word *cinema* appears to have for speakers in each of these two language communities, without ever being able to put my finger on the heart of the problem. I took the trouble of determining directly what this could be by asking Santiago Hidalgo,[5] one of my close collaborators who has been working for at least five years in a French-speaking environment at the Université de Montréal. Despite what his first and last names may suggest, my "subject" was raised speaking English in anglophone Canada. Hidalgo responded in the following manner to the question I asked him (by email) concerning the different connotations that the words *cinema* and *cinéma* could have:

> There is no question that "cinema" and "cinéma" evoke two different ... "domains of reference" since "cinema" evokes *multiple* things in each brain, some of which overlap, and others not. ... There is overlap, but some areas are distinct. But there is something else, and I can say this only came to mind now, for the first time. The English speakers that say "cinema" feel they are using a borrowed language. It feels a bit *foreign,* compared to "movies" or "film," as if they are trying to say something different than "movies" or "film" but they are not sure what. That has been my lifelong feeling on the matter. When the English speaker says "cinema" (when not in reference to a movie theatre), they are trying to say something "bigger" than "film," but rarely can they define this difference.[6]

"Something 'bigger' than 'film'"! The word *cinema* thus evokes something additional, something greater, something grander than the word *film,* not only in the sense in which it is used to speak of a single work (as in "a film by Martin Scorsese") but also in the sense in which it is used to speak of all works of cinematic art (as in the title of Rudolf Arnheim's book *Film as Art,* first published in 1932). This is also possible in French, for example, in the expression *histoire du film français,* which one encounters occasionally but is relatively rare compared to *histoire du cinéma français.*[7]

The word *cinema* in English calls to mind something greater than the word *film* and, it would seem, greater than the words *movie, flick, moving picture, motion picture,* and so on. This creation of a Gallicism to describe the *res cinematografica* has not always pleased everyone, as highlighted in an exchange between Orson Welles and Peter Bogdanovich in 1969 in Rome. In their discussion, the two pals mention several terms used to speak of film or cinema: *motion pictures, movies, films, cinema,* and, last but not least, a derivative of *photoplay.* What we can conclude from this exchange between the two is that the expression *motion pictures* comes across as "pompous," at least according to Welles, who, in addition, adjudges the word *film* to be acceptable, as is the word *movies* (which is rather "chic" but a "good English word"). Bogdanovich replies, "But I don't like [the word] 'cinema'!" To this, Welles responds, "I know what you mean," and then launches into a monologue that takes us back to the silent era, with a reference to a derivative of *photoplay,* a word the nascent industry had selected in 1910 among several others as part of a contest in the trade press in the search for a name that would give greater respectability to cinema:[8]

> In the library of Elèonora Duse's villa in a little town in Veneto where we've been shooting just now [*The Merchant of Venice*], I found an old book— written in 1915—about how movies are made, and it refers to movie actors as "photoplayers." How about that? Photoplayers! I'm never going to call them anything else.[9]

Moreover, questions around vocabulary used in cinema have been constant for a variety of people working in the field. It has even become something of an obsession (at least it has for the author of the present text!). Cinema would appear to be the ideal domain for implanting and overlaying such obsessions, which do not necessarily have to be linguistic in nature. So, for example, this well-known (and often recurrent) topic about the "death of cinema," which was somewhat "celebrated" in the conference from which this article originates. A few years ago, with my coauthor Philippe Marion,[10] I played about and compiled the most significant occasions in which "planet" cinema had mobilized to try to push back against such morbid portents that had overshadowed the medium. So, we put together a number of "deaths" (eight, to be exact) that had occurred since the beginning of cinema, which came, for the most part, at times of important technological transformations that shook the entire industry to its core (for example, the arrival of the talkie, the advent of television, and, most recently, the transition to digital). This is what we had to say about it:

> The crisis brought about by the emergence of digital media is not the first upheaval to rock the cinematic realm. It must be said and repeated over and over, tirelessly: *cinema's entire history has been punctuated by moments when its media identity has been radically called into question.* What people have called "cinema" for over a century has seen a series of technological mutations throughout its history. Whether when sound arrived or widescreen formats were introduced, to mention just those two examples, every new technology has, in its own way, gradually and lastingly turned upside down the way in which films are produced and distributed, along with their reception by viewers.[11]

This observation was made just a few years ago, and already another threat to cinema's survival has emerged in the wake of this transition to digital, at the last turn of the century: one such sign is that this new technology has indeed enabled the forming of new platforms that are so effective, popular, and lucrative that they threaten the survival of "cinema" as a medium, or at the very least the supremacy of cinemas as the preferred venue for the weekly release of new cinematographic material, for example, Netflix, which disrupted the world of film, including festivals, and is now, in a manner of speaking, rewriting the laws on it, as we will see later in this chapter. These laws are most certainly threatening to cinephilia, French cinephilia in particular, but to the economic interests at stake as well, most notably distributors and owners of *cinemas,* of *movie theaters.*

Let's return to our two friends sitting in a Roman restaurant and "listen in" on what Bogdanovich says next to continue the conversation: "I have a book from 1929, and they list 250 words to describe a talking picture, asking readers to write in their favorites. And 'talkie' was only one of them. Others were things like 'actorgraph,' 'reeltaux' and 'narrative toned pictures.'"[12] Indeed, since the very beginning (think of the battle between the "scopes" and the "graphs"), people have debated whether one term or another to describe "cinema" is correct: not only during the years of the industry's birth (such as the trade press contest in the early 1910s) but also, as we saw, at the time of the introduction of new applications of sound technologies that facilitated the advent of "talkies" (in the late 1920s and early 1930s). And this is true for each historical moment that has been witness to the introduction of new technologies likely to change the "nature" of the medium. This, moreover, has been our lot since the beginning of the transition to digital, a "revolution" that has made the question of nomenclature more crucial than ever. In fact, given today's blurring of the boundaries between media, the film studies milieu is constantly redefining itself, with each medium seeking its own specificity. However, it is not just those working in film studies who are trying to find themselves; the entire film culture has been doing so since the advent of the digital, because order has turned to complete disorder and practices have turned upside down. Orson Welles, I might add, would be turning in his grave if he could see what is happening today, and his buddy Bogdanovich, who is still alive, knows a thing or two about this. In fact, Welles and Bogdanovich were in the news recently because of an enormous kerfuffle within the "cinema" industry itself, when, at the 2018 Cannes Film Festival, Netflix decided to withdraw from the competition, refusing to screen the world premiere of Welles's last film, as had been planned. The film had remained unfinished and was completed by Bogdanovich, thanks to funding from Netflix.

It is truly outrageous what Welles and Bogdanovich have been subjected to. They have been the collateral victims in the war raging today around two different conceptions of what cinema *should* henceforth be: a new, multiplatform conception, under which watching a film in a movie theater is, in the end, just one form among others (an *application* of cinema in a sense), or a more "traditional" conception, under which multiplatform viewing is accepted, as long as movie-theater viewing is *preserved, protected, preferred,* and so on. This war[13] has recently pitted the champions of each camp against each other: in one corner, Netflix (represented by Ted Sarandos, chief content officer of the famous online broadcasting platform), and in the other corner, the no-less-famous Cannes Film Festival (represented by Thierry Frémaux, director of the festival[14]), which is said to receive more media coverage than any other film festival in the world.

During the 2018 edition of the festival, Netflix decided to boycott the event because of a decision by festival management to exclude films not meant for theatrical distribution from the competition. Netflix took its ball and went home, withdrawing its films from Cannes, even those being screened out of competition:

> In an interview with *Variety* published Wednesday, April 11, Ted Sarandos said that relegating Netflix films to the out-of-competition category could be perceived as "lack of respect" towards filmmakers. "The festival has chosen to celebrate film distribution rather than the art of cinema," he said, pointing out that Cannes is the only festival in the world that discriminates in this way. He is looking "to the future," while, as it currently stands, Cannes is "stuck in the history of cinema."[15]

Of the films excluded, two are of real interest in this discussion, both of which were to be screened out of competition: *The Other Side of the Wind*, Orson Welles's famous unfinished work, and *They'll Love Me When I'm Dead*, a documentary by Morgan Neville "about the eventful gestation" of Welles's unfinished film.[16]

The conflict between Netflix and Cannes raises important concerns for anyone doing research in film studies, notably in that it evokes the history of cinema. In short, it brings to mind the end of André Malraux's book, in which he sets art against the film industry; the Netflix chief content officer pits cinematographic art against Cannes's position defending "distribution," and therefore the industry[17]—it's like the tail is wagging the dog. Their positions represent two diametrically opposed ideas of cinema. On one hand, we have Sarandos's position on behalf of Netflix, which is concerned with the future of the medium (with no qualms about maintaining its cinematic trappings) and is looking toward the future. On the other hand is the position supported by Thierry Frémaux for the Cannes Film Festival, which seems to remain "stuck in the history of cinema," hesitating to recognize what appears obvious to its opponent. Not to put words in Sarandos's mouth, but we can imagine that he seems to believe that, given the range of platforms available, movies in theaters should be seen as only one of the possible "applications" for viewing a film. Here are two different views—two different philosophies, one could argue—in basic agreement on Frémaux's observation that his counterparts at Netflix "are people who love film, but don't have the same philosophical point of view."[18]

The fact that Netflix does not show its "films" (I voluntarily put quotation marks here, explanation to come) in theaters across France is a recurring source of tension between the online broadcasting platform and the Cannes Film Festival, the directors of which are closely linked to the world of film production, but also distribution and even exhibition. It was recently reported in the *Financial Times* that

> many French cinema owners, who are putting pressure on Cannes to resist Netflix et al, see the streamers' disruptive attitude as an incursion into their territory. "We have nothing against Netflix or new platforms," says Marc-Olivier Sebbag, chief executive of the Fédération Nationale des Cinémas Français. "The problem is that Netflix wants to have the benefits of the cinema industry without contributing to it."[19]

The reader will have noted the scare quotes I used in the previous paragraph around the word *film*. The intent was to highlight the fact that the Cannes kerfuffle, at least in French, seems to be shaking up traditions. What I referred to as *films* by Netflix are sometimes not even considered *films*, at least by some of the hardliners against broadcasting platforms. Guillaume Loison, whose article I cited earlier, put forward that "the Oscars, that will be Netflix's next objective. Like Venice—and unlike France—their features will be considered *films*."[20]

This highly publicized clash between Netflix and Cannes even unearthed some interviews between the two buddies to whom we referred earlier:

> In an interview in February 1969 with Peter Bogdanovich, Welles described the origins of his project before becoming bogged down in a long, unfinished film shoot from 1970 to 1976: "It's the story of an old film director and

his last job. It's about a big hairy-chested macho, based on John Ford, with a dash of Huston and Hemingway."[21]

The clash was also beneficial for the directors of the Venice Film Festival, who snapped up the world premiere of the two films in late August 2018, demonstrating that the Venetian event is "more flexible about the changing definition of film."[22] In his other role as director of Lyon's Institut Lumière, Thierry Frémaux has in part made up for it on France's behalf, because he screened *The Other Side of the Wind* as a premiere in France in mid-October 2018, a few months after the kerfuffle in Cannes, and a little over a month after it was screened in Venice. The "Netflix film," or, to put it another way, the version of Welles's film completed by Bogdanovich, was screened at Lyon's Festival Lumière 2018 (considered the world's leading festival devoted to the *legacy* of film—talk about history!), of which Frémaux is the delegate general. The festival is jointly organized by the Métropole de Lyon and the Institut Lumière, an institute that looks at the history of cinema and that Frémaux heads up as well. Also, the newsletter published by the Institut Lumière ends with an appropriate and honest "Thanks to Netflix and Filip Jan Rymsa," showing that the battle between these two views of cinema is far from over. The newsletter says of Welles's film that "its revival . . . is a major event for . . . film *historians*" (my emphasis) and that "Orson Welles got the idea for the film when he was talking about meetings between his friend Peter Bogdanovich and old directors forgotten by the amnesiac Hollywood machine."[23] Once again, this is a reference to the aforementioned discussions reported in *This Is Orson Welles,* during which Bogdanovich, supported by Welles, rejected the English equivalent of the favorite word of French cinephilia, *cinema.* Of course, we shouldn't see the two colleagues' frustration at Cannes as a fitting reversal of roles or a swing of the pendulum (perhaps we shouldn't go too far, but Cannes remains the pinnacle of the very idea of "CINÉMA"), so I will simply say that this is a striking, cruel irony.

One thing is certain: the "cinema" industry is in turmoil, and the advent of the digital has not finished sending huge shockwaves through it. The scare quotes used in the previous paragraph around the word *cinéma* are there to highlight the fact that the Cannes kerfuffle disrupted the entire industry of *images animées* or, again, *images en mouvement,* of which cinema is only one of the stakeholders. In fact, the concept of cinema no longer holds the high ground, even though it is highly resilient—nor does the word cinema. The use of a more encompassing substitute (*images animées, images* en mouvement, *moving images*) has become common practice since, with the "digitalization" of cinema, the boundaries between media have become so blurred that one no longer even knows if there are boundaries. Moreover, because of the downgrading of cinema's role in the concert of media, cinema itself has lost its luster and has fallen off the pedestal from which it reigned. In fact, today it no longer occupies the entire space, and one now strives to remember that it was once not just *one* of the audiovisual arts.

So how then should we, *in French,* speak of all audiovisual production (including cinema) using a simple expression which is as charged, handy and relatively "all-purpose" as the English expression *moving images*? It is not truly possible, and despite the fact (or is it for this very reason?) that the expression *moving images* can be translated in a thousand and one ways, none has unanimous support.[24] We should note that in English, there is effectively no hesitation to speak of *all audiovisual production,* of which cinema is just a part, because a fixed expression, *moving images,* rapidly took hold in English. Moreover, the expression in question, which had had a more or less secondary existence for a long time prior, has proliferated over the past twenty years, primarily in the world of film studies (particularly in the case of book publishing[25] and in the names given to university departments and programs where cinema is taught[26]). In French, the opposite holds. Even if we were to acknowledge that, generally speaking, French is a *fine* language, a *poetic* one even, it is a language so frozen that the French themselves (unlike French speakers in Quebec) have a staggering propensity to import a phenomenal quantity of English words rather than coining new words to describe new realities.[27] French speakers in France can then do just about anything with these newly imported words because, as these words have been imported, they don't have to follow the rules of the Académie française.[28]

From this we can conclude, however, that in some respects, French is less "handy" than English. While it is true that to identify the productions of the supposed seventh art, French has the (fine) word cinéma, there is no truly satisfying substitute for describing all audiovisual production of which cinema makes up only one part (the equivalent of *moving images*), because there is no fixed expression in French equivalent to the English *moving images* that could replace cinema when one needs to refer to all "images" that are "moving." There are of course the expressions *images animées* and *images en movement*, but each is imperfect, as we shall see. Hence the fully justified complaint of some, including Jacques Aumont, who reveals an unfortunate linguistic void when he asserts, "What is missing in the end, to express in simple terms this relatively simple situation [the fact that cinema is no longer the exclusive form of moving images], is a word—a single word which would say 'social uses of a variety of moving images.'"[29] For indeed, the word *cinéma* refers only to one of the "social uses" of the aforementioned moving images (which include television, video, holography, the internet, the transmission of operas in so-called movie theaters, museum installations, performance art with projection, etc.).

In the language of Molière and Duras, the two default French expressions, used interchangeably and which anglophones refer to as moving images, images *animées* (*animated* images, so to speak) and images *en mouvement* (images *in motion,* so to speak), therefore leave something to be desired. It is out of spite and, dare I say, due to a lack of anything better that francophones resort to them. They are probably too "reifying" and too strictly denotative for them to be used professionally, whereas the *moving* in *moving images* carries with it some connotation, however slight, that conceals its taking hold (brutally and directly) in reality (that of *les mains dans le cambouis* [getting one's hands dirty], to use the famous French expression). Hence we've found ourselves, for some time now, still in this "real" world, with *anglophone* university studies programs that use "moving images" in their departmental names and concepts, but there is no such *francophone* university program that uses *études de l'image animée,* nor are there programs in *études de l'image en mouvement.*[30]

Modeled after the archaic expression vues animées (animated views), the first of these expressions, images *animées,* could be considered inadequate and perceived as unnecessarily evocative of a distant past, bringing us back to the beginnings of cinema, yet without this stroll down memory lane having any pertinence whatsoever.[31] Furthermore, for obvious reasons, the expression is liable to cause an unfortunate misinterpretation with *animated* films, which did not stop the main cinematic institution in France, the Centre national de la cinématographie (CNC), from re-branding itself in 2010 as the Centre national du cinéma *et des images animées* (retaining its abbreviation). Adopting the phrase *cinéma et . . . images animées* (replacing the relatively dated *cinématographie,* used rather infrequently nowadays) clearly shows that the French institution was sensitive to the times and ready to "modernize" its brand image, not only to relativize cinema's place in the concert of media but to do so by putting forward an expression that was thought to be, I imagine, less inadequate than its rival. Indeed, one can only imagine that the governing bodies at the CNC preferred to avoid the English calque at the heart of the expression *images en mouvement* (do not forget, it is the Quebecers who value English calques, whereas the French, despite their propensity for importing terms from the English vocabulary, loathe them). Additionally, the expression *images en mouvement* lacks elegance and is ten times more reifying and descriptive than the expression *images animées,* which did not prevent another major francophone cinematographic institution, the Cinémathèque québécoise, from surreptitiously changing its name in the early aughts from a *musée du cinéma* (museum of cinema) to a *musée de l'image en mouvement,* which is less specific and even less glamorous.[32]

The French word *cinéma* is more evocative, appealing, and glamorous than the expression *image en mouvement.* It could even be said that the word *cinéma* offers a poetic touch and bears a hint of charm and mystery.[33] To me, this is even truer for an anglophone when he or she utters the Gallicism *cinema,* an abstract and highly evocative word, giving him or her the impression that the word is from (to go back to Hidalgo) a "borrowed language." It seems clear, to me at any rate, that it is the glamorous connotation of the French word *cinéma* that is at the origin of its importation and introduction, during the 1910s, into the English language. Today, the word is featured in the very name of the most important association of cinema scholars in the world, the Society for Cinema and Media Studies (SCMS), in which the recognized "discipline" is not "film studies" but rather "cinema studies," thus featuring the Gallicism discussed in this paper and which was imported into the English language from French more than one hundred years ago—a term which, as we've seen, has not garnered consensus. Yet the phrase that we most often see is *film studies*—by wide margins.[34] The discipline "cinema studies" had an even more significant presence in the name of the American association until 2002, when it was known simply as the Society for Cinema Studies. This was a response to a call—some might say a necessity—to broaden the sphere of activity and interest of this association, founded in 1959 as the Society of Cinematologists.[35] In this appellation, the word *cinema* is presented in the form of one of its derivatives, one unknown in French by the way, since it is the English adaptation of the concept of *filmologie*, a word that can be attributed to Gilbert Cohen-Séat, from the famous Institut de filmologie, and which enjoyed a rather good run in France during the 1950s[36] but did not survive past the original founders of the American association (among them was scholar Robert Gessner), since their successors did not find the word to be very glamorous, to say the least. In fact, we can assume that, some ten years after their association was founded (in 1969), the new officials found that the term, proposed most likely by Gessner himself, was a real lexical monster. It is, in any case, the feeling that can be surmised from reading the SCMS's declaration regarding this matter:

> The first name of the Society was always controversial. The term "Cine-matologist" was adapted by founding president Robert Gessner from the French "filmologie," a term coined by Gilbert Cohen-Séat in 1948 to give scientific credibility to his Institute of Filmology, established in 1948 at the University of Paris. In 1969, after Gessner's death, the Council voted *overwhelmingly* to change the name to the Society for Cinema Studies (SCS).[37]

This declaration implies an obvious sense of rejection toward the "monster." There is even a feeling, I think, of some buried emotional weight regarding how this part of the association's history has been described.[38] For example, the use of the word *overwhelmingly* (which means "predominantly" but can also mean "convincingly") perhaps hides a certain form of triumphalism. Furthermore, the reference to Gessner's death gives the impression that there was some wait before "finally" getting permission to change the association's name. It would be nice to believe that the "first name of the Society was *always* controversial," but without any reliable data, it is difficult to delve deeper into this. In any case, one could speculate that the association's name, which brought film scholars together under the banner of cinematology/filmology, did not give rise to controversy among the first three officials of the association.[39]

Even as I was readying myself to write right here that this "historical" note on the SCMS warranted an amendment, if only to honor Gessner's memory (a scholar who, it would one day be discovered, authored texts that deserve our total respect), I was overtaken by events! In fact, I realized that the revising process that I would have liked to set in motion was already under way: the "Executive Director's Note," signed by Jill Simpson and published in the last email sent to SCMS members, which I received while putting the finishing touches on the present text, reads as follows: "In 1961, the Society of Cinematologists, the forerunner of SCMS, started its first journal under the apt title, *The Journal of the Society of Cinematologists*. At that time, both the society name and the journal name were met with *mixed reviews* by the membership."[40]

To say that the association's name provoked mixed reviews is giving a more respectful, and slightly less absolutist, new version of the story.

Epilogue

Not only has the cinema conquered souls and invaded hearts over the past hundred years but the media has done the same. At least, this is my point of view from within the two linguistic communities in which I have taken an interest, a point of view that essentially straddles the two cultures in which both languages are rooted.[41] To speak like the "poet," I am from the land of *presqu'Amérique* (almost America), as goes the popular 1970s song by Quebecer songwriter Robert Charlebois.[42] "Almost America" is Quebec, a land in which a good portion of the population, though its experience is North American, remains irreducibly of French origin.[43] "Almost America" is populated with francophones who are not French and who inhabit this continent where English reigns supreme (I nearly wrote "where the English reign supreme"). And this may enable it to better understand, as a "distant observer,"[44] the soul of these Others who, to Quebecers, are the French, and at the same time the Americans, neither of whom, in a certain sense, speaks their language. My participation in the conference at the Center for 21st Century Studies at the origin of this text has allowed me bridge the two continents and the three cultures, all the more so since I made my way to the state of Wisconsin, which at one time itself was "almost America," since it was part of New France in the eighteenth century.[45]

And since I'm from the land of *presqu'Amérique,* and since the expression originates from the French idiom, it is because I am also, in a way, from "almost France," which is also what Quebec is in a sense . . .

Translated by Craig Lund

Notes

The work on which the present text is based has benefited from the financial support of the Social Sciences and Humanities Research Council of Canada, the Canada Research Chairs program, and the Fonds de recherche du Québec—Société et culture, through the intermediary of four university research bodies led by André Gaudreault under the aegis of the Laboratoire CinéMédias: the Canada Research Chair in Film and Media Studies, the Programme de recherche sur l'archéologie et la généalogie du montage/editing (PRAGM/e), the International Partnership for Research into Cinema Techniques and Technologies (TECHNÈS), and the Groupe de recherche sur l'avènement et la formation des institutions cinématographique et scénique (GRAFiCS). This text is an extensively revised version of my talk at the international Ends of Cinema conference at the Center for 21st Century Studies, University of Wisconsin–Milwaukee, in May 2018. The same conference paper, slightly adapted, was given in French, one week later, with the title "La résilience du [ouvrez les guillemets] cinéma [fermez les guillemets] . . . ," at the International Symposium on Innovation in Interactive Media, at the Universidade Federal de Goiás Media Lab, Goiânia (published in 2019), in the UFG Media Lab's electronic journal; see https://siimi.medialab .ufg.br/up/777/o/Andre-Gaudreault.pdf. Part of the new text, written by André Gaudreault and Philippe Marion, is titled "Le cinéma persiste et signe . . ." and was prepared for the international symposium Crise, quelle crise? Cinéma, audiovisuel, nouveaux médias, which took place in November 2018 at the Institut de recherche sur le cinéma et l'audiovisuel (IRCAV), Université Sorbonne Nouvelle—Paris 3 (forthcoming). The author thanks Martin Lefebvre for his advice and Dana Polan for his contributions via email as well as his authorization to let us cite some of his words. The author also extends his sincere thanks to Anne Bienjonetti, Marion Charroppin, and Marie-Ève Hamel from the Laboratoire CinéMédias.

1. See Ricciotto Canudo, "La leçon du cinéma," *L'information* 286 (1919): 2. Reprinted in Jean-Paul Morel, ed., *L'usine aux images* (Paris: Séguier/Arte, 1995),

41–43, which begins with these words: "The birth of Cinema was precisely that of a Seventh Art."

2. A shearing that is not an absolute rule when a word passes from French to English, if one thinks, for example, of the expression *mise en scène,* which, for its part, has preserved its accent (a grave accent on the letter *e*).

3. As is well known, a lexical unit often passes from one language to another without all the nuances accompanying that word in the original language migrating with it at the same time.

4. This is why I feel sorry for any translator who is tasked with tackling a text like this . . .

5. Affiliate professor and director of the research lab I founded at the Université de Montréal, Laboratoire CinéMédias, http://labocinemedias.ca/, and author of a PhD dissertation titled "The Possibilities of 'Film Consciousness': A Formulation in Search of a Theory" (Université de Montréal, 2015), https://papyrus.bib .umontreal.ca/xmlui/handle/1866/18467.

6. Email to the author, February 24, 2018.

7. Or in a "festival of films on art," like the one that exists in Montreal—the International Festival of Films on Art (FiFA).

8. See the introduction of Lee Grieveson, *Policing Cinema: Movies and Censorship in Early-Twentieth-Century America* (Berkeley: University of California Press, 2004), 1–2. See also the recent article by Louis Pelletier, which states, "As we have seen, photoplay and movie both appeared in 1910 in the MHDL data set, but photoplay initially spread more rapidly. Photoplay, however, went into a quick decline after its 1916–17 peak." Pelletier, "From Photoplays to Movies: A Distant Reading of Cinema's Eventual Legitimation from Below," *Film History* 30, no. 2 (2018): 23. I should point out that part of the ideas in the present text stem from a joint presentation I made with Louis Pelletier in Berkeley in February 2011, at the First International Berkeley Conference on Silent Cinema (Cinema across Media: The 1920s), whose title was "From Photoplays to Pictures: An Intermedial Perspective on the Names for 'Moving Pictures' in the Late Silent Era."

9. Quoted in Jonathan Rosenbaum, ed., *This Is Orson Welles,* with a new introduction by Peter Bogdanovich (New York: Da Capo Press, 1998), 23.

10. André Gaudreault and Philippe Marion, *The End of Cinema? A Medium in Crisis in the Digital Age* (New York: Columbia University Press, 2015).

11. Gaudreault and Marion, 2–3.

12. Ristorante Cesarina, a favorite restaurant not only of Welles but also of Fellini. Gaudreault and Marion, 21.

13. And it was a war, according to journalists, who keep reaching for martial metaphors to describe the conflict. See Laure Croiset, "Pourquoi la guerre est déclarée entre Netflix et le Festival de Cannes," *Challenges,* April 12, 2018, https:// www.challenges.fr/cinema/pourquoi-la-guerre-est-declaree-entre-netflix-et-le -festival-de-cannes_580389.

14. It should be noted that Frémaux is also the president of the Association Frères Lumière and director of the Institut Lumière in Lyon, which will be pertinent to my later discussion.

15. See Antoine du Jeu, "Cannes: Orson Welles exclu du festival à cause de la discorde avec Netflix?," *Les Inrockuptibles*, April 13, 2018, https://www.lesinrocks.com/2018/04/13/cinema/cannes-orson-welles-exclu-du-festival-cause-de-la-discorde-avec-netflix-111070826/.

16. See Guillaume Loison, "Mostra de Venise: l'OPA Netflix," *TéléObs*, September 10, 2018, https://teleobs.nouvelobs.com/actualites/20180910.OBS2100/mostra-de-venise-l-opa-netflix.html.

17. André Malraux, *Esquisse d'une psychologie du cinéma* (Paris: Gallimard, 1946).

18. François Léger, "Cannes 2018: selfies interdits, absence de Netflix... Les réponses du festival," *Premiere*, April 12, 2018, http://www.premiere.fr/Cinema/News-Cinema/Cannes-2018-selfies-interdits-absence-de-Netflix-Les-reponses-du-festival.

19. See Josie Thaddeus-Johns, "Netflix v Cannes: Inside the Battle for the Future of Cinema," *Financial Times*, May 9, 2019, https://www.ft.com/content/494e20b4-70b5-11e9-bf5c-6eeb837566c5.

20. See Loison, "Mostra de Venise," my emphasis.

21. Jeff Wilson and Ray Kelly, "Orson Welles Called 'The Other Side of the Wind' His Best Story," August 20, 2018, http://www.wellesnet.com/orson-welles-other-side-wind/. The quote from the interview comes from the audiobook edition of an augmented version by Peter Bogdanovich and Orson Welles, *This Is Orson Welles*, and is not included in the paper version.

22. And incidentally, for Alfonso Cuarón's *Roma*, another Netflix production that was never shown in theaters, Cannes also lost, and it won the Venice Festival's Golden Lion. Loison, "Mostra de Venise."

23. Filip Jan Rymsa is one of the producers involved in the film's completion. *Institut Lumière Newsletter*, October 1, 2018, http://r.newsletter.institut-lumiere.org/mk/mr/3jedbPMMPrlGuhfCiWQbnAbn4fz-gERbqmUdXmG4kGIpVk6I Vja8TvbUSiXB6iKGVYG8PIW9iM55mIsq1TRRvfDY9okItKrLQEs4nhXRPy vtkVp26sPETi8771zv. *They'll Love Me When I'm Dead*, the documentary about Welles that should also have been shown at Cannes, was screened as well.

24. Indeed, if one wants to express the idea of *moving images* in French, there is no shortage of possibilities: alongside the traditional *images animées* and *images en mouvement* is the expression preferred by Christian Metz, *images mouvantes*; he states, "We know that André Bazin attached great importance to this 'popularity' of the art of '*images mouvantes*'" (our translation). Metz, *Essais sur la signification au cinéma*, book 1 (Paris: Klincksieck, 1971), 14. There is also the expression found in Fernand Léger—*images mobiles*; he writes, "Building films without a screenplay by casting the '*image mobile*' as a main character." Léger, "Autour du

Ballet mécanique," in *Fonctions de la peinture* (Paris: Gonthier, 1965), 165. In addition, there is the neologism coined by Gilles Deleuze, "image-movement," which has a special meaning of its own. Deleuze, *Cinema 1: The Movement Image* (Minneapolis: University of Minnesota Press, 1986). It should be noted, as Benoît Turquety argues, that it is not at all certain that the concepts "image en mouvement, image mouvante or image animée . . . describe the same thing." Turquety, "Formes de machines, formes de mouvement," in *Ciné-dispositifs: spectacles, cinéma, télévision, littérature* (Lausanne, Switzerland: L'Âge d'Homme, 2011), 263. I would add that it is not certain that the same expressions in the singular and plural forms mean exactly the same thing. In the end, perhaps it is because there is too much vocabulary, in French, to describe the phenomenon of *moving images* that there is no fixed expression—in other words, that we have a poverty of riches.

25. In English there is a plethora of volumes with the expression *moving image* (or *moving images*) in their titles. These include, to mention just a few, Noël Carroll, *Theorizing the Moving Image* (Cambridge: Cambridge University Press, 1996); Wheeler Winston Dixon, *The Transparency of Spectacle: Meditations on the Moving Image* (Albany: SUNY Press, 1998); Vivian Sobchack, *Carnal Thoughts: Embodiment and Moving Image Culture* (Berkeley: University of California Press, 2004); Laura Mulvey, *Death 24× a Second: Stillness and the Moving Image* (London: Reaktion Books, 2007); Paul Wells and Johnny Hardstaff, *Re-imagining Animation: The Changing Face of the Moving Image* (Lausanne, Switzerland: AVA, 2008); Julia Hallam and Les Roberts, eds., *Locating the Moving Image: New Approaches to Film and Place* (Bloomington: Indiana University Press, 2013); and Andrea Sabbadini, *Moving Images: Psychoanalytic Reflections on Film* (Hove, U.K.: Routledge, 2014). One can also find a lesser number of older titles, such as Robert Gessner, *The Moving Image: A Guide to Cinematic Literacy* (New York: E. P. Dutton, 1968). On these questions, I take the liberty of referring the reader to André Gaudreault, "The Cinema Spectator: A Rapidly-Mutating Species Viewing a Medium That Is Losing Its Bearings," in *At the Borders of (Film) History*, ed. Alberto Beltrame, Giuseppe Fidotta, and Andrea Mariani, 191–97 (Udine, Italy: Forum, 2015). You may also want to check out this other publication, which has allowed me to address and develop certain issues in this article: Gaudreault, "The Future History of a Vanishing Medium," in *Technē/Technology: Researching Cinema and Media Technologies—Their Development, Use, and Impact*, ed. Annie van den Oever, 261–71 (Amsterdam: University of Amsterdam Press, 2014).

26. Such as the doctoral program at Concordia University (Montreal, Canada), founded in 2008 under the name "*Film* and *Moving Image* Studies" (my emphasis) in a department which is called, however, a "school of *cinema*" (the Mel Hoppenheim School of Cinema), a school where the dominant expression was hitherto "*film* studies" (see https://www.concordia.ca/finearts/cinema/programs/film-studies/film-moving-image-phd.html). To give just one other example:

another doctoral university program, this time in the United States, at Georgia State University, is also called "moving image studies" (https://communication .gsu.edu/moving-image-studies/).

27. In Quebec, an "electronic mail" or *courrier électronique* message is called a *courriel* (*courri-el,* similar to an "email"), while the French directly imported the word *mail,* pronouncing as it would be in English, because the word *mail* in French already exists, describing either a game with balls and a mallet or a covered pedestrian passageway between shops. Another example: a smartphone is called a *smartphone* in France and a *téléphone intelligent* in Quebec.

28. Once imported, these words do not even have to follow the rules of the language from which they came. An example: in the 1980s, the French imported the word *pin* to describe a kind of lapel pin or brooch, but they gave it a form that does not follow the rules of either French or English: *pin's*! The word is the English word *pin* with an apostrophe *s,* which usually indicates possession and thus makes no sense here. To an English speaker, the word *pin's* is truly barbaric, while for French linguists, it is a false Anglicism (or pseudo-Anglicism). That said, Quebecers are not "virgins" in this respect, as they use poor copies of English for an enormous number of expressions that are basically erroneous. An example: "Ce n'est pas la peine de *chercher pour* ce rapport, il a été détruit," an expression full of mystery for someone from France and which means "Don't trouble yourself to *look for* that report, it was destroyed." The person from France would say, and he would be right, that the expression *chercher pour* must be a copy of the English expression "to look for." See http://bdl.oqlf.gouv.qc.ca/bdl/gabarit_bdl .asp?id=2460.

29. Jacques Aumont, *Que reste-t-il du cinéma?* (Paris: Vrin, 2012), 59–60.

30. There is one exception to this, which can be found in Canada, or Quebec more specifically. It is presented as a specialized master's program at the Université du Québec à Montréal, a "specialization in 'Cinéma et images en mouvement,' within the master's in communications program." See https://communica tion.uqam.ca/cinema-images-mouvement/. Again, the expression is modeled on the nonequivocal relationship to *cinéma,* since the word is itself part of the formulation.

31. At the turn of the twentieth century, it was commonly said in French that one was going to *voir des vues animées* (see animated views).

32. Let's remember that the Cinémathèque québécoise belongs to the same linguistic community as the Université du Québec à Montréal. This is what can be read on the Cinémathèque québécoise's website (http://www.cinema theque.qc.ca/fr): "La Cinémathèque québécoise, c'est le musée de l'image en mouvement à Montréal" (The Cinémathèque québecoise is Montreal's museum of moving images). See http://www.cinematheque.qc.ca/fr/cinematheque/com muniques/la-galerie-de-luqam-et-la-cinematheque-quebecoise-preparent-sou levements-ex. Some traces of the old naming can be found on the site's archives:

"La Cinémathèque québécoise/Musée du cinéma a 25 ans 1963–1988" (La Ciné-mathèque québécoise/Musée du cinéma is 25 1963–1988). See http://www.cine matheque.qc.ca/fr/programmation/projections/film/cinematheque-quebec oise-musee-du-cinema-25-ans-1963-1988. To find out more about the subject, see Gaudreault and Marion, *End of Cinema?*, 144.

33. Whereas, for its part, the word from which it is derived, *cinématographe*, was deemed ugly by the bard of the "seventh art" himself as early as 1908. Ric-ciotto Canudo wrote, "Le Cinématographe—il est inutile d'en changer le nom, mais il n'est pas beau" (The Cinématographe—it's pointless to change its name, but it's not pretty). Canudo, "Lettere d'arte. Trionfo del cinematografo," *Il nuovo Giornale illustrato*, Florence, November 25, 1908, French translation by Jean-Paul Morel, "Triomphe du Cinématographe," in *L'usine aux images* (Paris: Séguier/Arte, 1995), 27; underlined in the text. As for Louis Delluc, he wrote in 1917, "Nous manquons de mots, je veux dire de mots brefs et précis . . . pour remplacer *ciné-matographe* qui est lourd, interminable, laid, et ne s'applique plus très bien à ce qu'il est chargé de désigner" (We lack words, I mean short and concise words . . . to replace *cinématographe*, which is cumbersome, never-ending and ugly, and is not very well suited to what it has been tasked with describing). See *Le Film*, November 12, 1917.

34. A simple test in the form of a Google search is convincing enough. Look-ing up the phrase "cinema studies" yields 626,000 results in 0.34 seconds, whereas "film studies" yields 6,220,000 in 0.59 seconds. We don't really know why Welles and Bogdanovich rejected the word *cinema*, but what we do know is that Welles found the expression *motion pictures* "pompous" and the word *movies* rather "chic." We can only imagine that they found *cinema* to be even more pompous and chic.

35. "The late 1990s saw the debut of digital media as a growing field of study. During the last decade the number of Scholarly Interest Groups (SIGs) has expanded, reflecting the growth of subfields in Cinema and Media Studies, many intermedial and interdisciplinary. In 2002 the 'M' for Media was added to SCS to reflect these changes and create the Society for Cinema and Media Studies." See https://www.cmstudies.org/page/org_history.

36. Please see the issue of the Canadian (Québécois, to be exact) film journal *Cinémas* dedicated to this topic ("La filmologie, de nouveau," under the direction of François Albera and Martin Lefebvre): https://www.erudit.org/fr/revues/cine/2009-v19-n2-3-cine3099/.

37. https://www.cmstudies.org/page/org_history.

38. I asked a colleague from New York University (where Gessner taught), Dana Polan, who wrote me the following in an email on November 5, 2018: "I think though the reaction is not to a French idea per se (Cinema) but to the -ology part of it. As US film studies was starting up again in the late 1950s, -ology was a way of making a soft branch of humanities (lettres, even belles-lettres) seem

scientific and hard and therefore respectable. That's the case with 'filmology' in France too (let's make this field a science) but it's a different battle in the US: film study comes out of English (that's where Gessner started) and out of Theater Arts but also out of Communication—a social science. By giving the name 'ology,' you make film studies seem more rigorous and more social science. But that's what the humanities people didn't want. And they didn't want public journalists like Pauline Kael to attack attempts to make a theory of film—whether Kracauer and the realist theory, or Sarris and the auteur theory." It may not be pointless to point out that Polan teaches in a department of "cinema studies" (instead of "film studies"): the Department of Cinema Studies at the NYU Tisch School of the Arts, the same one in which Gessner worked and founded the Society of Cinematologists. He started teaching cinema in 1935 and in 1941 founded the aforementioned department, but under a connotatively different name: the Motion Picture Department. To give a relative (and not scientific) idea of the difference in popularity between the two designations for departments in which cinema is taught, I did a Google search and obtained the following results: 67,600 results in 0.39 seconds for "Department of Cinema Studies" and 345,000 in 0.48 seconds for "Department of Film Studies."

39. President Robert Gessner (New York University); secretary Hugh Gray (University of California, Los Angeles); treasurer Gerald Noxon (Boston University).

40. The email was sent on October 16, 2018 (my emphasis). See http://campaign.r20.constantcontact.com/render?m=1121577869045&ca=fa01f3ca-087d-4f81-b0f5-f727a6c90844. It should be noted, however, that the old version of this account is still on the website and is paired side by side with the new, more respectful way of putting things.

41. So as to not complicate things, I avoided including England in this text. But there is much to be said for the "kinematographers" from Albion and their predilection for the word *kinematograph*. See Gary D. Rhodes, "'Movie': How a Single Word Shaped Hollywood Cinema," *Film History: An Interdisciplinary Journal* 46, no. 1 (2016): 43. Rhodes argues, "During the early cinema period, preferred nomenclature became an important issue. Published in Great Britain and read by some industry members in America, the *Optical Magic Lantern and Kinematograph Journal* noted in 1906 its preference for the generic term 'kinematograph,' the word having originated with the Lumiere exhibitions in Europe. The trade also bemoaned that the letter 'k' was rapidly being replaced with a 'c,' as in 'cinematograph,' a corruption they viewed with contempt, as the 'correct' use of the 'k' followed such Greek terms as 'Kinema,' 'Kinematic,' and 'Kineo.'"

42. The lyrics to Charlebois's song can be found here: http://www.robertcharlebois.com/default.asp?p=3&sl=1&chanId=29.

43. Who are still nonetheless subjects of Her Majesty, the Queen of England . . .

44. To use the expression in the title of Noël Burch's work: *Pour un observateur lointain. Forme et signification dans le cinéma japonais* (Paris: Cahiers du cinéma/ Gallimard, 1982).

45. Traces of this heritage can be found, just to give an example, in the joint publication between the presses from the Université Laval and the University of Wisconsin of the work *The Seigneurial System in Early Canada,* by R. C. Harris (several editions: 1966, 1968, 1984), available at http://www.deslibris.ca/ID/40 0975 (see p. 7).

9

& Mediation

Television's Partial Visions

Amy Villarejo

This chapter was written amid, and I have to say also *against*, a very specific anxiety felt by the discipline of film studies, namely, the death or end of cinema. By this death, we mean, of course, transformations in the industry, technology, organization, and social function of moving images and the demise of a certain version of shared experience, taste, and culture embraced under the sign of a largely masculine cinephilia (which Thomas Elsaesser shows to be itself a retroactive temporality of deferral, inherently bound up with loss and mourning[1]). To be sure, other media than cinema feel their lives cut short: Amanda Lotz, in her short treatise on nonlinear television, *Portals,* notes how pervasive is the argument that so-called new media have arrived to kill off the old ones like TV, an argument that, as she demonstrates, obscures how media really work and in fact persist.[2] And in my book *Ethereal Queer,* I begin with the death of television's broadcast era only to herald another beginning: "Analog television is dead. Long live analog television!"[3]

I initially wrote a piece of this chapter for a graduate student conference at the University of California, Berkeley that was meant to interrogate the implications of their change in department name from "Film" to "Film & Media." (We undertook our own name change at Cornell from "Theatre, Film & Dance" to "Performing & Media Arts.") Amid the more general anxieties sparked by crises in public education, the likelihood of underemployment, and a national, if not international, climate increasingly hostile to the humanities, the students worried about their objects and methods of study as well as the historicity and legitimacy of their discipline. Was it OK to write a dissertation on TV? On YouTube? How would they demonstrate their capacities in this still-emerging field? A year or two later, I adapted and extended these reflections for the Ends of Cinema conference and its proceedings published in this volume. In the conference's call for papers, the climate for the kill, the transformations I have just referenced, had quite a particular name: the "digital." "Whatever the cinema was, it seems to have been summarily executed in the digital era." It's not clear who was *doing* the killing, but blood flowed in the digital nonetheless. These University of Wisconsin–Milwaukee conference organizers, however, also envisioned alternatives to this death, to the universal analog canon built on default ideologies, a set of new beginnings that might be glimpsed in new modes of production of moving images and recorded sound, new technologies of distribution and exhibition, and greater access to all three by diverse makers, artists, and audiences. This was a version of endings I could get behind! But what *is* this new conglomeration, and how might we capture its form as it takes shape? Ultimately, this chapter is just a start at answering this question.

Ampersand

Let's begin with the ampersand, that little pesky bit of typography that had the Berkeley graduate students worried. The word *ampersand* derives from the practice of speaking the alphabet aloud, adding the phrase *per se* after those letters that are themselves also words (such as the article "a" or the pronoun "I") to emphasize their dual function. *A, per se, B, C, D,* and so on: this was the earliest technological melding of the structure of the alphabet (in Latin as it gave way to English, as a signifying system) and the human voice. This vocal technology gave rise to the practice of writing "and" (*et* in Latin) to designate this proliferation of *significance: a* is a letter AND means "a" as an article, which is a word. That "AND" is written first as "et" and then as what is called a ligature, where the two letters of "et," the *e* and the *t,* are conjoined typographically in a single glyph to create a new entity that literally comes to signify "and." When I say "new," as I will emphasize in a moment, I mean that this practice emerged in the first century A.D., and it became more widespread by the fourth century in New Roman cursive, and while other ligatures diminished under the script known as Carolingian miniscule during the ninth century, the *et*-ligature persisted. This I learned from Wikipedia but then verified through some completely spectacular histories of typography, such as the definitive 1953 work devoted to the ampersand, *The Ampersand: Its Origin and Development*, by the eminent historian and designer Jan Tschichold.

When the practice of writing the *et*-ligature became widespread, finally, the ampersand symbol was added to the end of the alphabet as a kind of twenty-seventh letter *itself*, so that the end of the recitation was "X, Y, Z, and *per se* and." And the latter, if slurred or otherwise corrupted by the situation of the human voice, can sound like "ampersand," giving us the modern name in English for this way of writing "and." The word doesn't enter the *Oxford English Dictionary* until the nineteenth century, which might be symptomatic of the pedagogy of rote recitation that involved schoolchildren chanting the alphabet aloud, or it might just be that the *OED* didn't know what to do with something that isn't really a word at all but, variously, a letterform, a semantic designator, a character, or, as Marc H. Smith puts it in his elegant postface to Tschichold's book, "an ornament of the written page."[4]

It is in fact in Smith's postface that we learn that the French word for the *et*-ligature, *esperluette*, essentially has the same history as the English *ampersand*. While French schoolchildren were taught to recite "and by itself and," they said "*et par lui, et*" (with the last *et* pronounced in Latin, voicing the *t*), which, when slurred into a word, might sound like "esperluette."[5] From Smith, we also gain an insistence that what Tschichold sees as a series of *formal* transformations in the *et*-ligature, interested as he is in its typographic history, might more profitably be understood as reflecting fundamental changes in both its form and its function. That is, the *et*-ligature evolves precisely as a practice of writing, beholden to rules and habits followed by scribes; as the *et*-ligature in its many forms became solidified as the abbreviation or logograph of the conjunction itself, it proliferated and transformed from the Renaissance onward according to changing rules, codes, and conventions.

What's interesting to me about this history, a history dating back to the first century A.D. (as opposed to the history of, say, the hashtag, which is by contrast only about a decade long), is that the ampersand is already all about whatever we might talk about when we talk about media. It is about the relationship between formal systems and popular adaptations, between written structures and oral tradition (between *la langue* and *la parole*). And, it is also about the displacement of ontology (*per se,* by itself, being) by conjunction: and, *per se,* and. And, it is also about the endless process of concatenation or thought: to be Deleuzian about it, it's the rhizomatic "and and and" (film, television, video art, informatics, digital media, and, and, and).

And, finally, the ampersand interpellates us into language *and* image: it insinuates itself into our habits and *habitus,* into our ways of speaking and methods of inscription. In a word, it itself *mediates.* It forms a link; it becomes a means of conveying. It takes the letters of the alphabet and shows us their instability, their capacity to point beyond themselves, as well as their elemental importance. Alphabet is after all the chosen name of the parent company of both Google and YouTube. It adds (plus one, and, and, and), proliferating linkages and likenesses. In proliferating, it finds new spaces and methods. As Peggy Phelan puts it, trying to find a word that might be ampersand, in the context of confronting the dual deaths of her teacher Richard Poirier and the superstar Michael Jackson, "what we need is *and*: close readings of performances and poems, more muscular math for calculating oversound, the thing not in the words, not in the melody, not in the dance, not in the meter."[6]

Let me be clearer, then, about what the ampersand enables or suggests. It concatenates, but it is not only additive. It involves the body and the voice. It is imperfect (the product of a slur) and yet functional. It conjoins, but there is no end to what it can bring together. It is visual, but it is also linguistic and alphabetic, confounding domains that often remain separable. It is internal to the history of the alphabet, but it also marks the limit of that system, a limit that oscillates historically. It is, in short, a species of critical figure or concept-metaphor we have come to know as deconstructive, and it allows, for my purposes here, a way of reframing an incessantly ontological focus on cinema (including its ontology as indexical) that partakes of the drive toward death with which I opened.

In taking a cue from the ampersand, then, I want in this chapter to speak less about which objects might belong to the discipline of cinema and media studies (i.e., films, television programs, web series, or whatever) and more about processes of mediation themselves. I want to jettison the question of ontology for what I think are richer questions about media history, cultural authority, and partial knowledge. By "partial," I mean both senses of the word: that is to say crosshatched with power and also never total. And and and. Most of all, I want to raise some specters in this land of death and ends: Whose deaths can we absorb, tolerate, or accommodate? What would it mean, instead, to insist upon life, not just by multiplying or diversifying what we mean by cinema or the moving image but by changing the aperture and ambition of the question itself? Let me offer an example of partial vision I've been learning about recently that has galvanized some of my questions, before turning to further theorization of the ampersand through two very different thinkers, Bernard Stiegler and Bifo Berardi. I conclude with a second bookend example from the artist Bruce Nauman.

The visual anthropologist Jennifer Biddle has written on Australian Aboriginal art, particularly art from the Western and Central desert or "remote" communities, in a wonderful book called *Remote Avant Garde*. The cover image for her book—the first image that frankly comes to my mind in thinking about what the ampersand provokes—is of a woman named Pantjiti Ungkari Mackenzie posing with artist Niningka Lewis's artwork titled *Tjanpi Film Camera* (Figure 9.1).

There are a number of layers required to understand this image, layers that Biddle gently yet insistently and elegantly unfolds in her book (which I recommend heartily). Biddle's overall argument involves understanding Australian policy since 2007 regarding Aboriginal communities as a form of occupation and genocide, where communities are pathologized as delinquent and dysfunctional, and art in response to those degradations is in turn understood as a practice of survival, of life, a *technē* of social intervention *and* aesthetic invention.

Remember, the ampersand brings together formal systems and techniques of embodiment. It bridges domains. It does not insist on ontological content; it welcomes rhizomatic movement. This image on Biddle's book cover mediates, and it records a history of cinema, too. The artwork plus the image, the artwork & the image, demand certain kinds of questions, questions not of essential being or of ends but of—you guessed

Figure 9.1. Cover of *Remote Avant Garde,* by Jennifer Loureide Biddle, published by Duke University Press in 2016.

it—mediation. These are questions we should bring to any artwork, as Jacques Derrida has taught in *Droits de regard*.[7] Who has the right to look at this artwork and this photo and this woman, and who has the right to circulate it? Who or what authorizes the right to look and, subsequently, to interpret? How does the collective work of the Tjanpi Desert Weavers, the cross-community group of mostly women who have developed this art form of weaving/coiling, become intelligible and through what art historical, cultural, linguistic, and geopolitical rubrics? How does the Western conception of an avant-garde—with all of its baggage having to do with high art, with modernism and modernity, with urbanism, with artistic and intellectual genealogies, with masculinity, and so on—transmute when applied to this kind of artwork, which leaves no doubt about its inventiveness and departure from received traditions? Through what collaborations and partnerships does this work speak to Whitefellas such as the readership for Duke University Press or Rutgers Press books?

Although it's the cover image for her book, Biddle doesn't spend any time generating questions specifically through *this* image, but we can. Is it, for example, a film camera, or a representation of a film camera, or something else entirely, and what difference lies there? Does this camera record the history of industrial modernism, through which Aboriginal communities have now passed, or does the camera convey an abstraction of mechanized vision, a capacity for storytelling in the present? Biddle shows us that the process of the artwork's construction, in which grasses are coiled, matters as an act of tracing Ancestral stories. This artwork conjoins the visible world, a world of machines and technologies of the moving image, with the Ancestral world through the process of its very making. What may appear to us as the conjunction of a form of traditional women's fiber-art handicraft, that is, basket making—a Third Worldy craft ready for "fair trade" and multiethnic fetishization—and a banal object (a machine, like a truck or a TV or other objects rendered by the Tjanpi Desert Weavers) holds worlds within it that reveal themselves not through the annotation of a story of Dreaming (as with the highly commodified Aboriginal acrylic dot paintings) but through the material, embodied, affective life of these sculptures themselves. They contain, in her words, "the capacity to engender an encounter of tangible lifeworld exigencies, providing a speculative analysis of the banal, the everyday, as itself a radical site of Indigenous-specific ontological experimentation and politics."[8]

Almost as an aside, Biddle further notes that this introduced experimental art form arrived at precisely the same time that mobile phone technologies saturated these desert communities. She asks, "what new public intimacies and assemblages of handheld technologies and techniques can travel with people whose lifeworld is defined by mobility, transmigration, movement?" I am interested in capturing the holding (of a device) that we see in this photograph, not a phone next to the ear but a camera traveling on the shoulder of a woman. She holds it "as if" it is recording, and indeed it is: those Ancestral worlds that are part of its making. This camera, then, signifies and embodies but does not *appear* to record in the indexical way we have imagined for decades since our friend André Bazin. What theory of "film and media" can recognize and embrace the bodies of Aboriginal women that make their mark in this holding, and what history of "film and media" can encompass ties to Ancestral worlds?

Biddle's work thus introduces a way of homing in on a certain problem of mediation I have named with the ampersand: what happens when minoritarian or marginalized intellectuals and artists take up a new medium, let's say, image-making, when they have been subject to an ethnographic or racist or misogynist or homophobic gaze engendered by that very medium? How do artists and intellectuals inhabit new media forms and, as the slogan goes, speak truth to power within new assemblages of publicness and intimacy, within new formal and technological systems? What forms of critical thought and writing can attend deeply to these assemblages? How do history and theory combine in them? These are the questions that animate my research.

Misery and Phenomenology

In fact, I keep asking the same questions. How can critical theory be lived today, especially with regard to the power of art and aesthetic experience? How can the ways that capitalism works on the sensorium, or the sensible, be registered and opposed? One important phenomenological approach to this question is exemplified by the work of Bernard Stiegler, one of the most provocative heirs to the Frankfurt School and to the work of his teacher Jacques Derrida.[9] In his many writings, Stiegler has sought to explain a generalized sense of misery in hyperindustrial society, a misery that for him results from the synchronization of consciousness with mass-produced culture. In hypothesizing how a culture of mass consumption—particularly of images, symbols, and sounds—produces passive and impoverished subjects, Stiegler extends critical theory's philosophy that emphasizes the impersonal logic of economic productivity and the standardization of experience under what his predecessors Adorno and Horkheimer called the "culture industry." But in Stiegler's revisions to the Frankfurt thinkers' treatment of the psychodynamics of capitalism and the negative dialectics that opposed them, hyperindustrial culture (media–informational–digital) is seen to put at risk our very capacity to develop as individuals through the mechanisms of primary narcissism. In his view, our impoverished and standardized culture inhibits our ability to individuate, to attach to singularities, to recognize singular objects; it inhibits, that is, our capacity for *aesthetic* engagement.

In the realm of the aesthetic, Stiegler finds the resources for those singular identifications or attachments to singularities: the artwork affirms and promotes processes of primary narcissism insofar as it permits both identification and differentiation, processes I will want to connect to the idea of proliferation through Berardi. In place of negative dialectics, then, Stiegler, like the Tjanpi Desert Weavers, proposes a revolution at the level of the interface between the body and technics, between one's sensorium and a technological extension or prosthesis. He argues, interestingly, that mass culture does not simply need to be negated but rather *invigorated*: since we share so much in common, from YouTube to national archives, we have to find ways for our own singular bodies to encounter and enliven aesthetic objects. Such a revolution would be *organological,* what Stiegler sometimes calls a critical project of general organology, insofar as it would interrogate and specify sites of interaction between the body and technics that allow for intervention, action, contestation, struggle, indeed, revolution. Like other key thinkers of the intersection between technologies and bodies (Herbert Marcuse, Gilles Deleuze and Félix Guattari, Wilhelm Reich), Stiegler links the refunctionalization of

the aesthetic to a reconstitution of libidinal energy, so that our unconscious as well as embodied rhythms escape synchronization by the society of control and can be rerouted into new forms.

Such an ambition is echoed in Franco "Bifo" Berardi's book *And:
Phenomenology of the End,* a raucous and idiosyncratic self-described
"aesthetic genealogy of capitalist globalization" (according to the back
cover). In sync with other phenomenological studies of the digital universe, particularly the third volume of Stiegler's *Technics and Time,* Bifo,
too, locates a certain malaise or set of pathologies arising from the mis-
match between digital transmission interfaces with the organic world of
reception, among them panic, overexcitement, hyperactivity, attention-
deficit disorder, dyslexia, information overload, and so on.

He says this over and over and in a number of inventively paranoid
ways. In one of his more environmentalist-inspired formulations, a semiotic ooze "spread by the media" is seeping into the infosphere, "pollut-
ing the psychosphere and provoking disharmony in psychic breathing."[10]
Another version emphasizes, horror-movie style, the monstrous growth
of the infosphere:

> The technological composition of the world changes, but cognitive appro-
> priation and psychic reactivity do not follow in a linear manner. The muta-
> tion of the technological environment is much more rapid than the changes
> in cultural habits and cognitive models. The stratum of the infosphere grows
> progressively thicker and denser, and informational stimulus invades every
> atom of human attention.[11]

For Bifo, then, "and" (the "and" of his title) is doing a number of things
simultaneously. It names the *acceleration* of what he calls semiocapital-
ism, an acceleration that has been a diagnostic feature of most, if not
all, versions of postmodernism. For him, the problem, so to speak, is
not with acceleration per se, or some version of time/space compression,
but with the fact that the human sensorium changes much more slowly,
through neuroplasticity, than the stimulus of the infosphere. In addition
to speed, then, "and" names this *proliferation*: a mutation or transformation that seems to be describable through every material property or
dimension (thicker, denser, faster, bigger, and so on). "And" also designates

transformations that are captured less readily through science fiction metaphors of environmental degradation and monstrosity that I've cited: reversals of internality and externality, for example, leading to wholly mysterious sentences such as this one: "the colonization of the mind and of perception is based [now] on an interior acceleration in the perception of time."[12] This might mean something Foucauldian: what was external in power is now automatism, but it might just as easily designate a more phenomenal fracture in the body itself, a reformulation of its rhythms and sensations.

The latter corresponds to Bifo's emphasis on a transition from a sphere of conjunction, valued now as positive, to connection, valued now as negative. Here is his summary of what conjunction enables:

> Collectivity happens in conditions of conjunction, while a swarm is a connective body with no conjunction, with no conscious affective collectivity. Conjunction emerges from an unmotivated, logically necessary attraction whose purpose is not implied in its pattern. Conjunction is a random concatenation, whose only rule is desire.

Furthermore, he continues later,

> conjunction has nothing to do with belonging. While belonging entails a necessary implication and presupposes the fixing of an identity, on the contrary, conjunction does not refer to something embedded and natural. Conjunctive acts do not presuppose any meaning, since meaning is *created* in the acts of conjunction. In conjunction, knowledge is creation, not recognition.[13]

Let me propose that behind Stiegler's differentiation and Bifo's conjunction, we can see the palimpsest of our ampersand, the motor for a certain proliferation and linkage. All three terms—*ampersand, differentiation, conjunction*—designate a rhizomatic mode of linkage that is *generative, aesthetic,* and *capable of bringing together what usually remains separate.* What I furthermore like about all three, while acknowledging their differences, is that they arise in and refute abstract categories: language, body, media, philosophy, image, history. In taking these philosophical resources

freely, I aim myself to animate the history of media and to stimulate reflection on their theoretical domains. These phenomenologists are trying to
capture the entanglements of the ampersand: embodied, historical, complicated relations within systems that are structured and technical but
also collective and shared. Let us turn to a final artwork to try to eluci-
date these reflections on mediation.

PheNAUMANology

I didn't make that up. It's the title of a famous essay on the conceptual
artist Bruce Nauman that was first published in 1970.[14] Its epigraph from
Rene Dubos essentially summarizes the definition of the ampersand I
offer in the preceding paragraph: "Experience shows that human beings
are not passive components in adaptive systems. Their responses commonly manifest themselves as acts of personal creation." Let me propose
an example of video art, an act of creation, that showcases the range of
the conceptual field that I have been outlining through the ampersand,
Stiegler, and Bifo. Nauman may feel like a surprising choice. He is by
no means a marginal figure; indeed, he is one of the most prominent,
influential American artists to emerge in the late 1960s and has been
at the forefront of a postminimalist conceptual practice for fifty years
(his peers in range and insight might be John Baldessari, Ed Ruscha,
James Turrell, maybe Yoko Ono). What attracts me to his work, particularly the video work, is its philosophical reflection on the "and." Look at
One Hundred Live and Die, a neon sculpture from 1984. It showcases his
love of wordplay, his interest in combining the essential and the vulgar
(the flippant and the tragic), his indebtedness to popular culture (neon
signs), and the sociopolitical commentary that arises from conjunction
and juxtaposition.

One Hundred Live and Die recombines different abstract and usually
separable domains of human life and understanding into an iterative force
field. Every act and affect (rage, hate, sleep, love, fuck, speak) combines
with the horizons of human being (live, die), but they congeal into fascinating subpatterns and resonances, too. A range of colors (black, white,
red, yellow) mingles with verbs that find tensions and relationships among
themselves: oppositions like come and go and sick and well and fall and

rise, but also more attenuated relations like those between smile and think and pay, or play and kill and suck. The "and" stands in for all of those relations formally, but it concatenates in ways that generate unexpected and powerful feelings and responses. An algorithm drives the piece, which lights up a phrase, then a column, then finally the entire piece, which people wait to see in its full splendor in the gallery (the piece was part of the New York Museum of Modern Art's [MoMA] 2018 Nauman retrospective titled *Disappearing Acts*). In its combinations of life and death, it recites a field of possibility.

The curators of the MoMA show note how both neon and video as different forms play with physical space, human emotion, and textuality, and so I would agree with them that it's not a leap to the video work, which has been part performance art, part conceptual study, since Nauman's early practices in the late 1960s. In the video piece *Good Boy Bad Boy*, from 1985, actors Joan Lancaster and Tucker Smallwood each recite the same text five times, yet with a slight time delay and different vocal gestures, generating a theoretical force field for the play of gender, language, presence, absence, reference, and affect (Figure 9.2).

The script goes like this (and I regret that space prevents me from reproducing it in its entirety):

Figure 9.2. Bruce Nauman, *Good Boy Bad Boy* (1985). Screen grabs from online circulating version of the video.

I was a good boy, you were a good boy, we were good boys, that was good
I was a good girl, you were a good girl, we were good girls, that was good
I was a bad boy, you were a bad boy, we were bad boys, that was bad
I was a bad girl, you were a bad girl, we were bad girls, that was bad
I am a virtuous man, you are a virtuous man, we are virtuous men, this is
　　virtue
I am a virtuous woman, you are a virtuous woman, we are virtuous women,
　　this is virtue
I am an evil man, you are an evil man, we are evil men, this is evil
I am an evil woman, you are an evil woman, we are evil women, this is evil
I'm alive, you're alive, we're alive, this is living
. . .
I play, you play, we play, this is play
I'm having fun, you're having fun, we're having fun, this is fun
I'm bored, you're bored, we're bored, this is boredom
I'm boring, you're boring, we're boring, this is boring
I have sex, you have sex, we have sex, this is sex
I love, you love, we love, this is love
. . .
I like to eat, you like to eat, we like to eat, this is eating
I like to drink you like to drink, we like to drink, this is drinking
I like to shit, you like to shit, we like to shit, this is shitting
I piss, you piss, we piss, this is piss
I like to sleep, you like to sleep, we like to sleep, this is sleeping

The structure and effects of this video have been described in a number
of different ways that miss its complexity. The MoMA curators describe
it this way:

Nauman has often parsed the categories of the virtuous and the immoral.
In the two-channel video *Good Boy Bad Boy* (1985), for example, a black
man and a white woman repeat five times, with fluctuating emphasis, a
sequence of twenty declarations ranging from the commendatory to the
accusatory. The certainty of each of these attributes is abandoned over the
work's hour-long duration. This shifting script mirrors the centuries-old
definitional drama about the philosophical character of good and bad, as

well as the related problem of how to ascertain the necessary proportions of each to live decently.[15]

"Commendatory" and "accusatory"? How were we certain of anything, from the first couplet (I was a good boy, I was a good girl) switching gender to the first quatrain switching values (good to bad)? The singular "you" who is the viewer, moreover, responds not to a single recitation but to two, Lancaster and Smallwood, which increasingly overlap in complicated ways. Let me have a go at more careful description.

The formal elements of this video belong to the simplest and most elegant vocabulary. A static camera, a key light, a single microphone, and a black studio isolate the talking head. Nauman knows that we know that talking heads stand in for philosophical universalism, and he gives us instead of the anticipated European white guy an American woman and African American man. Filmed separately, Lancaster and Smallwood establish relationships only with the camera, until the two-channel artwork is mounted for exhibition (where a more complex relay takes place). The form of the script mimics the conjugation of verbs in a foreign language (I verb, you verb, we verb) until the final line of each segment, "that was adjective" or "this is noun." Immediately, however, many things start to get complicated and conjunctive, ampersand-y, through this seemingly repetitive and simple linguistic game.

From the start, the "I" and the "you" are suspect, as Joan Lancaster recites, "I was a good boy," "I was a good girl," "I was a bad boy," "I was a bad girl," "I am a virtuous man," "I am a virtuous woman," and so on. From boy to girl, man to woman, good to bad, virtue to evil: these are the binary poles that have preoccupied Nauman throughout his career. Here they are put to work in the fundamental relationship between "I" and "you" that direct address establishes. The actor shifts between genders and identities in her and his almost-affectless recitation, nonetheless provoking an affective storm in the spectator, who is addressed as, or interpellated as, male, female, good, bad, virtuous, and evil, in a concatenation that is as unassimilable as it is funny.

In these swings from pole to pole, the viewer also starts to glimpse a field of reference outside of the I, you, and we. "This" and "that," as readers will know, are deictic indicators, pointer words, that gesture to a place where truth lies: "this is boring," "this is sex," "that was bad." Neither belonging to that suspended intersubjective space constituted through address nor to the phenomenal world, which is almost entirely excluded from the space of the video, "this" and "that" provide a kind of conclusion reached by the conjugation, an inevitable landing point for each refrain, yet they also compile impossible truths side by side: good, bad, virtuous, evil, bored, boring, and so on. "This" and "that" also, of course, point to the artwork itself and the experience of it: I'm having fun, you're having fun, we're having fun, *this* is fun. What I'm calling this field of reference "outside" is precisely the deconstructive *effect* of generative, aesthetic, affect force.

The critical literature on Nauman emphasizes the effects of these tensions, where Nauman plays with and disrupts the norms of human perception. In a compilation on video art, *Film and Video Art,* Nauman's work is celebrated as an early instance of art that is especially true to the medium of video:

The unique properties of video, and specifically the Portapak, introduced in 1966, had up until this point rarely been investigated. Unlike images shot on film, those made on portable video are immediately available for viewing. Furthermore, they can appear on a monitor while simultaneously being recorded. This reflexive quality of the video camera in relation to performed activity was exploited by each artist in different ways. It allowed for an investigation into the complex schism between live and recorded image, between illusion and reality, raising disquieting ontological questions: Am I there or here? Is this me now or then? The camera-monitor-circuit acted as a kind of mirror; it turned practices inwards, involving at least one degree of removal. Nauman took advantage of this to create an antagonistic or at least disquieting effect on the audience, as in his works with disembodied voices or bodiless heads.[16]

Let me continue to think about these bodiless heads in relation to one another, on monitors side by side. Nauman stages something other than a conversation. Each head recites a script to the camera, but the precise timing of the piece creates resonances, both verbal and gestural, rather than intersubjective engagement, at least not between the two channels or the two actors. Let's say that it displaces, disenchants, or dissolves subjectivity. It is difficult but not impossible for the viewer to watch both screens at once, if you stand far enough back from the monitors, listening to the layers of key terms piling up on one another, sometimes in hilarious juxtaposition, sometimes in antagonistic tension. *Good Boy Bad Boy*, however, unfolds in a more complicated temporality than the neon sculpture *One Hundred Live and Die*, asking the viewer to explore an affective and phenomenal encounter with minimally communicating human others but to do so in a space/time that Nauman has disrupted in all possible formal ways. This space/time, I would conclude, is that of the ampersand, a figure for mediation that enlists our affinities and potential collectivities and offers an invigorating energy to media. It's not "new media," it's not old media, it's not cinema, it's not television: it's a way of thinking, opening the spaces in between.

Notes

1. Thomas Elsaesser, "Cinephilia; or, The Uses of Disenchantment," in *Cinephilia: Movies, Love, and Memory*, ed. Marijke de Valck and Malte Hagener, 27–44 (Amsterdam: Amsterdam University Press, 2005).

2. Amanda Lotz, *Portals: A Treatise on Internet-Distributed Television* (Ann Arbor, Mich.: Maize Press, 2017), 1.

3. Amy Villarejo, *Ethereal Queer: Television, Historicity, Desire* (Durham, N.C.: Duke University Press, 2014), 1.

4. Marc H. Smith, postface to *A Brief History of the Ampersand*, by Jan Tschichold (Paris: Zeug Press, 2017), 30.

5. Smith, 27–28.

6. Peggy Phelan, "Just Want to Say: Performance and Literature, Jackson and Poirier," *PMLA* 125, no. 4 (2010): 942–47.

7. Jacques Derrida, *Droits de regard/Right of Inspection: Photographs by Marie-Francoise Plissart* (New York: Monacelli Press, 1998).

8. Jennifer Biddle, *Remote Avant Garde: Aboriginal Art under Occupation* (Durham, N.C.: Duke University Press, 2016), 110.

9. See Bernard Stiegler, *Technics and Time 1: The Fault of Epimetheus*, trans. Richard Beardsworth and George Collins (Stanford, Calif.: Stanford University Press, 1998), and Bernard Stiegler, *Symbolic Misery Volume 1: The Hyperindustrial Epoch* (London: Polity Press, 2014).

10. Franco "Bifo" Berardi, *AND: Phenomenology of the End* (New York: Semiotext(e), 2015), 171.

11. Berardi, 187.

12. Berardi, 170.

13. Berardi, 226.

14. Marcia Tucker, "PheNAUMANology," reprinted in *Bruce Nauman,* ed. Taylor Walsh (Cambridge, Mass.: MIT Press, 2018).

15. Kathy Halbreich, "Disappearing Acts Appear," in *Bruce Nauman: Disappearing Acts,* ed. Kathy Halbreich with Isabel Friedli, Heidi Naef, Magnus Schaefer, and Taylor Walsh (New York: MoMA, 2018), 26–27.

16. Stuart Comer, ed., *Film and Video Art* (London: Tate, 2009), 81.

Conclusion

At the End of the Ends of Cinema

A Dialogue

Richard Grusin and Jocelyn Szczepaniak-Gillece

RICHARD GRUSIN: Here at the end of the *Ends of Cinema* volume, it might be worth reflecting on where we began. When I approached you in August 2017 to invite you to co-organize the spring 2018 conference of the Center for 21st Century Studies (C21), whose directorship I had just resumed, my idea was that we could do a conference on "post-cinema." In part I imagined that this conference would inaugurate the Center's fiftieth anniversary year in 2018. Because cinema played a crucial role in the Center's first decades, and because the Center itself was instrumental in establishing film studies as an academic discipline in the United States and abroad in the 1970s and 1980s, I felt that it would make great sense for C21 to host the first major international conference on post-cinema.[1] By the end of our conversation, you had agreed to co-organize, but the theme of the conference had morphed from "post-cinema" to "ends of cinema." How did that happen?

JOCELYN SZCZEPANIAK-GILLECE: I was so excited to sign on to this conference and gather some of the field's major figures and new stars. Plus, it meant we could think together (you, me, and eventually all of the conference attendees and readers of this volume) about the discipline's past and future. But I think the terms we use in our chosen fields sometimes restrict us. The term *post-cinema* made me think about a defined historical moment and a definitive break. This reminded me of the seemingly inter-minable debates around the end of cinema in the digital age and, ironically, how such a sharp and polemical moment never ended up resolving itself. I liked the idea of looking once more at a con-troversial (if a bit dated) term and teasing out its historiographic implications for the discipline's *longue durée*. And the double—triple?—entendre satisfied my love for humor in the midst of seriousness: When did cinema end? How many times? And what are its ends in terms of its limits or even perhaps its overarch-ing goals? Maybe what at first glance seems tired and worn could be reoriented from a straight and severe line into the kind of squiggly, meandering web of tangents that my favorite histories tend to indulge. You and I come from different methodological approaches, but I think we share a fascination with the scrambled narrative and a belief that there is not one single end to anything. What was it like for you to imagine this conference and its resul-tant volume as something both of a local and historical basis—the Center's history, film studies—and methodologically vast?

RG: There is so much to unpack in your delightful response. Scram-bled narratives indeed! Perhaps I'll begin with your closing ques-tion and work backward.

Of course you would want me to think locally and histori-cally, since this is in fact very much of a piece with your meth-odological approach to theatrical exhibition and screening, an approach I love and admire.[2] And while I share your commitment to local and historical particularity, my work as a media theorist (and, before that, as an American cultural theorist) also aims to tease out logical or conceptual patterns often submerged or concealed among the particulars of media or other cultural tech-nologies. As you note, my idea for the conference began precisely from the local and historical situation of the Center's fiftieth anni-versary. By first imagining the conference in terms of post-cinema, I wanted to try to tease out a pattern or through-line across the Center's history, from its vital role in the 1970s and 1980s in fos-tering the emergence of film studies as an academic discipline in the United States to my own more recent efforts as C21 director to help give names to emerging concepts like the nonhuman turn, the dark side of the digital, or Anthropocene feminism. Because I saw post-cinema as such an emerging concept—marked by works like Steven Shaviro's *Post-Cinematic Affect* (2010) or the massive, open access 2016 volume, edited by Shane Denson and Julia Leyda, *Post-Cinema: Theorizing 21st-Century Film*—I thought that a conference focused on interrogating this concept would be a fitting counterpart to the Center's international film conferences from the late twentieth century.

In addition, to scramble the narrative a bit more, I have been thinking about the questions of post-cinema and the ends of cinema for more than twenty years. When, in *Remediation* (1999), Jay Bolter and I took up the double logic through which new media refashioned older media forms, film stood in as the predominant twentieth-century medium that digital media were remediating. A few years later, at the Domitor conference in 2002, I asked in a keynote lecture if we could now say that we found ourselves in the late age of early cinema.

My Domitor talk was prompted by the digital production, distribution, and screening of *Star Wars: Episode II—Attack of the Clones*, which media and industry voices had proclaimed as marking a historical moment in the history of cinema, heralding the future of Hollywood and the death of actual "film" making. For media and industry types, digital cinema improved on and would eventually supplant celluloid filmmaking by both improving on the presentation of realistic or naturalistic transparent immediacy and allowing for better special effects, cinema of attractions, and other forms of hypermediacy. In light of such claims, I asked the question, What would it mean to argue that new digital media signal an end to the late age of early cinema?[3]

To approach this question, I took up the similarities between the double logic of remediation at the beginning of the twenty-first century and at the beginning of the twentieth, contending that, like digital media, cinema from its inception functioned as a medium for creating a transparent window onto a world elsewhere and for projecting and screening images and eventually sounds that circulated among other sounds and images in the space of our world. In thinking about new media in the late age of early cinema, only one thing seemed certain: that new digital media, like cinema in the past, and like all new technological media to come, will never succeed in erasing mediation even as it will never cease wanting to try. Or, to put it in the terms of this book, the end of cinematic mediation was always already present in its earliest beginnings.

JSG: To start again, at the end, "the end of cinematic mediation was always already present"—not only in terms of immanence but also in terms of temporality. An end, therefore, is not only ahead of us but with us and at our backs as well, like Paul Klee's Angelus Novus moving backward. If there is a prophet of film studies, it's Walter Benjamin. Though Benjamin wrote relatively early in film's development, his love for the ruin and elegiac tone ensured that cinema's end was a foregone conclusion even near its beginnings. What I'm getting at here is that the ends of cinema are a function not only of mediation's unstoppable implements of inscription and erasure but also of the discipline itself. If Benjamin was a guiding light, he set the stage for generations of film studies scholars and their lapsarian tendencies. What is there will never be perfect and thus is always doomed to end. Per Bazin, cinema has yet to be invented, but it's already gone.

Your observations on the "late age of early cinema" are prescient both for the moment you spoke about them and for emerging scholars who grapple with the tripled legacies of film itself, film's relationship to its new container the digital (both lifeboat and coffin), and the accumulating decades of film studies as a discipline. I think of the recent, excellent anthology *New Silent Cinema* (2015), edited by Katherine Groo and Paul Flaig, which included pieces by several of our authors gathered in this book. James Leo Cahill's fine essay on YouTube as bestiary is a particularly relevant object for our discussions; in it, he looks at online animal videos both contemporary and (cinematically) foundational, such as the Edison Manufacturing Company's *Electrocuting an Elephant* (1903). This famously horrifying short that shows Topsy the elephant killed by electrical current makes for another fascinating example of cinema's ends: the spectacle of animal death as icon, reiterated and replayed on film's new delivery mechanism, an end that never reaches completion or at least lumbers up from its legs to repeat its throes as many times as the viewer desires.

I wonder, then, about the idea of being "post-cinema"—if, with apologies to Latour, we have always been postcinematic in that the medium has always anticipated its own ends. Sound, color film, widescreen, television, home viewing, digitality—film dies over and over again, certainly in industrial rhetoric, sacrificed always for something better, whether that's more immersion, more realism, more convenience, or more spectacle. I think it's not for nothing that the debate around cinema's end in the wake of the digital came alongside a swelling of discourse on film's inherent deathliness, as in Laura Mulvey's *Death 24× a Second* (2006). It often seems like cinema has a privileged relationship to its own conclusions. Perhaps that makes it a little different from other media. I'm curious about your thoughts regarding media writ large and its relationship to ends. Is remediation an avoidance of deathliness/ends, or is it something else entirely? And what, then, of premediation—do news media and journalism and digital urgency represent some version of film's central anxieties, or have we entered a new era?

RG: You aver, "If there is a prophet of film studies, it's Walter Benjamin." I would add that if there is a prophet of media studies, it's undoubtedly Benjamin as well, with his messianic approach to technical reproduction. And although Benjamin died well before what McLuhan understood as electronic media, and what we now understand as the digital, his concern for the newness of photography and cinema (note how often he writes "for the first time" in the artwork essay) offers a rhetorical template for so much of the work on digital media over the past half century.

My work has countered this exuberance for newness for twenty-five years, when I first challenged claims that electronic authorship marked a radical break with the author function as it operated in a technical regime of print.[4] With *Remediation,* Jay Bolter joined me in taking on enthusiasts for the fundamental newness of digital media when we argued that the only thing consistently new about digital media was their refashioning or remediation of prior media forms. *Remediation* acknowledges the centrality of cinema as the dominant medium of the twentieth century, what Jonathan Beller terms "the cinematic mode of production." But cinema's specificity as a medium must always be seen as historical—as in some sense no more or less specific than any other medium, but also distinct from other media in its historical particularity. The particularity of cinema is inseparable from, but not identical to, its photographic origins, insofar as photography, too, entailed an elegiac deathliness that can be traced back at least to the daguerreotype. But cinema was from its origins equally concerned with newness and beginnings, with animating images and bringing them to life, as much as with their inevitable ends.

Because of the deep historical ties between cinema and photography, the transition at the end of the twentieth century from filming and editing on celluloid film stock to editing and then capturing images through digital cinematography prompted what I think we would both agree was the most extensive and profound expression of the end of cinema in the medium's history. But from the perspective of media history and theory, the digital death knell for cinema looks very much like the digital death knell for other media—like photography or print or vinyl records or magnetic recording—or in the dangerously disruptive rhetoric of crisis capitalism, the impending end of museums or libraries or schools or universities brought about by networked digital media. So for me, while the end of cinema takes a variety of forms specific to the medium of film, the recent and ongoing digital instauration impacts not only cinema but other media as well.

So does this mean we have entered a new era of digital mediation? Insofar as changes of dominant technical formations have real and significant consequences not only for the ontology of inscription but also for the circulation and exhibition of texts, sounds, and images, the answer to your question would have to be yes—just as the era of print marked a fundamental shift from the age of writing, copying, and transmitting manuscripts by hand. But like all new eras, the current era of radically digital mediation does not put an end to earlier forms of mediation or reproduction but sometimes remediates those forms and sometimes leaves those earlier forms in place. As Latour (whom you have also invoked) reminds us, technical mediation is never only modern but always "polytemporal."[5]

Thus, to return to the question of news media and journalism with which your last exchange ended, we can see the same polytemporality at work. Print newspapers still carry out the functions of the Roman *acta diurna,* which were carved in metal or stone, just as televisual and internet news formats still perform the functions of print newspapers in reporting on the prior day's news, weather, sports, and market transactions. But the immediacy of live television (and, later, globally networked live video) altered the temporality of news from reporting on *what had happened* to *what was happening* at the moment. And the advent of data modeling, simulations, and digitally networked formats has now shifted much of the focus of journalism and news from recording the past or streaming the present to premediating potential futures. Most recently, as people have begun to claim that we find ourselves in a post-truth era with the explosion of "fake news" surrounding the election and administration of Donald Trump, one might also say we are in a post-news era as well.

But in responding to your provocative questions, I have wandered quite far from the ends of cinema into more generalized media temporalities. To bring our exchange back to film studies, and to the disciplinary turf on which you more usually engage, I wonder if you see an altered temporality in cinema itself in response to the new potentialities and futurities enabled by digital mediation. Insofar as the transience of cinema was also tied to earlier practices of theatrical exhibition, in which not only individual screenings but theatrical runs were marked by their impending ends, how do you see new digital technologies of distribution and exhibition altering cinema's ends, in all of the senses we intended for our conference? Should the kinds of emergent formats taken up by Amy Villarejo and Michael Gillespie, for example, in their contributions to this volume, still be considered cinema? How do you see the relationship of the medium specificity of film and film studies to the proliferation of new formats of audiovisual media encouraged by digital technology? With apologies to Dylan, could this really be cinema's end, to be stuck watching a video on your iPhone with the movie palace blues again?

JSG: While we have wandered far afield in looking back on the conference and volume, I think that the breadth of your response illustrates the impossibility of declaring a single "end" (as in conclusion, but maybe also as in goal—what media want from us is as manifold as, per W. T. J. Mitchell, what pictures have always wanted from us) of any media form. In turn, this highlights a struggle in film studies as well: how to define the borders of the discipline.

I think about how film studies is still an "emerging discipline," compared to history, English, art history, and so on. Film studies is something I've experienced as set, since I arrived in it well after its establishment in university settings. But the newness of film studies is linked to the time of its birth, which is, in the academy's terms, very recent. Caetlin Benson-Allott, whose urgent and incisive work is in this collection, has recently spearheaded an effort to change the title of the Society for Cinema and Media Studies' journal from *Cinema Journal* to the *JCMS: Journal of Cinema and Media Studies*. By renaming the journal, the editorial board asserted that the discipline's ends—here, its limits— should be properly expanded to include television, digitality and games, and other media forms. That this constitutes a relatively significant move tells us quite a bit about how polytemporal disciplines themselves can be, and how what is perceived as "new" is always up for debate. *Newness*, as you note, is a term that should never be taken at face value. I'm reminded of the undergraduate tic of calling a film "realistic." Much as the dimensions of realism shift over time and space, so too does what is new.

If I think about film's privileged relationship to time, I turn first to Mary Ann Doane's remarkable book *The Emergence of Cinematic Time*. What Doane shows us there is not only that film captures duration in a groundbreaking, era-defining manner but that it also aids in structuring the modern experience of time. Time as something both captured and lived is the domain of Henri Bergson, another hierophant of film studies. In keeping with these two essential—polytemporal—theorists of the discipline, then, I am hard-pressed to argue that the emergent formats discussed by Villarejo and Gillespie (among many, many others) are not film or not cinema (and that is another topic to take up: the interchangeability or specificity of those two terms). Both capture the experience of lived time, and especially of time as it is represented and lived at a particular historical moment.

But as the chapters in this volume have shown, cinema's relationship to temporality does not only imply duration of a film or the capturing of lived time on-screen. There is also the place and time of exhibition. When I think about the heyday of "end of cinema" conversations in the first decade of this century or so, the conversation revolved around digitality in terms of the erosion of 35mm film production and projection. Looking back, one of the ironies that now becomes exposed is that while such changes were lamented, the discipline hadn't always put that much stock in the necessity of material conditions of viewing for an understanding of text. It's only in its impending absence that its salvation becomes necessary. Certainly exhibition studies has a long history in the larger fields of film and media studies, but it's always been somewhat of a niche. And one question I regularly come up against is whether film studies without film is still, well, film studies. I think, yes, of course, because film is much more than a two-hour feature; it's an ideological vehicle, but it's also a vector for discourses of civil conduct, sociality, and citizenship that reach far beyond the screen. Its material traces—its theaters, for one, but also the urban (and suburban and rural and even natural) spaces it shapes, even the modes of religiosity and transportation it aids in shaping, as in Erica Robles-Anderson's work on the mediated megachurch and the drive-ins that dotted mid-century America—physically exist.

I wonder, then, how the chapters in this volume have helped us think about materiality beyond analog and digital: the theater, the home, the breaths and bodies (or lack thereof) that make up a shared experience. One functional difference between analog and digital circuitry is continuous transmission versus discrete signals. What if we consider the impact of physicality and materiality past transmissions and signals, past messages and representations? If the material of film—even its waste, like the giant Sphinx head from De Mille's first *Ten Commandments* (1923) found in the Guadalupe-Nipomo Sand Dunes in California in 2017—is inarguably extant, as is the material of the digital, as much as it seeks to efface itself, can there be a method for discussing both?

RG: I have never put much stock in hyperbolic claims for digitality or its fundamental difference from the analog. The technology of cinema—its illusion of motion—operates precisely from the differences between discrete frames. And digital media only emerge and have their eventfulness within the materiality of our analog bodies and world. So for me the method for discussing either digital or analog, or both, would be "mediating" in all of its variants.

What are the remediations, or what Karen Barad calls intra-actions, through which cinema is always emerging and already ending?[6] To think these mediations and intraactions is to think across materialities and scales, as both Mary Ann Doane and Francesco Casetti have done in this volume. In the case of cinema, one might think about electromagnetic intraactions of light and sound waves being remediated across technical recording, projection, and display devices or how light and shadow move across screens through social and economic networks and practices. What are the countless mediations and remediations, collaborating as well as conflicting, technical, economic, social, and formal, that give us a classical genre like the western, for example, or make possible the experimental irruptions of the avant-garde?

In thinking about mediation, then, the distinction between analog and digital makes no methodological sense. Of course, different technologies provoke different techniques, styles, and logics of mediation, because mediation is always material—light is recorded differently on a daguerreotype or glass plate, on photographic film or electronic image sensors. Editing and reproduction happen differently with filmic, video, or digital images, and the particularities of those mediating differences matter, are what create the opportunities and problems for scholarly investigation. For me the interesting questions are both how cinema (understood broadly) emerges from these intraactive mediations and, in a cinema that is always already ending, what gets lost or left behind.

JSG: If we fixate too intensely on categories, like a definite end of something, we can lose sight of the value of what you point to here: the question of what it means to mediate. I think that's part of why those three days in May 2018 ended up being so thrilling. Maybe it was a bait and switch on our part as the organizers, but I think many of us came in assuming there would be a standard conversation about, say, the digital murdering the analog but walked away with something else entirely.

What is lost or left behind was ultimately at the forefront of the conference's concerns. From Casetti's counter-genealogy and its insistence on what has been ignored in a focus on the text, to André Gaudreault's recouping of "cinema" and its etymology, to Mark Paul Meyer's curatorial detritus and the gemlike qualities of the discarded, to Jennifer Lynn Peterson's precarious visions of the wild captured on film, to the work of other marvelous contributors we've included here, Ends of Cinema turned out to be about the risk of a foregone conclusion when we stop allowing for regeneration. As James Leo Cahill explains, cinema and waste have always walked side by side. Cinema is an object of the living and the dead as well as the end and the beginning.

Let's hope this volume is a reason to keep sifting through that waste, returning to what was left behind and filtering through what gets tossed aside. It turns out that it's not just about the ends of something—it's about the category of an end itself. All our contributors know that if you get your hands a little dirty with something that seems dulled and broken, new edges start to emerge, and the brilliance begins to shine through. Thanks for being willing to grant the space and time for that kind of rigor and play and for understanding that what seem like old questions still have the capability to make us think in new ways.

Notes

1. Almost every year from 1975 to 1985, the Center for 20th Century Studies hosted a major international film conference. These conferences served to put the Center on the map as among the leading sites for film studies in the United States and helped to institutionalize film studies as an academic discipline. The list of presenters at these conferences reads like a who's who of major film and media scholars and critical theorists. To give you a sense of the intellectual traffic coming through the Center in this decade, following is a nonexhaustive list of participants from that period: Dudley Andrew, Raymond Bellour, Herbert Blau, David Bordwell, Noel Carroll, Jean-Louis Comolli, Manuel De Landa, Teresa De Lauretis, Mary Ann Doane, Thomas Elsaesser, Shoshana Felman, Jane Feuer, Sandy Flitterman, Jane Gaines, Douglas Gomery, Miriam Hansen, Stephen Heath, J. Hoberman, Fredric Jameson, Marsha Kinder, Annette Kuhn, Jean-François Lyotard, Gerald Mast, Judith Mayne, Patricia Mellencamp, Christian Metz, Annette Michelson, Laura Mulvey, Bill Nichols, Ruby Rich, David Rodowick, Kaja Silverman, Kristin Thompson, Linda Williams, and Peter Wollen.

2. Jocelyn Szczepaniak-Gillece, *The Optical Vacuum: Spectatorship and Modernized American Theater Architecture* (Oxford: Oxford University Press, 2018).

3. Richard Grusin, "Remediation in the Late Age of Early Cinema," in *Early Cinema: Technology and Apparatus,* ed. André Gaudreault, Catherine Russell, and Pierre Véronneau, 343–60 (Lausanne, Switzerland: Payot Lausanne, 2004).

4. Richard Grusin, "What Is an Electronic Author?," *Configurations* 2, no. 3 (1994): 469–83.

5. Bruno Latour, *We Have Never Been Modern* (Cambridge, Mass.: Harvard University Press, 1973), 75.

6. Karen Barad, *Meeting the Universe Halfway: Quantum Physics and the Entanglement of Matter and Meaning* (Durham, N.C.: Duke University Press, 2007), 97–185.

Acknowledgments

This book originated in the conference End(s) of Cinema, which was hosted at the Center for 21st Century Studies (C21), University of Wisconsin–Milwaukee, on May 3–5, 2018. Although she came on board after the conference, our greatest debt of thanks is first and foremost due to Maureen Ryan, C21 deputy director. Dr. Ryan's disciplinary rigor, superior organization, careful eye, and exemplary editing skills made this book the excellent object it is; it simply would not exist without her. UWM is lucky to have her dedicated leadership and powerful intellect at the Center. We would like to thank the other members of the conference organizing committee: Lauren McHargue, C21 business manager, and C21 graduate fellows Molly McCourt, Kyle Miner, and Cami Thomas. Together the committee proved essential to the success of the conference in so many ways, including the selection of papers, the formation of panels for End(s) of Cinema's breakout sessions, and the overall organization and administration of the conference. For their support of the conference and dedication to intellectual community at UWM, we thank Johannes Britz, provost and vice chancellor for academic affairs; Dave Clark, interim dean of the College of Letters and Sciences; Jasmine Alinder, associate dean of the College of Letters and Sciences; Marija Gajdardziska-Josifovska, dean of the Graduate School; and Mark Harris, interim vice provost for research.

We offer continuing thanks to Doug Armato, director of the University of Minnesota Press, for his role in bringing the Center's book series to

Minnesota, and to Danielle Kasprzak, former acquisitions editor at the Press. Thanks also to Zenyse Miller at the Press for her dedication to the project and all her work in getting it together in the final stages. Finally, we send our deepest thanks to our plenary speakers from End(s) of Cinema and to all of the book's contributors, without whom this volume would not exist.

Contributors

CAETLIN BENSON-ALLOTT is Provost's Distinguished Associate Professor of English and film and media studies at Georgetown University. She is the author of *Killer Tapes and Shattered Screens: Video Spectatorship from VHS to File Sharing* and *Remote Control* and the editor of *JCMS*, the scholarly publication of the Society for Cinema and Media Studies.

JAMES LEO CAHILL is director of the Cinema Studies Institute and associate professor of cinema and French at the University of Toronto. He is author of *Zoological Surrealism: The Nonhuman Cinema of Jean Painlevé* (Minnesota, 2019).

FRANCESCO CASETTI is the Thomas E. Donnelly Professor of Humanities and Film and Media Studies at Yale University. Among his books are *Inside the Gaze: The Fiction Film and Its Spectator*; *Theories of Cinema, 1945–1995*; *Eye of the Century: Film, Experience, Modernity*; and *The Lumière Galaxy: Seven Key Words for the Cinema to Come*.

MARY ANN DOANE is the Class of 1937 Professor of Film and Media at the University of California, Berkeley. She is the author of *The Emergence of Cinematic Time: Modernity, Contingency, the Archive* and *The Desire to Desire: The Woman's Film of the 1940s*.

ANDRÉ GAUDREAULT is professor at the Université de Montréal, Canada, research chair in cinema and media studies, and director of the

TECHNÈS International Research Partnership on Cinema Technology. His publications include *From Plato to Lumière: Narration and Monstration in Literature and Cinema* and *Film and Attraction: From Kinematography to Cinema.* He is coauthor of *The End of Cinema? A Medium in Crisis in the Digital Age* and *Le récit cinématographique.*

MICHAEL BOYCE GILLESPIE is associate professor of film at the City College of New York, CUNY. He is author of *Film Blackness: American Cinema and the Idea of Black Film* and coeditor of *Black One Shot,* an art criticism series on *ASAP/J.*

RICHARD GRUSIN is director of the Center for 21st Century Studies and distinguished professor of English at the University of Wisconsin–Milwaukee. He is author of *Premediation: Affect and Mediality after 9/11* and *Culture, Technology, and the Creation of America's National Parks* and coauthor of *Remediation: Understanding New Media.*

MARK PAUL MEYER worked as a film restorer and curator for thirty years and is senior curator at the Eye Filmmuseum in Amsterdam. He is a staff member of the MA course Preservation and Presentation of the Moving Image at the University of Amsterdam and coeditor of the book *Restoration of Motion Picture Film.*

JENNIFER LYNN PETERSON is professor of the Department of Communication at Woodbury University in Los Angeles. She is the author of *Education in the School of Dreams: Travelogues and Early Nonfiction Film.*

JOCELYN SZCZEPANIAK-GILLECE is associate professor of English and film studies at the University of Wisconsin–Milwaukee. She is author of *The Optical Vacuum: Spectatorship and Modernized American Theater Architecture.*

AMY VILLAREJO is the Frederick J. Whiton Professor of Humanities at Cornell University. Her most recent monograph is *Ethereal Queer: Television, Historicity, Desire,* and she is coeditor of *The Oxford Handbook to Queer Cinema.*

Index

affect: of archival materials, 59–60, 187; embodiedness as, 150; of endangerment, xi, 54–55; as performance, 191–93, 195; production of, 16, 59; and race, 133, 135; spectatorial, 14, 196–97; structures of, 55; as textual quality, 143–44, 193. See also *Post-Cinematic Affect*; spectator: and affect

Afrofuturism, 147, 151

Aitken, Doug, 7

ampersand: linguistic function, xiii, 182–84, 195; as mediation 184, 188, 192, 197; as rhizomatic, 184–85, 191

analog. *See under* celluloid; technology

animation: direct, 143–46; film as, 90, 204; as form, 134; stop motion, 135, 138. *See also* film: animated

Anthropocene: and capitalism, 56, 58; as emergent concept, 53–54; feminism, 201; historical epoch, xi, 56–59, 70, 157n46; material precarity, 100; as reception context, 69–70, 72

Anthropocinema, 149

apparatus: cinematographic, 20n16, 27, 37, 41–42, 79; theory, viii, 12, 36–37, 82. *See also* spectator

architecture: as media 6–7; theory, 4. *See also* screen: as architectural space

archive, xi, 134, 143; film preservation, 80–82; films, 54–55, 59–60, 72–74, 83; Hugh M. Hefner Moving Image Archive (HMIA), xi, 54, 61, 65, 70; national, 146, 189; photography as, 88, 92; as remediation, 54, 56. *See also* Derrida, Jacques: "archive fever"

audience: antiracist, 107; crossover, 115, 118; popular, 63; as racialized groups, 108–9, 114–16, 120–21, 125, 130n42, 140; receptivity, 27, 29–30, 40, 196. *See also* spectator

Aufhebung. *See* Hegelian

avant-garde, 90, 100, 151, 187, 208

Bahng, Aimee, 147

Bataille, Georges: on cinema, 100, 102–03; "Figure Humaine," 87, 91, 95–97; on photographic media, xi, 86–87, 91–93, 95–97

Baudry, Jean-Louis, viii, 12, 36, 44n6. *See also* apparatus

Bazin, André, 67, 174n24, 188, 202

Belton, John, viii, 8

215